D1551671

LITERACY, PLACE, AND PEDAGOGIES OF POSSIBILITY

"Barbara Comber's new book is generative, accessible, timely and incredibly important for literacy educators. Drawing on three decades of rich, powerful and collaborative work with teachers, children and researchers, it offers a vision of hope for children who are often denied such pedagogies of possibility. Drawing on collectively designed pedagogies of belonging and radical optimism together with a direct engagement with the situated expertise and ways of knowing of teachers, children, and researchers, this book is a gift to the field of literacy education. We have been waiting a long time for this book and it surpasses expectations. It was worth the wait."

Kate H. Pahl, Sheffield University, UK

"At a time of increasing global educational reform through standardization, where the lived experiences of students and teachers are discounted, we are fortunate to receive this gift from Barbara Comber. After reading the illuminating collection of social justice-driven pedagogical stories assembled from decades of research, you can't help but imagine possibilities for taking up everyday places as dynamic spaces in which to enable children to develop critical, action-oriented, social justice perspectives on the world. This book has the potential to shift our thinking for years to come about students' histories and life-worlds as assets and productive resources in the design of powerful curriculum and critical pedagogy."

Vivian Maria Vasquez, American University, USA

How can teachers ensure pedagogies of possibility underpinned by social justice, and what has literacy got to do with this? This book explores the positive synergies between critical literacy and place-conscious pedagogy. Through rich classroom research, it introduces and demonstrates how a synthesis of insights from theories of space and place and literacy studies can underpin the design and enactment of culturally inclusive curriculum for diverse student communities, and illustrates how making place and space the objects of study provides productive resources for teachers to design enabling pedagogical practices that extend students' literate repertoires. The argument is that systematic study of and engagement with specific elements of place can enable students' academic learning and literacy.

Literacy, Place, and Pedagogies of Possibility

- is informed by critical literacy, place-conscious pedagogy and spatial theory
- is richly illustrated with examples from classroom research, including teacher and student artifacts
- provides new directions for classroom practice in critical literacy.

This novel combination of multidisciplinary theory and classroom research extends previous work in critical literacy pedagogy, drawing on three decades of ethnographic and collaborative inquiry in culturally and linguistically diverse classrooms. At this time when the relationships between the local and the global are shifting in sometimes unpredictable ways, and the need to care for the planet can no longer be ignored, the social and negotiated nature of places and spaces can provide a central and meaningful focus for students' learning and their work with multiliteracies.

Barbara Comber is Research Professor, Faculty of Education, Queensland University of Technology, Australia.

Expanding Literacies in Education

Cynthia Lewis and Jennifer Rowsell, Series Editors

Visit **www.routledge.com/education** for additional information on titles in
Expanding Literacies in Education

LITERACY, PLACE, AND PEDAGOGIES OF POSSIBILITY

Barbara Comber

Routledge
Taylor & Francis Group

NEW YORK AND LONDON

First published 2016
by Routledge
711 Third Avenue, New York, NY 10017

and by Routledge
2 Park Square, Milton Park, Abingdon, Oxon OX14 4RN

Routledge is an imprint of the Taylor & Francis Group, an informa business

© 2016 Taylor & Francis

First edition published by Routledge

Library of Congress Cataloging-in-Publication Data
Comber, Barbara.
   Literacy, place, and pedagogies of possibility / by Barbara Comber. —
First edition.
      pages cm. — (Expanding literacies in education series)
   Includes bibliographical references and index.
   1. Literacy.   2. Place-based education.   I. Title.
   LC149.C65 2016
   302.2′244—dc23
   2015008346

ISBN: 978-1-138-82979-4 (hbk)
ISBN: 978-1-138-82980-0 (pbk)
ISBN: 978-1-315-73565-8 (ebk)

Typeset in Bembo
by Apex CoVantage, LLC

This book is dedicated to my family, especially to John, Tom, Laura, Lachlan, Jack and Oliver, to my parents Tom and Joan and my brother Kevin. From all my family, I have learned so much.

CONTENTS

FOREWORD

Looking Forward by Looking Back

Late in the 19th century, a young woman who described herself as 'an upstate country woman' abandoned (at least for a while) her goal of becoming a kindergarten teacher (Pratt, 2014, p. 17). This life decision was a response to a teacher training class at Teachers College–Columbia in New York City. Young children gaining some mystical insight into the unity of human kind by sitting in morning circle was too much balderdash for her. A bunch of grown women fluttering around like butterflies upon command just made her feel silly.

Eventually, Caroline Pratt went out into New York neighborhoods, recruited children, and founded her own school, which started with 5-year-olds and, under her leadership, eventually stretched from nursery school through eighth grade. Key traits of Pratt's envisioned school, begun in 1914, bring to mind those of Barbara Comber's vision, which infuses this rich account of teaching in and for the world in formation. Their visions are not identical, nor are the circumstances in which they worked. But strong beliefs undergird the writing of both—the need for inclusive classrooms where all have the respect of, and a responsibility towards, others; the agency of teachers and children as key to schooling; and the necessity of children's reflection on, replaying of, and inquiry about dynamic spaces that are everyday places. I comment briefly on Miss Pratt because her work, and its fate, construct a stage upon which shared and, moreover, unique qualities of Comber's work stand out boldly, as does the unique role of Comber herself in supporting pedagogical possibilities for *our* times.

When Miss Pratt began her school, she recruited young children whose parents, often immigrants, were 'hardworking members of the humbler professions' (p. 58). In her own childhood, Miss Pratt had learned both from engagement with her hardworking farm family in its daily work, and from her explorations with friends into the community; she knew, for example, the workers at (and the work of) the flour and paper mills on a nearby stream and the local shop keepers and their particular labor. Now, as a city resident, she worried that her children, living in crowded apartments on busy streets, had narrowed lives—no open spaces to explore, no involvement with parental work. So Miss Pratt used their city surroundings as curricular material. She and the children visited workers in lively neighborhood spaces—among them, the dock workers with their boats, the bakers and their shops, the crews at the railroad tracks. The children learned to follow their curiosity, to wonder, for example, about where the boats had been, what cargo they carried to the city, and where the wagons that met those boats took the cargo. The workers became Miss Pratt's fellow teachers, their daily grind the source of important information that led to the world beyond the neighborhood. Back in the classroom, the explorations led to multimodal composing (not, of course, a phrase Pratt used)—maps, block building, dramatic play, dictated stories—as the explored neighborhood places were analyzed and reconstructed through the children's own actions.

Now, a century later, Barbara Comber draws on decades of research projects with teachers to bring us vivid illustrations of children who are also venturing into the local, led by lively and masterly educators. But the work has a sociopolitical urgency that befits the times and spaces. Pratt's school has survived with its philosophy intact. But it is now a private school, with a 5 to 1 student/ teacher ratio; it has substantial tuition costs and serves primarily white children from educated families (Find the Best/A Research Engine, 2014). All children, of course, deserve an education that exploits both available cultural and spatial resources and collective and independent agency. But local spaces of economically poor children too often are dehumanized, dismissed as 'ghettos', 'slums' or 'the bad part of town' (Haymes, 2003). Like their homogenized surroundings, the children of these spaces are also dismissed, seen as lacking in resources and, thus, in need of rescue. This is not the standpoint of Barbara Comber and the talented teachers with whom she has worked over the years. To play with Doreen Massey's (2005) words, children 'thrown together' in a classroom must negotiate a common place where they all belong. With their teachers' guidance, the children reach out from their sociocultural, familial and personal experiences and interactively make a place of multiplicity, of diverse experiences and perspectives. The children's negotiating may well happen through their joint inquiries about local places, including the school itself (a place of memories, relations, hidden nooks and celebrated corners).

Pratt verbalized a distrust of language as a medium of instruction, a distrust grounded in silent classrooms where children, denied the right to play and explore, learned the surface structure of school basics. Nonetheless, talkative, text-producing children were the norm in her school, as language figured into their explorations, their representations and their performances.

Barbara Comber is also committed to creating intellectual and social elbow room for children stuck on their timed curricular pathways, experiencing schooling as a series of skills to be mastered. Her collaborating teachers too began with children's local spaces and their reflections on their pleasures and desires relative to those spaces. But Comber explicitly illustrates that such explorations entailed new ways of talking, new vocabularies and, most importantly, new ways to harness language and other symbolic modes (model buildings, images, digital displays and new sorts of text genres) for critical ends. In the classrooms featured herein, those new symbolic ways were aided by children's engagement with locally available experts—for example, experts in building design, in particular animals' habitats and in media use—and Indigenous Aboriginal citizens, especially artists and other storytellers; the latter shared the stories that made environmental features meaningful and regulative in their lives.

In this way, Comber's teachers went far beyond the usual rote 'pedagogy of poverty' (Haberman, 1991) low-income and minority children regularly receive. Indeed, in relation to Pratt's school, these teachers led their children to a more critical, action-oriented perspective on the world. Inviting children, for example, to share their special places in their school could lead to their desires for improvement and, indeed, to efforts to design a new, child-friendly school building. Or, a study of local flora and fauna could give rise to concerns about disappearing habitats. In their efforts, children 'thrown together' in a classroom could become collaborating contributors to texts of varied genres and modes, as well as classroom members who negotiated relations as playmates and learners. Comber and her collaborating teachers thus were about changing assumptions about what 'those kids' can do.

As I read Barbara Comber's book, I thought of 6-year-old Tionna and her peers, all low-income students in a multiracial school (featured in Dyson, 2013). The children had no qualms about critiquing a required social studies text. One day, with that text, the student teacher was busy guiding the children to designate an abandoned building, with a large parking lot, as a site for an urban garden (the book's solution to an empty lot). Their city did not need more gardens, the children said; it needed buildings, 'houses for people that don't have 'em'. 'For *free*', stressed Tionna's peer, Jon. There was no place in their class for the children to explore the homeless problem in their city (although at least one child was indeed homeless). The lesson marched on. In a class Barbara Comber might study, the children might interview parents and relatives about the problem of homelessness; they might talk with city officials about what was being done for homeless people; after studying with an urban planner, small groups might design an ideal apartment building that could house families with kids.

Tionna and her peers knew about hard times. Moreover, homelessness was visible on the streets of their neighborhood. Tionna also worried about kids without grandmas, moms and dads to take care of them, perhaps because her grandmother—her 'mom'—was quite old; she thought about how a school could be organized to serve as a home for these kids. What could matter more to children than a home, a building that becomes a place they belong? Gaining some control over worries through their own actions—playing with, and learning about, design concepts with construction blocks, paper and colors, and digital images, and sharing their thinking as citizens—this is what I imagine after reading Barbara Comber's book.

It is time for you, dear readers, to enter the book proper and begin your own pedagogical imagining. This imagining of possibilities, particularly for marginalized children, is exactly what Barbara Comber is aiming for in this book, and so she has aimed through three decades of work that culminates herein. We are in her debt.

So let the imagining begin.

Anne Haas Dyson
Department of Education Policy, Organization and Leadership
College of Education
University of Illinois at Urbana-Champaign

References

Dyson, A H 2013, *ReWRITING the basics: Literacy learning in children's cultures*, Teachers College Press, New York.

Find the Best/A Research Engine 2014, *Education-private schools*, retrieved from http://private-schools.findthebest.com/1/130072/City-and-Country-School

Haberman, M 1991, 'The pedagogy of poverty versus good teaching', *Phi Delta Kappan*, vol. 73, pp. 290–294.

Haymes, S N 2003, 'Toward a pedagogy of place for Black urban struggle', in A. Darder, M. Baltodano & R. D. Torres (eds.) *The critical pedagogy reader*, Routledge/Falmer, New York, pp. 211–237.

Massey, D 2005, *For space*, SAGE, Los Angeles.

Pratt, C 2014, *I learn from children*, Grove Press, New York. (Original work published 1948).

PREFACE

Note to Readers: You will notice that this book is written in terms of 'we'. This is not the 'royal we'; indeed just the opposite, as this text is the product of the collective wisdom of various people working together over time (see acknowledgments for full explanation of contributing researchers). 'Our' research agenda across a number of projects takes a socio-cultural approach to literacy studies informed by feminist and critical theory. Writing as 'we' recognizes that this is not an individual account, but a faithful record of practices accomplished by many.

Why This Book?

In ongoing research with early career teachers, many express their desire 'to do the right thing'; that is, the right thing by their students, the right thing by their colleagues and school leadership, the right thing by the goals they graduated with, the right thing theoretically. This book provides accounts of experienced teachers across their careers doing exactly that: trying to be true to the right thing as they currently understand it.

The aspiration is that it might inspire other teachers and researchers to collaborate to get their stories out. In brief, this book aims to:

- demonstrate what particular teachers working in particular places with particular students have made use of in designing and operationalizing curriculum and pedagogy in situ over an extended period of time
- document some of the most enabling literacy pedagogies we have witnessed in a range of school contexts over an extended period of time where teachers have in various ways made place the object of study

- show how spatial theory can inform literacy pedagogy and research, especially that related to high poverty contexts
- indicate the affordances of longitudinal research with teachers
- provide catalysts for teachers working in other unique places.

Why This Book *Now?*

We have worked as teachers, teacher educators and researchers in the field of English and literacy education in high poverty contexts for over three decades. So what motivates this book now? What, if anything, do we have to say to literacy researchers, teacher educators and teachers given that the world of literacy education is vastly transformed from the world we entered as elementary students in the 1950s and as teachers in the 1970s? What might be the legacy associated with our long-term privilege of conducting collaborative inquiry?

Recently, we have begun to explore the productive possibilities of linking spatial theories with critical literacy, especially for designing creative pedagogies that make sense in high poverty locations. Theoretically, and in practice, we are interested in exploring the possible pedagogical relationships between places and textual, spatial and learning practices. This may be more important than ever in this era of global educational reform, which aims to standardize curriculum, pedagogy and assessment and bracket out the lived experiences of students and teachers.

To situate this book in the contemporary moment, we recently completed a study focusing on mandated literacy assessment and the reorganization of teachers' work as an international phenomenon (see acknowledgments: *Mandated Literacy Assessment and the Reorganisation of Teachers' Work*, an Australian Research Council Discovery Project, No. DP0986449). Most troubling was that the emphasis on high stakes testing closed down teachers' opportunities for innovation and creativity in connecting curriculum with children's lives and interests. Especially worrying is that the impact was greatest in high poverty contexts, in schools with culturally and linguistically diverse communities, and in schools in rural areas. In other words, children in communities who have already experienced social and educational disadvantage are more likely to receive a reduced and narrowed curriculum in the wake of poor results on standardized literacy measures. They are likely to be offered what might be seen as 'fickle literacies' (Comber & Woods, in press, 2015)—rote learning, repeated test preparation, copying, coloring-in and other time-filling, challenge-free, thought-less activities, which will not build their capacity for academic learning and complex literacies.

With high stakes assessment significantly impacting on schools, it is no surprise that literacy and leadership is a central focus for professional development in the USA, Australia, and elsewhere. In a current project (see acknowledgments:

Educational Leadership and Turnaround Literacy Pedagogies, an Australian Research Council (ARC) Linkage Project, No. LP120100714), we are exploring educational leadership, pedagogy and literacy in schools located in poor and working-class communities. We recently visited a school to observe a teacher development day focusing on incorporating Information and Communication Technologies (ICT) into curriculum and pedagogy. During the day, keywords included Scootle, connectivity, calibration, settings, projector alignment, firmware and similar technical jargon. The tools, technologies and vocabularies of the teaching trade are clearly changing. But what of the everyday work of educators in schools serving communities in poverty?

When we returned the following week to observe again, this time to focus on how leadership team meetings were conducted, we found that two team members were away sick, including one whose major responsibilities included behavior management. Within the first half an hour of the school day, already two boys had been sent to the office: one for purportedly having slapped another student across the face, and another for having thrown a chair. As we watched, one of the boys left the office without permission, hopped on his scooter and headed out of the school grounds. The other boy was trying to convince the assistant principal not to call his parents and send him home. The school principal and another teacher were at the local shopping center rounding up some students who were truanting.

The next day, when the principal had time, he discussed how long-term poverty impacts the work of school leaders and teachers in myriad ways. While some things such as the use of ICT have changed in education, the dilemma of moving beyond deficit discourses for schools located in poor communities is as visible as ever. Being a school leader (or a teacher) in such contexts is different work than what is done in more affluent locales. The materiality of poverty matters, and poverty is situated in particular places. Some would argue that massive open online courses and other web-mediated learning platforms are changing the local nature of teaching and learning, but it remains the case that with all our new tools and technologies, the actual work of learning and teaching is accomplished locally and materially whether that be in schools, libraries, clubs, centers, homes, or malls. And this work of teaching and learning involves real and embodied people, negotiating relationships and resources in complex and dynamic ways in particular places.

Despite the competing policy and material pressures on teachers, some do maintain their optimism and courage and find ways of offering opportunities for students to aim high, and to assemble academic dispositions and sophisticated literate repertoires. Some teachers accomplish this through engagement with place and space as this book will demonstrate.

Recent events across the globe also provide strong motivation to foreground place and space in our research and pedagogy. For example, recent severe weather events, natural disasters, and ongoing wars mean that some communities are even more vulnerable than ever. As Cindi Katz wrote after Hurricane Katrina:

> Landfall is not just a physical question. Geography is always socially produced. And so every landscape can reveal sedimented and contentious histories of occupation; struggles over land use and clashes over meaning; rights of occupancy; and rights to resources.
>
> *(Katz, 2008, p. 16)*

Why does it take disasters, such as Hurricane Katrina, to fully expose injustice? The delays in responding to natural disasters in places of poverty are indicators of the ways in which people in poor places everywhere are often left out of sight, out of mind. It is easy to ignore poverty when it is not seen. It is easy to blame people for their poverty, when one does not encounter the reality oneself. Ironically, the global financial crisis may have been educative in demonstrating to the middle and upper classes how wealth and poverty are produced.

Those of us as educators who have grown up in working-class areas, playing and learning with culturally diverse peers and their families, as children, experienced everyday norms of low family incomes and a melting pot of cultures, languages and religions. With little disposable money, and no cars until late in childhood, lives were lived largely within the neighborhood. Going by bus to other schools to play sports revealed school grounds, surrounding houses and neighborhoods were in stark contrast. For example, poorer neighborhoods lacked parks, trees and footpaths. The houses, schools and churches were made of fibro materials that were easily erected, incredibly cold in winter and stiflingly hot in summer. The school grounds were largely asphalt and gravel, with ageing knees bearing the scars to prove it! There were no trees of enough size to provide shade and no grass to sit on.

Schools on the other side of town enjoyed landscaped grounds, green lawns, huge trees, changing sheds, and so on. Some school buildings looked like castles. Such memories indicate that school lives are embodied experiences that occur in particular places. Those places and the people that populate them are in relation to other places, other histories, other trajectories. We did not know we were poor until we entered other spaces and were confronted by comparisons with those we routinely inhabited.

Our histories have led us to interrogate claims made by educators, policymakers and educational researchers that explain unequal educational outcomes by referring to children's 'backgrounds' (Comber, 1998). Such correlations too easily consign children of the poor and working class to continued educational failure. When deficit discourses are rampant in the wider community, including the press, and indeed in educational research, teachers can explain away a lack of learning by referring to children's family backgrounds. There is an ongoing need for educators at all levels to contest the common assumption that poverty equals a lack of learning capability. In saying this, we do not mean to bracket out the material realities of poverty as lived experience, nor its impact on children, their families and indeed their wider school communities. However, as we will show throughout this book, because place, or even places, are defined by poverty, this does not need to limit in any way children's literacy learning when teachers are able to design curriculum that opens opportunities for inquiry and imagination.

Literacy development in the elementary years is contingent on a number of interrelated factors, both in the home and school environments. A lot has been written and said about the effects of children's home lives on children's literacy learning. Children's home lives do need to be taken into account, and, in particular, the possible effects of poverty must be anticipated. Illness, family dislocation, unemployment and so on do make a difference in the lives of families and to children's learning. Yet equally important is to work against deficit equations about poverty and illiteracy (Comber, 1997; Freebody et al., 1995; Gregory & Williams, 2000). Hence, educational systems must work on at least two fronts: first, ensure that students are provided with all the resources they need to engage with and learn from the program and second, design and deliver programs that are both culturally responsive and futures driven. That is, they must both work with what students bring, and offer them new discursive resources and literate practices that they do not yet have.

In terms of school related factors that affect children's literacy development, our research shows the profound effects of both school and classroom practices. Of particular note are school structures designed to facilitate one-to-one and small group interactions, and teachers' classroom discourses designed to develop particular literate dispositions. Our earlier longitudinal studies of children growing up in poverty (Comber & Hill, 2000; Comber, Badger, Barnett, Nixon & Pitt, 2002) indicate that the following factors at school make a difference to what children learn:

- the resources factor (the extent to which schools have the human and material resources they need)
- the curriculum factor (the quality, scope and depth of what is made available)
- the pedagogical factor (the quality of teacher instructional talk, teacher-student relationships and assessment practices)
- the recognition factor (the extent to which what children can do counts and that they can see that it counts)
- the take-up factor (the extent to which children appropriate literate practices and school authorized discourses)
- the translation factor (the extent to which children can make use of and assemble repertoires of practice which they can use in new situations) (Comber, Badger et al., 2002).

It is the relationship between what schools and teachers provide, and what students are able to do with that, which makes a difference in the literacies children assemble at school. Hence, it remains crucial to understand teachers' work in poor communities. This means working collaboratively with teacher-researchers. Over several decades, we have undertaken such work with colleagues to consider questions such as the following:

- What can we learn from pockets of redesigned pedagogies, where literacy curriculum is not stripped to simulation by its school context?
- How is it possible to broaden and sustain inclusive teaching in times of increased stipulation of standardized literacy?
- How can teachers productively make place the object of study in ways that are generative for assembling complex literate repertoires?

Our standpoints as literacy researchers have been informed by our childhoods and educational histories, and also by our work as classroom teachers and decades of collaborative inquiry with teachers (Comber, Nixon, Ashmore, Loo & Cook, 2006; Comber, Nixon, Grant & Wells, 2012). While it is essential to avoid simplistic equations that poverty means poor literacy (Comber, 1997), at the same time, the reality is that teachers' work in schools in poor communities is different from the work of teachers in more affluent communities. Indeed, it is complex and challenging and that is why documentation, of the innovative and imaginative pedagogy that some teachers are able to accomplish in schools serving poor communities, is so crucial. The teachers featured in this book explicitly recognize that each school they work in is located in 'a particular material place' (Thomson, 2002, p. 73) and their work is always local, embedded and contextualized.

Because a school and its community form the arena in which the pedagogical practice of the teacher plays out (Reid & Green, 2009), systematic inquiry into contextualized practice is an important part of 'the larger process of imagining alternatives for students who have been most vulnerable in our schools' (Campano, 2009, pp. 332–333). In times such as these, when 'public money and status are again linked with large-scale impersonal research' (Zeni, 2009, p. 265), it is especially important for teacher-researchers and their university collaborators to make specific places the object of study and to foreground the 'local and little stories' (Griffiths, 2009, p. 31) of the people who move through and live in those places. A primary purpose of this book is to collect and tell illuminating pedagogical stories emerging from research.

We conclude this preface on a positive note about the goals of this book to shift readers' thinking about literacy, place, and pedagogies of possibility. It is not only bad news that shifts people's thinking. Rather, the dynamism of place and change, such as the case with some aspects of urban regeneration and renewal, can provide the impetus and the motivation for considering new possibilities, and for imagining how things might be otherwise. Here is one example:

Early in the 2014 school year, a group of elementary school teachers met after school in Christchurch, New Zealand, to consider innovative literacy strategies to manage redevelopment and change in their classrooms. The city and surrounding suburbs were still reeling from the long-term effects of the February 2011 earthquake and after-shocks and more recent storms, immanent school closures, urban redevelopment and recent or planned reconstruction of 'superschools'. Superschools were first introduced to South Australia in 2010 when newly built, larger schools drawing students from a larger geographical area replaced smaller local primary or secondary schools. Four schools have been built to replace a number of smaller local primary or secondary schools. The New Zealand teachers were able to consider the documented work of experienced Australian teacher-researchers focusing on place as a resource for learning. The Australian research does not provide a blueprint for pedagogy but it does illustrate some pedagogies of possibility and in so doing is a positive catalyst for thinking about how things might be otherwise. The power of collaborative research, which is situated and illustrated richly with teacher and student artifacts, is that it can unleash alternative imaginings, practical optimism in the face of real despair—small beginnings of different conversations, new ways of knowing and more hopeful action.

This book features the work of some very talented and committed teachers, with whom we have worked, who have designed literacy curriculum around place and space that has engaged students and also provided high quality educational outcomes for them. We believe their work has much to offer other educators. This book is written for the teachers starting out, the people preparing to teach, the next generation of educators and literacy researchers who may not have wise, creative and inspiring teachers in their building or available to do collaborative research.

How This Book Is Organized

Chapter 1 introduces the key theories upon which the book is based, including the conceptual synergies between critical literacy, a relational conceptualization of space and place-conscious pedagogy. It explains how it is underpinned by principles of social justice or education in the interests of the disadvantaged and begins to demonstrate how critical literacies can be situated in place and why this might matter for schools in high poverty locales.

Chapter 2 expands notions of critical and inclusive literacies to incorporate the idea of pedagogies of belonging. Massey's (2005) notion of 'throwntogetherness' is appropriated as a helpful spatial metaphor for thinking about classrooms. Through a longitudinal study of the practices of one teacher, we demonstrate how working overtly with space and place can allow for the design and enactment of enabling pedagogies, where children are able to make their placed identities resources for learning literacy at school.

Chapter 3 argues that developing different knowledges about place can provide an important bridge for children to assemble academic literacies. In other words, learning in depth about local phenomenon (through various knowledge systems; for example, ecological, historical, architectural) provides the necessary field knowledge upon which complex reading and writing practices can be built. Learning to speak and write like scientists, for instance, requires time and purposeful learning opportunities to build key conceptual understandings. Proficiency in producing a scientific report is not only about a linguistic repertoire, but also about ways of thinking and knowing. This chapter contends that place is an ideal object for school students to study as a way of developing literacy.

Chapter 4 returns to the social and spatial nature of literacy. Rather than seeing the development of literate repertoires as an individual accomplishment, we assert that designing the classroom literacy curriculum as collective social practices affords different opportunities for children to work together as a collective. Once again, shared spaces and places can be pivotal in such activities. Through an examination of collaboratively produced student artifacts about space and place, we demonstrate the pedagogical possibilities of place to make new meanings together and imagine different ways of being.

Chapter 5 asks what might happen if we imagined school literacy as a collective accomplishment. Taking on board the particular challenges of standardized curriculum and high stakes assessment, we argue that attending to place now is more urgent than ever, both in terms of children's needs to identify with communities and environments and the needs of the planet to be cared for. While this chapter is a conclusion, it also wants to open out to future possibilities and, for this reason, hopeful accounts of current and emerging classroom practices are included. This is work in progress. Nevertheless, as the final chapter, a summary of key principles for enabling literacy pedagogical practices is provided.

References

Campano, G 2009, 'Teacher research as a collective struggle for humanization', in M. Cochran-Smith & S. Lytle (eds.), *Inquiry as stance: Practitioner research for the next generation*, Teachers College Press, New York and London, pp. 326–342.

Comber, B 1997, 'Literacy, poverty and schooling: Working against deficit equations', *English in Australia*, pp. 22–34, 119–120.

Comber, B 1998, 'Problematising 'background': (Re)constructing categories in educational research', *Australian Educational Researcher*, vol. 25, no. 3, pp. 1–21.

Comber, B, Badger, L, Barnett, J, Nixon, H & Pitt, J 2002, 'Literacy after the early years: A longitudinal study', *Australian Journal of Language and Literacy*, vol. 25, no. 2, pp. 9–23.

Comber, B & Hill, S 2000, 'Socio-economic disadvantage, literacy and social justice: Learning from longitudinal case study research', *Australian Educational Researcher*, vol. 27, no. 3, pp. 79–98.

Comber, B, Nixon, H, Ashmore, L, Loo, S & Cook, J 2006, 'Urban renewal from the inside out: Spatial and critical literacies in a low socioeconomic school community', *Mind, Culture and Activity*, vol. 13, no. 3, pp. 228–246.

Comber, B & Nixon, H with H. Grant and M. Wells 2012, 'Collaborative inquiries into literacy, place and identity in changing policy contexts: Implications for teacher development', in C. Day (ed.), *International handbook on teacher and school development*, Routledge, London, pp. 175–184.

Comber, B & Woods, B in press 2015, 'Literacy teacher research in high poverty schools: Why it matters', in J. Lampert & B. Burnett (eds.), *Teacher education for high poverty schools*, Springer, Dordrecht.

Freebody, P, Ludwig, C, Gunn, S, Dwyer, S, Freiberg, J, Forrest, T, . . . Wheeler, J 1995, *Everyday literacy practices in and out of schools in low socio-economic urban communities: A descriptive and interpretive research program: Executive summary*, Curriculum Corporation and the Department of Employment, Education and Training, Carlton, Victoria.

Gregory, E & Williams, A 2000, *City literacies: Learning to read across generations and cultures*, Routledge, London.

Griffiths, M 2009, 'Action research for/as/mindful of social justice', in S. Noffke & B. Somekh (eds.), *The SAGE handbook of educational action research*, SAGE, London, pp. 85–98.

Katz, C 2008, 'Bad elements: Katrina and the soured landscape of social reproduction', *Gender, Place and Culture*, vol. 15, no. 1, pp. 15–29.

Massey, D 2005, *For space*, SAGE, Los Angeles.

Reid, J & Green, B 2009, 'Researching (from) the standpoint of the practitioner', in B. Green (ed.), *Understanding and researching professional practice*, Sense, Rotterdam, pp. 165–183.

Thomson, P 2002, *Schooling the rust-belt kids: Making the difference in changing times*, Trentham Books, Stoke-on-Trent.

Zeni, J 2009, 'Ethics and the 'personal' in action research', in S. Noffke & B. Somekh (eds.), *The SAGE handbook of educational action research*, SAGE, London, pp. 255–266.

PERSONAL ACKNOWLEDGMENTS

The work that is reported in this book is the result of decades of collaboration. I want to acknowledge here just how much I have enjoyed learning from all of my literacy education colleagues, too many to mention. In particular, I want to thank my long-term fellow researchers and friends—Helen Nixon, Phil Cormack, Rosie Kerin, Bill Green, Jo-Anne Reid, Lyn Kerkham, Rob Hattam, Pat Thomson, Courtney Cazden, Jackie Marsh, Kathy Hall, Barbara Kamler, Allan Luke and Peter Freebody. With these folks in particular, I have learned about literacy, place, poverty, race, class, gender and pedagogy.

I thank my colleagues at Queensland University of Technology for their support and encouragement, in particular Annette Woods, Val Klenowski, Susan Danby, Kerry Mallan, Cathie Doherty and Wendy Patton. I thank also my fellow feminist institutional ethnographers, Dorothy Smith and Alison Griffith, from whom I learned so much about how people's work is organized and coordinated. Their insights make the work accomplished by teacher-researchers in ordinary schools even more extraordinary.

I also want to recognize just how much I have learned from working with teacher-researchers for over three decades. Once again, there are too many to list here. However, as will be clear, long-term collaborators are Marg Wells, Helen Grant and Ruth Trimboli. They are truly inspiring teachers who really understand what difference place, race, class and gender make in children's literacy learning trajectories.

Finally, this book would never have appeared at all without the patience, feedback and encouragement of Naomi Silverman, Vivian Vasquez, Hilary Janks, Jennifer Rowsell and Cynthia Lewis. These women have had faith in this project when I most needed it. A particular thanks to Anne Haas Dyson, who has always inspired me to look in classrooms and who agreed to write the foreword for this book.

The limits of this book are, of course, down to me.

Barbara Comber

PROJECT ACKNOWLEDGMENTS

This book draws from research conducted over three decades. The main sources of data and findings are taken from those projects listed here.

Urban Renewal from the Inside Out was a project funded by the Myer Foundation (http://www.myerfoundation.org.au/main.asp), a philanthropic foundation in Victoria, Australia. The Myer Foundation works to build a fair, just, creative and caring society by supporting initiatives that promote positive change in Australia, and in relation to its regional setting. Chief investigators are Barbara Comber, Helen Nixon, Stephen Loo and Jackie Cook. Louise Ashmore provided research assistance. The views expressed in this book are those of the author only.

Mandated Literacy Assessment and the Reorganisation of Teachers' Work is an Australian Research Council (ARC) Discovery Project (No. DP0986449) with the University of South Australia, Queensland University of Technology and Deakin University in Australia and York and Victoria Universities in Canada. The chief investigators are Barbara Comber, Phillip Cormack, Helen Nixon, Alex Kostogriz and Brenton Doecke. Partner investigators in Canada are Dorothy Smith and Alison Griffith. The views expressed in this book are those of the author only.

River Literacies is the plain language title for 'Literacy and the environment: A situated study of multimediated literacy, sustainability, local knowledges and educational change', an ARC Linkage Project (No. LP0455537) with the University of South Australia, Charles Sturt University, and The Primary English Teaching Association, as the industry partner. Chief researchers are Barbara Comber, Phil Cormack, Bill Green, Helen Nixon and Jo-Anne Reid. The views expressed in this book are those of the author only.

Investigating Literacy 4–9 was conducted by Helen Nixon, Rosie Kerin and Barbara Comber in 2009. It was funded by the Department of Education and

Children's Services, South Australia. The views expressed in this book are those of the author only.

New Literacy Demands in the Middle Years: Learning from design experiments was an ARC Linkage Project (No. LP0990692) with the Department of Education and Children's Services and the Australian Education Union, South Australia, conducted between 2009 and 2012. Chief investigators were Barbara Comber and Helen Nixon (Queensland University of Technology), Peter Freebody (University of Sydney) and Victoria Carrington (University of East Anglia). The research fellow was Anne-Marie Morgan (University of South Australia). The views expressed in this book are those of the author only.

Educational Leadership and Turnaround Literacy Pedagogies is an ARC Linkage Project (No. LP120100714) between the University of South Australia and the South Australian Department for Education and Child Development (DECD). The project was undertaken between 2012–2014. The chief investigators are Robert Hattam (University of South Australia), Barbara Comber (Queensland University of Technology) and Deb Hayes (University of Sydney). The research associate is Lyn Kerkham (University of South Australia). The views expressed in this book are those of the author only.

1
LITERACY, PEDAGOGY AND PLACE

Introduction

As educators, our work is to foster learning and to produce learners: people who know how to go about learning beyond the classroom, to transfer understandings, develop dispositions and practices that will allow them to pursue questions, solve problems and imagine different ways of doing things.

Theories of learning and teaching offer explanations about ways of improving processes and activities, and help us attend to what matters in learning for different children. Ultimately though, the explanatory power of theories matters less than what teachers actually do with theories in negotiating everyday classroom practices. How do theories play out in relationships with students, curriculum design and pedagogical activities?

- *How* do they see the children sitting before them, running on the playground, playing with classmates?
- Who do they see?
- In what ways do they *know* the community?
- What do they see as they travel to school?
- How do they understand the *place* in which they teach?
- *Why*, *where* and *how* and *when* do they communicate and relate to families?
- What do they understand about *these* children and their educational needs and aspirations?
- What *messages* do they send through their ways of speaking and their ways of organizing the classroom spaces?
- When they *design* the curriculum and the tasks for children to do, what underpins that work?

- When they assess, moment by moment, and later report on children's achievement in report cards, what guides their grades and choice of words?

These are the theories that count—those that frame the world and make it knowable, name populations, constitute students as assessable subjects and so on. Teaching is fundamentally theoretical and semiotic work because it depends on communication in one form or another for the work of learning to proceed. Teachers' educational theories are assembled over time from their own experiences of learning in and out of schools, their academic engagement in teacher education programs, and ultimately in situ learning on the job in classrooms and staffrooms, conferences and courses. Yet how teachers learn across their careers, and how they put such learning into practice, is beyond what we can usually track as educational researchers. This book draws from over three decades of collaborative research with classroom teachers to provide a unique time-scale on the productive relationships between literacy learning and place-conscious pedagogy, particularly in schools located in high poverty locales. The intention is to leave a little legacy of these cumulative inquiries to literacy educators and researchers by bringing emerging insights together in the pages of one volume.

Teaching is an intellectual profession where theories, with their associated vocabularies, are generated within classrooms and in collaboration with peers and academics. Teaching is also cultural and political work. The search for conceptual frameworks is continuous and cumulative, enabling us to understand and address the intransigent problems of education: the inequity of education outcomes, reproduction of class, gender and racial differences, and the alienation of marginalized students. Post 9/11 and the global financial crisis, there may be new forms of inequities that threaten democratic practices on which free public education is based. Economist Thomas Piketty warns that today's market economies contain:

> powerful forces of divergence, which are potentially threatening to democratic societies and to the values of social justice on which they are based.
> (Piketty, 2014, p. 571)

The potential risks associated with out-of-control economies, out-of-control climates and out-of-control conflicts means that we need to attend closely to questions about the relationships concerning people, poverty, places and education. While poverty is experienced by particular people living in particular places, it should not limit anyone's access to powerful and enabling pedagogies. Driven by commitments to social justice, yet needing the optimism that generates the energy to innovate and experiment, educators and researchers seek out opportunities and situations to think creatively and critically. Collectively, teachers and researchers have become gleaners of generative vocabularies, collecting words that hold out hope for the educational project: *cultural capital, virtual school bags, funds of knowledge, resourceful families, permeable curriculum, talk story, culturally responsive instruction, critical multiliteracies, place-conscious pedagogy* and so on. These key words signify complex theoretical ensembles, and it is teachers who grapple and experiment with these within their day-to day practices.

Selected key theories, such as those signaled in these keywords and phrases, that inform teachers' work for social justice through literacy pedagogy, are explored in this chapter. Acknowledging that there are gaps and omissions, readers are invited to reflect on these theories, and those that underpin their own approach to pedagogy and their interpretive repertoires, or those they witness in the work of colleagues who may inspire them. In the chapters that follow, interpretations of these same theories in action are illustrated through the exemplary curriculum planning and pedagogies of a number of teacher-researchers engaged in projects in urban and regional settings.

The conceptual synergies between theories of critical literacy, space and place-conscious pedagogy are particularly generative for designing and research-ing pedagogies of possibility in places of poverty. In brief, both share a set of common assumptions about learners, including:

- that all young people can make a positive contribution in the world
- that all can assemble semiotic repertoires for full participation
- that places and texts are socially and materially constructed, and could be made differently in the interests of particular social groups
- that representations of people and places are open to question
- that communication involves spatially located and material power relations.

How these assumptions underpin pedagogical practices and curriculum designs and the subsequent affordances for children's learning and classroom artifacts will become clear in the accounts of teachers' work in this book. In this chapter, and others to follow, a spatial lens is applied to literacy research, and illustrations of practice show how an explicit place and space focus can be incorporated into primary classroom critical literacy pedagogy. It often seems to be forgotten that teachers' work and children's learning is accomplished across time and space by particular people in specific places. Just as children's literacy learning involves rich engagement with material objects (Pahl & Rowsell, 2011), so too does the work of teachers. Because culturally inclusive curriculum and pedagogy attend to the embodied and situated nature of students' lives, this lends itself to making local places and communities the object of study and action.

First, a brief introduction to social justice and education is provided, as prin-ciples of social justice underpin all of what follows. Second, aspects of spatial theories that we have appropriated to understand social justice and the contingent and situated nature of critical literacies are outlined. Next, the chapter consid-ers how different approaches to critical literacy have emerged with particular attention to the emphasis of each approach. A discussion of place-conscious pedagogy, its synergies with critical literacy and relevance in the contemporary world concludes the menu of theories introduced here.

Social Justice and Literacy Education

Literary researchers working for social justice are committed to understanding how schools can begin to address some of the well-recorded and long-term unequal outcomes of schooling, especially as experienced by the children of the poor and working-class. A necessary, but not sufficient, starting point is to adopt an assets rather than a deficit model of learners and communities. According to this way of thinking, the linguistic and cultural resources of students and their families and wider communities can serve as important resources for teaching and learning (Ashton-Warner, 1963; Dyson, 1993; McNaughton, 2002; Moll, Amanti, Neff & Gonzalez, 1992). This means that the embodied and situated nature of students' lives is not forgotten or ignored. On the contrary, students' histories and lifeworlds are understood as material, productive resources in the design of curriculum and pedagogy.

Similarly, our work in literacy studies is framed by a concern with social justice and education and was very much influenced by Australian sociologist R. W. Connell. Connell wrote a number of seminal papers (Connell, 1994) and books (Connell, 1993; Connell, Ashenden, Kessler & Dowsett, 1982) during the 1980s and 1990s that theorized the complex relationships between poverty and education. Importantly, unlike some sociology, Connell maintained careful consideration towards the whole question of teachers' work (Connell, 1985) in schools located in working-class and low socio-economic communities. In other words, Connell was interested in the relationships between teachers, curriculum and class, and developed the notion of curricular justice, which identified three areas for examination in designing a just curriculum:

1. starting from the perspective and the interests of the least advantaged
2. the goal of full participation in a common schooling
3. the need to heed the historical production of inequality in education.

Connell argued the need to consider how curriculum privileges the knowledges and practices of advantaged groups within society and to think about ways in which it might be changed to consider knowledge from the standpoint of the poor and working-class, women, and culturally marginalized people. Connell wanted to interrogate the valued knowledge of school curriculum and consider other ways of knowing and ensure that all students were supported to learn a common curriculum, and were not subjected to the negative effects of high stakes testing and unequal access to learning.

Connell's emphasis on considering the standpoints of most disadvantaged groups of students (for example, Indigenous and poor students) in considering curriculum, assessment and pedagogical fairness influenced the conceptualization of critical literacy and how it was theorized with the teacher-researchers featured in this book (Comber, 1994). In this context, critical literacy, based on curricular justice, involved three key moves:

- repositioning students as researchers of language
- respecting student resistance and exploring minority culture constructions of literacy
- problematizing classroom and public texts (Comber, 1994, p. 661).

The assumptions are that all students could research how language works, that all cultural groups have significant contributions to make to our understandings of literate practices, and that all texts should be subject to question. Some teachers are able to work with students' diverse cultural capital, or what Thomson (2002) calls their 'virtual schoolbags', and within the context of the challenges and opportunities of the local environment (under construction, built and 'natural'). Such teachers are able to educationally exploit and build upon the diverse and contrastive resources of the classroom collective and the affordances of the place at that time.

Our work with early childhood teacher-researchers (Comber, Thomson & Wells, 2001; Luke, Comber & O'Brien, 1994; Vasquez, 2004) indicated that when teachers positioned children as researchers and incorporated their everyday ways of participating in talk around texts, even young children were able to take agency and produce texts which questioned the status-quo. In other words, they assembled the semiotic resources to argue for fairness. This early approach to critical literacy is mentioned here in order to indicate the kinds of conceptual resources that were shared with teacher-researchers whose work we draw upon later. The key point is that this formulation of 'critical literacy' was motivated by a desire to start from the standpoints of the most disadvantaged and to design curriculum which would ensure a just approach for the children of the poor.

In a recent discussion of critical literacy, Luke (2014, p. 21) also revisits the whole question of social justice and draws upon Fraser's (1997) conceptualization of justice: namely, as redistributive, recognitive and representative. Redistribution is akin to Janks' (2010) view of access, whereby all students would have opportunities to assemble valued literate practices, such as dominant academic genres. A recognitive aspect would value the literate practices marginalized and that minority youth bring to school, such as their home languages and capabilities with popular culture and vernacular literacies. Representative justice means promoting uses of literacy to fairly represent the standpoints of different groups. We can see in these versions of social justice through literacy education a strong commitment to giving students access to understandings and capabilities that matter here and now, even as educators work to change what counts in the interests of diverse and disadvantaged groups. This is a long-term project and the responsibility is beyond what can be expected of individual teachers and even schools.

The explanatory potential of theories of social justice has been challenged by the impact of globalization. As Fraser explains, it is now increasingly difficult to work out the 'who' and the 'how' of justice.

> [T]he forces which perpetuate injustice belong not to 'the space of places', but to 'the space of flows'. Not locatable within the jurisdiction of any actual or conceivable territorial state, they cannot be made answerable to claims of the state-territorial principle.
>
> *(Fraser, 2009, p. 23)*

These risks are associated with the interests of economic capital that are not bound by the rules and practices of the state. Hence, in considering social justice and critical literacy in contemporary times, we increasingly need to take space and place into account. Writing several decades ago, Michel Foucault (1984) speculated that:

> The present epoch will perhaps be above all the epoch of space. We are in the epoch of simultaneity: we are in the epoch of juxtaposition, the epoch of the near and far, of the side-by-side, of the dispersed.
>
> *(p. 1)*

He went on to explain that it is the relationships between sites which define them and that are crucial to the ways people live and the specific functions of places and institutions. Given the constitutive nature of space in organizing relations and trajectories of populations across places, theories of social justice and education must attend to the where and how, as well as the who and the what. And such theories need to be dynamic and account for continuous movement and the translocal organization of people's work and everyday lives.

Spatial Theories: The Affordances for Literacy Pedagogy

Over the past decade, educational scholars have noted a 'spatial turn' in educational studies (Fenwick, Edwards & Sawchuck, 2011; Green & Corbett, 2013; Gulson & Symes, 2007; Leander & Sheehy, 2004). These writers have argued that in the past, space and place in comparison to other factors, such as historic or economic, have not received adequate attention. Yet space, along with discourse, gender, class and race, is productive of subjectivities, relationships and practices. Recent theorizations of space in the social sciences emphasize this produced nature of space (Lefebvre, 1991; Soja, 1996). Schools are 'placed' institutions with architectural divisions and furniture within their spaces that contain and prescribe activities and bodily habitus for specified groups. Through particular spatial regimes, people are contained in schools in a Foucauldian sense (Foucault, 1979). Yet as Foucault also pointed out, people are 'freer than they feel'. Similarly, social geographer Doreen Massey has argued that because any place must be negotiated, when people with different trajectories arrive, there is the possibility for something new. It is this possibility that offers pedagogic potential. Because we are committed to reimagining schools as different kinds of places—both materially and metaphorically—the spatial turn holds out promise. We see this as aligned with Kress's observation (2003) about the 'stuff' of meaning-making—the physicality and materiality of the resources humans use for semiosis.

To return to the earlier theme of social justice, it is the relationships between people and places that produce poverty and inequities. Massey (2005, p. 157) points out that it is the 'success' of some places—'power-geometries'—such as large cities like London, that produce poverty and exclusion in other areas (see also Harvey, 2009). Massey's attention to how poverty is produced in particular places through political and economic decisions means that educational policy, including school reform, always needs to be understood within a broader material analysis of what is going on beyond the school, beyond the neighborhood, indeed beyond the state. What are the activities that produce underemployment and unemployment, pockets of extreme and persistent cross-generational disadvantage and the associated problems of ill health, crime and so on? Teachers' work, and what might be accomplished in schools, always needs to be considered in relationship to, and with proper attention to, all the priorities of everyday living. Yet on a positive note, Massey stresses that the unpredictable nature of places and the people who come to populate them creates the continuing need to negotiate something new. We cannot simply take places for granted as a backdrop to the real action. Places are constitutive of relations.

Schools, as material places located in particular geographic sites, with different social, cultural and physical histories and characteristics, are dynamic and subject to change. Schools are also places in the sense that they are purpose-built (or adapted) structures for educating children and youth. That is, they have the materiality of built environments that include purpose-built structures and landscaped grounds. These in turn are located within the distinctive built environments of local areas, regions and neighborhoods. However, schools are also social *spaces*; people enter into and leave and interact in the social spaces of schools and the areas around them. In these purpose-built places, people mix with diverse others and enter into social and educative relationships. For these reasons, the work of critical and social geographers is very generative for thinking about enabling pedagogies.

The typical experience of children in postindustrialized nations is attendance at a designated elementary school, often a neighborhood school. Yet international research suggests that the *neighborhood school* is being erased as the result of neoliberal educational forces (Lipman, 2011; Lupton, 2003; Sanchez, 2011). The physical and metaphorical significance of 'the school' as a particular kind of place captures people's imaginations, as evidenced by the popularity of the genre of school stories across ages and cultures, such as the Harry Potter phenomenon, which is built upon an 'imaginary materiality' (Cresswell, 2004, p. 7). The dominance of the school as a particular kind of built (or adapted) environment in a particular location leads us to take it for granted, yet children's (and teachers') everyday experience in school spaces is embodied, psychological, emotional and specific. The work of geographers may offer a fresh perspective in helping us to see the school as a particular kind of place, offering specific kinds of spaces: social, cultural, physical, semiotic and so on.

Massey's approach nudges us to think further about schools and classrooms as meeting places; places where people are forced to negotiate ways of being, relationships, ways of acting and indeed ways of knowing. Massey posits that place can be thought of as 'an ever-shifting constellation of trajectories', a constellation that in turn 'poses the question of our throwntogetherness' (Massey, 2005, p. 151). For those of us who work in educational institutions, this insight confronts us at the beginning of each new academic year as cohorts of students appear in our classrooms and lecture halls, each group unique and distinctive as a result of who comes to be there and the life histories they bring to our spaces of learning. Such a framing situates literacy teaching and learning within the socio-material world of schooling and acknowledges the political nature of the diverse, and placed, trajectories and histories that participants bring to school sites. It is also imbued with a sense of possibility, dynamism and movement. As Massey notes:

> Place . . . does change us . . ., not through some visceral belonging . . . but through the *practising* of place, the negotiating of intersecting trajectories; place as an arena where negotiation is forced upon us.
>
> *(Massey, 2005, p. 154)*

This is not chaos where nothing can be done; rather, there is the sense that something must be done. Negotiation is not feared as a problem, but instead is seen as an opportunity. This approach avoids the determinism that is so often associated with educational discourses about working-class or poor areas, and also the hopelessness wrought by some theories of globalization. Hence, being constituted as an 'urban school' or a 'disadvantaged school' can only be understood in relation to the wider economics and politics that produce poverty in particular areas of a city or in rural or regional places. This is relevant to literacy education in that understanding the politics of representation of people, a key objective of critical literacy, is contingent upon understanding the politics of places: the dynamic, situated and historical nature of relationships between people and places.

Massey (2005, p. 130) understands places as relational, changing, '*spatio-temporal events*' which require ongoing negotiation. She sees space 'as an arena for possibility' which 'leaves openings for something new' (Massey, 2005, p. 109). Educators can take responsibility for making school/places 'community spaces' in the sense that all spaces are socially negotiated. This approach allows a reimagining of the positive potential of schools, as institutions always under construction in terms of social relations which must be continuously negotiated, where different people are thrown together in a space located in a place and expected to not only to get on but also to learn together. Massey contests views of globalization which defend place as a victim, and which assume territorial traditions are unproblematic. She challenges versions of place that see it as a surface and ignore its ongoing dynamism. Her approach is to consider the specificities, and how local-global politics and power relations are constructed in different places and situations.

Foregrounding the politics and relational dynamics of place reminds us that spatial dimensions should not be overlooked when it comes to considerations of social justice, nor can environmental considerations be consigned to context. In addition, the whole question of who is educated where and with what effects is fundamental to thinking about poverty and education and ways in which educators might work for social justice. In terms of designing curriculum and pedagogy, spatial theories are an important additional theoretical resource for literacy researchers and educators to explore. It reminds us that the contexts in which pedagogical relationships are negotiated are not only social, cultural, political and historical, but also profoundly geographical and spatial. Lupton and Thrupp (2013) argue that in order to change schools for the better, educators need to understand school contexts in more complex and critical ways, less framed by middle-class individualized assumptions and more by more nuanced sociological understandings of local economies and conditions. School leaders' and teachers' understandings of their school contexts are fundamental to the ways in which they design interventions and programs in response to their student cohorts. The work of teaching and learning is accomplished by actual people in particular places (Smith, 2005); this is not to ignore what is achieved through and in virtual spaces but to understand those spaces are also ultimately materially constituted though people's actual and embodied doings with texts, somewhere. How textual practices can be made the object of study is the particular province of critical literacy—an evolving and contingent concept, as discussed below.

Critical Literacy

Critical literacy is an 'evolving repertoire of practices of analysis and interrogation which move between the micro features of texts and the macro conditions of institutions, focusing upon how relations of power work through these practices' (Comber, 2013, p. 589). More recent developments in critical literacy have noted the need to balance pedagogical attention not only to the analysis of texts but also to the design and production of texts by students themselves (Janks, 2010; Kamler, 2001; Luke, 2013). A full review of models of critical literacy is not included here; however, a brief outline of key concepts is included to provide a sense of how the spatial and place elements of critical literacy suggested in this book have emerged in relation to the work of key contributions.

The political nature and democratic potential of education is a central principle of 'critical' approaches to pedagogy inspired by Paolo Freire (Campano, Ghiso & Sanchez, 2013; Freire, 1972; Freire & Macedo, 1987; Luke, 2013; Souto-Manning, 2010). This work suggests that, despite seemingly intractable structural inequalities in a society, it is possible for oppressed social groups to become literate and politically active about issues that matter in their daily lives in particular places and that some of this political work can be achieved in educational institutions (Gregory & Williams, 2000; Janks, 2010; Vasquez, 2004; Woods, Dooley, Luke & Exley, 2014).

Critical approaches to pedagogy position students as active agents in their own learning and the social and political life of their schools and communities. Yet despite Freire's famous adage about proper literacy involving 'reading the word and the world', his focus was less on the materiality and sustainability of places and more on the political economy associated with workers' rights (Bowers, 2005). While the politics of people in particular places, and the politics of places themselves, have not been central in most versions of critical literacy, the impact of climate change and associated severe weather events, terrorism and globalization is beginning to turn attention to place and space, as futures cannot be taken for granted. Questions of sustainability of the planet are now firmly on the agenda (Gruenewald, 2008; Somerville, 2007).

Socio-cultural approaches to literacy demonstrate that literacy involves situated practice: that meanings are made in the historical and cultural contexts of situations. As such, literacy is always more than a skill, always more than an operational or functional matter. The critical dimension of literate practice focuses on the ways in which representations, namings, accounts, narratives and so on always work to serve particular interests (Green, 2012b; Luke & Freebody, 1997) and thereby position readers, hearers and viewers in specific ways. No texts are neutral; the discourses that shape them constitute particular versions of the world. Hence, critical literacy theorists point out that language practices are always invested with power relations. Texts work to impact on the actions and thoughts of readers, a fundamental principle of what has come to be known as critical literacy.

Critical literacy has a long history and has been informed by different traditions of scholarship, including Freire's critical pedagogy; approaches emerging from critical linguistics, especially critical discourse analysis (Fairclough, 1992; Janks, 2010); and those from feminist poststructuralist theory (Davies, 1993; Gilbert, 1991; Luke, 1991). While critical literacy defies definition (Comber, 2001; Luke, 2014), in school education, it is usually concerned with young people learning about how texts work for and against interests of different people. As we have discussed elsewhere, our work has been informed by these overlapping and mutually informing traditions of critical literacy (Comber, 2001; Comber & Nixon, 2014), as described below:

- 3D model of literacy pedagogy
- Four Resources model
- Multiliteracies pedagogy
- Janks' integrated model of critical literacy.

Originally, these approaches did not foreground the spatial dimensions of critical literacy; however, the researchers who developed these models have increasingly noted the need to attend to the politics of place in conceptualizing and enacting pedagogy.

The 3D Model of Literacy

Another way of conceptualizing literacy that also argues the necessity of paying attention to questions of agency and power has been proposed by Bill Green. Known as 'the 3D model', it provides 'a multidimensional framework for understanding and conceptualizing literacy practice and pedagogy' and argues that there are always three aspects or dimensions of literacy simultaneously in play: the operational, the cultural and the critical (Green, 1988; 2012b). That is, these three dimensions are conceptualized as always 'working together within a distinctive, textually mediated social-semiotic practice' (Green & Beavis, 2012, p. xvii).

In early formulations in the 1980s, the first dimension, the operational aspect, focused on the importance of the written language system and how adequately it is handled. Green's model in this regard emphasizes the importance of attending to the *technical* and *material* aspects of literacy. In the contemporary world, this means paying due attention not only to the technical and material aspects of *language*, but also to these aspects of *technology* because it has become very important as a means of communication (Green, 2012a).

The second dimension of the 3D model is the cultural dimension. This 'involves what may be called the meaning aspect of literacy' and refers to 'competency with regard to the meaning system' (Green, 2012b, p. 5). Green emphasizes the

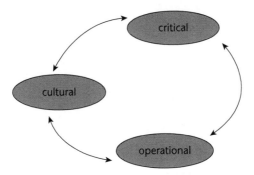

FIGURE 1.1 Green's 3D model (Durrant & Green, 2000)

need to take account of the fact that 'literacy acts and events are not only *context-specific* but also entail a specific *content*' (Green, 2012b, p. 5, original emphasis). An important point here is that learning language (and learning to use technology) is a form of enculturation into certain practices and systems of meaning. It enables people to become functioning participants in culture as they draw on language and technologies as resources for meaning. In the formalized school context, cultural learning involves (but is not confined to) subject-area learning: for example, learning how language is used in the meaning-system of mathematics, and how this is different from its use in history; or how technologies are used to make meaning in geography, and how this is different from their use and meaning in art and design. This conceptualization highlights how 'school learning is highly dependent on and closely related to literacy' (Green, 2012b, p. 6) and points to the close relationship between the operational and the cultural dimensions of subject-specific literacy, in which the development of specific reading, writing and technology competencies are developed in order to foster the enculturation of students into specific learning areas or domains of human knowledge as authorized by the school curriculum.

The third dimension of the 3D model of literacy is the critical dimension. The operational and cultural dimensions work to enculturate or socialize the learner into dominant forms of cultures (e.g. what counts as history, English literature and so on). However, like Freire (1972), Janks, Luke and others, Green also argues the need to give individuals access to 'the grounds for selection and the principles of interpretation' that underpin such meaning systems. That is, individuals need to understand that meaning systems are 'always selective and sectional; they represent particular interpretations and classifications' (Green, 2012b, p. 7). This is an important aspect of enabling 'individuals not simply to participate in the culture but also, in various ways, to transform and actively produce it' (Green, 2012b, p. 7).

Green has gone on to significantly develop his work in literacy studies and to pioneer interdisciplinary research and theorizing concerning literacy practices and place-conscious pedagogies (Green, 2013; Green & Corbett, 2013). In particular, he has drawn attention to 'rural' education, problematizing the term 'rural', but also acknowledging the specific challenges of sustaining high quality education and, indeed, literacy education in rural communities. Green (2013, p. 26) calls for more consideration of '*geographical* dimensions of context' in literacy studies.

The Four Resources Model

A seminal classroom approach to critical literacy, often known as the four roles of a reader—was developed by Allan Luke and Peter Freebody, and updated later as the Four Resources model of literacy (Luke & Freebody, 1997). Luke and Freebody's heuristic conceptualizes literacy as practices that involve participants

TABLE 1.1 Four Resources Model (Luke & Freebody, 1997)

Code Breaker	Text User
Meaning Maker	Text Analyst

in text analysis, text use, meaning-making and decoding, and argues that these are always socio-cultural and political practices (see Table 1.1).

People develop repertoires of textual practices orchestrated in specific contexts—everyday, academic, work and so on. Psychological models of literacy previously ignored how texts work politically. As Luke (2013, p. 144–146) recently argued, all models of critical literacy imagine 'a particular kind of cultural and political subject'. Referring to climate change and related ecological threats and changes, Luke points out that 'reality still looms large in everyday life'. For educators, the key question remains: *What are the real and material consequences of texts and discourses?* In our current work, we are shifting the lens towards the *real and material* in the sense of attending to the ways in which discourses and texts have effects in particular places. Similarly, Freebody (2013) has also recently added to the Four Resources model of literacy, to incorporate ways of dealing with discipline knowledge and ways of taking transformational action. Hence, there is wide recognition that critical literacy needs to be put to work in actual sites to tackle contemporary problems using complex emergent knowledge.

Multiliteracies Pedagogy

In the mid-1990s, at about the same time as the four roles of the reader approach was becoming known in Australia, Allan Luke was one of a small group of English-speaking literacy educators who met in the city of New London, New Hampshire, in the United States. Their objective was to consider and debate what definitions of literacy and models of literacy teaching would be appropriate to prepare young people for the rapidly changing world of the 20th and 21st centuries, which were so different from the 19th century, when mass schooling began in England and elsewhere. They argued that significant change had arisen from two important features of the contemporary world: local diversity and global connectedness.

As a result of their deliberations, the group published an influential paper in the *Harvard Educational Review* using the author name the New London Group (New London Group, 1996). This paper became known as the 'multiliteracies' manifesto, and the approach to literacy education it implies is generally referred to as 'multiliteracies'.

The multiliteracies approach to literacy education aims to address two main themes of social change. First, it acknowledges the fact that the world has become increasingly socially diverse. This means that literacy education has an important

TABLE 1.2 Multiliteracies Pedagogy (New London Group, 1996)

Multiliteracies Pedagogy
Situated Practice: *Connecting with experiences, familiar and new*
Overt Instruction *Conceptualising and teaching through naming and theoretical connections*
Critical Framing *Analyzing through critical and functional approaches*
Transformed Practice *Applying creatively and knowledgably according to context*

role to play in honoring and working with the multilingualism and multicultur-alism that comes with such diversity. Second, the multiliteracies approach takes account of the fact that, even though many communities might be culturally diverse, there is a significant amount of global connectedness via travel, the Internet and other forms of digital communications, whether this connected-ness takes place in minority languages or in a globalized language like English. So both local diversity and global connectedness exist side by side, and literacy is connected with both of these. At the same time, we now live in a world in which meaning is increasingly made not only with language, but in *multiple* modes and media. This means that literacy education has an important role to play in addressing the new significance of multimodality and multimedia in the changing landscape of communication (Cope & Kalantzis, 2000; Kress 2003; New London Group, 1996) (see Table 1.2).

Yet there is recognition also that in order to learn and to appropriate aca-demic discourses and design resources, students need to have a sense of belonging (Kalantzis & Cope, 2008) in their learning settings, and to the content and the ways of knowing being employed. Learner identity and place are irrevocably connected.

Janks' Integrated Model of Critical Literacy

Hilary Janks' (2010) integrated model of critical literacy is based on critical dis-course analysis (Fairclough, 1992; Janks, 1993). Unlike many approaches emphasiz-ing deconstruction only, Janks puts as much attention on the productive aspects of critical literacy in her focus on writing and multimodal design (see Table 1.3).

Janks' model argues that different approaches to critical literacy tend to fore-ground orientations which are, in fact, all necessary and interdependent. For example, some approaches, such as genre theory, tend to emphasize the dominant genres and discourses as the most important for students to acquire in order to access powerful literacies. Janks complicates this picture and argues that critical literacy educators need to consider questions of domination, diversity, design and access together.

TABLE 1.3 Janks' Model (Janks, 2010)

Domination without access	This maintains the exclusionary force of dominant discourses.
Domination without diversity	Domination without difference and diversity loses the ruptures that produce contestation and change.
Domination without design	The deconstruction of dominance, without reconstruction or design, removes human agency.
Access without domination	Access without a theory of domination leads to the naturalization of powerful discourses without an understanding of how these powerful forms came to be powerful.
Access without diversity	This fails to recognize that difference fundamentally affects pathways to access and involves issues of history, identity and value.
Access without design	This maintains and reifies dominant forms without considering how they can be transformed.
Diversity without domination	This leads to a celebration of diversity without any recognition that difference is structured in dominance and that not all discourses/genres/languages/literacies are equally powerful.
Diversity without access	Diversity without access to powerful forms of language ghettoizes students.
Diversity without design	Diversity provides the means, the ideas and the alternative perspectives for reconstruction and transformation. Without design, the potential that diversity offers is not realized.
Design without domination	Design, without an understanding of how dominant discourses/practices perpetuate themselves, runs the risk of an unconscious reproduction of these forms.
Design without access	Runs the risk of whatever is designed remaining on the margins.
Design without diversity	This privileges dominant forms and fails to use the design resources provided by difference.

Students do need access, but they need to be able to question dominant discourses and take up diverse positions to produce different and innovative textual designs. Janks' model allows for change to what counts as proper literacy without ignoring the power relations already invested in preferred academic and cultural forms. She asks:

> How does one provide access to dominant forms, while at the same time valuing and promoting the diverse languages and literacies of our students and in the broader society?
>
> *(Janks, 2010, p. 24)*

This question allows for both contestation and creativity, for humor and desire to be considered as teachers plan their curriculum. These affective attributes are especially important in primary school classrooms in high poverty contexts where children may have low motivation to attend school and to engage with the complex demands of schoolwork. As Janks (2010) points out, questions of language and identity go beyond rational logic. Learning English literacy practices needs to have some here-and-now payoffs in order for students to invest in the work they require. Making space and place the object of study affords opportunities for shared experiences and collective learning.

In a recent paper on why we need critical literacy now and into the future, Janks (2014) takes the case of bottled water and the textual practices associated with its production and marketization as a focus. As Janks notes, water has always been a precious resource and related in powerful ways to questions of poverty, people and place. Who has easy access to clean, fresh water can be seen as a marker of privilege and power. Janks illustrates powerfully that critical literacy—being able to interrogate words, images and numbers and whose interests they serve, along with the capacities to construct and argue for alterative views of reality—is essential in ensuring a just and sustainable world.

Critical Literacies in Place

Our collaborating teacher-researchers, located in culturally diverse and poor communities, have been driven by strong commitments to social justice and wanting to ensure that their students understand how power is exercised through language and other semiotic resources, so that they can both interrogate the way things are and also work towards equitable change, even while still in primary school (see also Comber, Thomson & Wells, 2001; O'Brien, 2001; Vasquez, 2004). It is the teachers' location in particular schools that has led us to think more about place as we explain further. It is also that we have sometimes found it easier to initiate discussions about critical literacy by starting with familiar and somewhat taken-for-granted everyday texts, rather than with academic material or even advertising.

At one level, making place the object of study in literacy education may involve noticing the ways in which everyday texts work in the world (Scollon & Scollon, 2003), and so this involves an examination of the semiotics of place. Scollon and Scollon, for example, in *Discourses in Place*, demonstrate that the meanings of signs and symbols is typically contingent on where they are located in time and place, and the communities of practice for whom they are designed. Their book provides an analysis of the semiotics of five street corners around the world: Hong Kong, Beijing, Washington DC, Vienna and Paris. Making sense of the semiotics of a place requires a great deal more than the ability to decode the orthography of the language in which signs are displayed. Scollon and Scollon (2003, p. 167) coined the term 'semiotic aggregate' to explain 'the intersection of the interaction order and the built environment in which social interaction takes place'.

The materiality of texts in terms of socio-spatial relationships has to date received little attention in educational research (but see Burnett, Merchant, Pahl & Rowsell, 2014; Nichols, Rowsell, Nixon & Rainbird, 2012; Pahl & Rowsell, 2010; Scollon & Scollon, 2003). In a project exploring how parents assemble information about early literacy, the research team used a similar approach to investigate the kinds of material educational resources accessed by different families in different places (Nichols et al., 2012).

Local Signage and Critical Literacy

In a project with teachers from a bio-region of Australia known as the Murray-Darling Basin, critical literacy was situated and connected to the textual practices of teachers' lives, rather than an abstract academic exercise. Exploring the affordances of discourses in place is often the first productive step in introducing teachers to critical literacy. Working explicitly with everyday texts from local neighborhoods and inviting teachers to collect and bring texts from their own places can illustrate the 'semiotic aggregate' of places. The figures below are representative samples of such texts.

The sign attached to the gate of this public playground in Adelaide, South Australia, serves a functional purpose. The 'keep out' message is clear; however, various possible sub-texts based on our wider cultural knowledge become possible. We can ask ourselves, who is the intended reader of such a message? Which adults do the council want to exclude? How would the placement of this sign work to exclude particular groups? Or, to have certain readers of this sign exclude themselves? This interest here is in texts that portray and attempt to authorize particular relationships between different

FIGURE 1.2 Public playground sign

people, spaces and places. When texts are located in a place, represent a place or people in and of a place, or direct the actions of people in a place, it is possible to recognize how they work relationally, ideologically and materially rather than just linguistically.

Just across from this playground is a public swimming center, also displaying signs concerned with entry. On this occasion, the purpose concerns wearing appropriate dress in this place (see Figure 1.3).

FIGURE 1.3 Sign at a local swimming center

Everyday texts such as the sign on the playground gate and the sign in the foyer of the pool attempt to exclude certain kinds of people from certain kinds of places. They also attempt to regulate behaviors according to social norms that are often implied rather than explicit. Through the imposition of a dress code, this sign attempts to exclude particular groups of youths—the kind who might prefer to wear denim and people who might think it is appropriate to wear nonspecific pool attire, such as underwear. Of course, these may include people for whom the purchase of pool attire is not affordable.

The semiotics of texts such as these demonstrate elements of critical discourse analysis and the framing of critical questions about texts. For example, the sign outside the swimming center might be interrogated by asking the following:

- What does the list of 'acceptable swim wear' have in common?
- Why might these products be listed as 'acceptable'?
- Why would 'rash vests' be worn at a swimming center?
- How localized is the term 'rash vests', and would some swimmers be confused by the term?
- What do the items listed as 'inappropriate swim wear' have in common?
- On what grounds could these items be considered 'inappropriate' for swimming?
- Who are the intended readers of this sign?
- For whom might this sign create a problem?
- For which pool attenders might this sign be unproblematic?

Local Media and Critical Literacy

Teachers engaging in the Murray-Darling Basin project were invited to examine such everyday texts, and then bring texts from their own places, and the research team began to collect texts that were telling stories about people and places in the broad bio-region in which project teachers were situated. This included a number of townships located along the largest river system in Australia. The page from the newspaper (Figure 1.4) was typical of the kinds of journalism to be found in the pages of local and regional newspapers and held significant potential for exploring issues of representation, politics and places.

Critical questions that could be explored by teachers and young learners living in this region include the following:

- How are different people inserted into place (on the river, on the farm)?
- How are people presented in relation to each other and in relation to the environment/places?
- What stories are told about places (and people) in tourist brochures, on Council web-sites, TV news and soaps, in the national and local press?
- Do certain situations, people and problems regularly appear?
- How and why might we question these?

FIGURE 1.4 *Murray Pioneer*, August 22, 2003, p. 10

A closer examination of the semiotics of the page, reproduced in Figure 1.4 and taken from a local newspaper, reveals competing narratives of rural life. In particular, we can see Foucault's insight—that discourses construct the objects of which they speak—at work in these texts. Different subjects are produced in these accounts. This page concerns the actions and activities of different groups of men and boys living in the riverland area: politicians, irrigators, sportsmen and Indigenous men. Although the groups represented presumably include women, since they include an agricultural association and youth groups, only men are reported and represented visually on this page. Further, the men and boys represented on this page in the different articles are shown as engaged in particular kinds of activities including politics, farming, music and sport. These are men taking action, having a say and having fun. The absence of women and girls is stark. Nevertheless, in other ways, these articles represent a positive framing of rural life with active involvement in democracy; environmental issues; engaging cultural practices, including Indigenous perspectives; healthy living and positive representations of the young. This is not always the case with rural places and people frequently being represented in troubling ways (Green & Corbett, 2013).

Countering Deficit Discourses of Places of Poverty

Like rural communities, people living in poverty are also often likely to be negatively represented in the media. Our horror at the pervasive representation of the poor as deserving blame and as dangerous has fueled our work in critical literacy and, more recently, place-conscious education. Recognizing the ways in which texts and places are constitutive means that we see texts such as the one reproduced in Figure 1.5 as dangerous.

For decades, we have witnessed the complicity of the press in producing deficit discourses that are tied to particular parts of the city and beyond. Rappaport (2000) describes such accounts as 'texts of terror'. Newspaper reports like these blame poor people for their poverty and create divisions between those who are judged and those who judge (see Figure 1.5). In contrast, 'optimistic narratives' that contest dominant cultural narratives and reposition children and teachers as positive agents, as people who can make a difference, are crucial (Rappaport, 2000).

> We cannot remake the world through schooling but we can instantiate a vision through pedagogy that creates in microcosm a transformed set of relationships and possibilities for social futures; a vision that is lived in schools.
>
> *(Cope & Kalantzis, 2000, p. 19)*

Research has proven time and again that constructing counter-stories is fundamental work for teachers who work in such communities. In the words of Maxine Greene (1988):

> When people cannot name alternatives, imagine a better state of things, share with others a project of change, they are likely to remain anchored or submerged.
>
> *(p. 9)*

The goal of this book is to demonstrate ways in which teachers can enable children growing up in poverty not only 'to imagine a better state of things', but to learn how to represent their designs for better places and how to take action to improve the places and spaces they inhabit.

Residents living in fear of the neighbours

By State Political Reporter
GREG KELTON

STAR Group police officers are regularly called to handle disruptive Housing Trust tenants in the western suburbs, a parliamentary inquiry has been told.

Many of the people involved have been described as "clearly mentally ill".

Figures given to the Statutory Authorities Review Committee inquiry into the trust show that so far this financial year there have been 1077 complaints about disruptive tenants.

The trust figures show 30 per cent of complaints were lodged against single males and 21 per cent against single females, with only 4 per cent of complaints involving couples with children.

Labor MP John Rau, who gave evidence to the committee, said the worst area for complaints was The

Parks, with Kilburn and Blair Athol also having a high rate of complaints.

Mr Rau, whose electorate of Enfield takes in the areas affected, said he was talking about people who were "not fully in connection with what is going on on this planet".

He said some trust residents were living in "genuine fear and distress".

Many of the people caus-

ing this fear wound up coming to the attention of police.

"We have STAR (Group) officers brought out quite regularly to ... calm these characters down and take them away (for) ... treatment," he said.

"And all too often these people are returning back to the same environment and the cycle repeats itself."

The committee was told:

PEOPLE were afraid to come forward and complain, fearing being victimised.

THE trust has residents under surveillance.

ONE tenant had two people turn up at his door and say they were taking over his room. The tenant had to sleep on the lounge room floor and was given "pocket money" from his benefit payments.

"RATBAGS" who understand the system very well "finesse their position of abusing a neighbour to the nth degree and pull back a millimetre before they are

booted out". Mr Rau said no one should seriously suggest an 80-year-old woman who had "20-year-old yobbos living next door who are making her life a misery" was going to paint a big target on herself by applying to have the trouble makers removed.

Trust general manager Malcolm Downie said only a very small minority of trust tenants disrupted the lives of their neighbours.

Eviction was pursued only when necessary but so far this financial year there had been eight evictions.

TROUBLE IN THE TRUST
Number of complaints since July this year

Type of problem	Number of complaints	% of total
Abusive behaviour	177	16%
Alleged illegal activity	44	4
Communal property dispute	31	3
Noise and nuisance	716	66
Physical assault	27	3
Threatening behaviour	82	8
TOTAL	1077	100

DISTURBANCE: STAR Group police officers are called in regularly to calm down neighbourly strife in trust areas.

Mental health spending up 128pc

By ANDREA STYLIANOU

FEDERAL funding for mental health increased by $643 million between 1993 and 2002, a national report shows.

This increase of 128 per cent was well above the 40 per cent increase by state governments in the same period, parliamentary secretary for Health and Ageing, Christopher Pyne, said.

The National Mental Health Report 2004 showed that the Federal Government was responsible for more than one third of total spending on mental health.

State Health Minister Lea Stevens said the 1993-2002 period referred to was when the Liberal Party was in government.

"We know that mental health services were run down for a decade under the previous State Liberal government, and that has now been confirmed by one of their own senior federal colleagues," she said.

"In contrast, since the Rann Government came to office we have boosted annual spending on mental health services by $20 million a year – that's a 15 per cent increase in two years." She also pointed to an $80 million capital works program.

FIGURE 1.5 *The Advertiser*, November 30, 2004, p. 13

Permission Provided, November 10, 2014

Space and Place

In this book, space is defined as relational and as always under construction. Massey (2005, p. 9) imagines 'space as a simultaneity of stories so far'. Space is inherently social and political. For Massey, it is a 'sphere of possibility'. Classrooms (virtual and actual) are spaces that must be negotiated by participants.

While space and place were key elements in ethnographic studies of literacy practices, which considered power and difference (for example, Lewis, 2001; Moje, 2000), these concepts were not foregrounded in conceptualizations of classroom approaches to critical literacy. Leander and Sheehy's 2004 edited collection gave a new prominence to spatial approaches to literacy education research. Conceptualizing space as a 'social product and process' and informed by theorists such as Foucault, Lefebvre and Soja, they encouraged literacy researchers to complicate their understandings of the real, or contexts, and of identities to foreground how people navigate discursive relationships in time and across spaces. This understanding of space also informs teachers whose work is showcased here. They position their students as people who need to negotiate learner identities and classroom relations. They do not fear this dynamism, the openness of space.

Massey writes of 'the event of place', in that she does not see place as predetermined, unchanging, or as coherent or populated by homogeneous populations. School would seem to be the epitome of place in terms of it being a site of trajectories and negotiation. That does not mean that schools are not located somewhere, nor that they have no history, nor that their communities are not distinctive. And each school is always located in relation to other schools, other communities, other neighborhoods. These relations are neither accidental nor innocent, and to some degree, they are subject to change. This book is based upon the work of educators in school communities who embrace a complex but open and relational sense of place. That is, the situatedness of their school in its economic, social, cultural, historical, political and ecological environment matters to their curriculum and pedagogical program. These educators also understand that students' sense of belonging affects the extent to which they can embrace and negotiate the school as a learning space.

To conclude this chapter, our own experience of the spatial turn as it impacted our work is briefly introduced.

Urban Renewal and Representations of Space

After undertaking collaborative research on critical literacy with educators in the culturally diverse and poor areas of Adelaide for several decades, we understood in a very embodied sense that poverty is organized spatially. Schools were often located in pockets of poverty. Government housing policies seeking to change these patterns were being implemented in the nineties and continue today, often badged as 'urban renewal'. In one school, a teacher and a school principal were interested in the affordances of 'urban renewal'—a major redevelopment that was occurring in the neighborhoods surrounding the school—for children's learning and had been working with the developers so that children could have some input into the design of new parks and playgrounds. In discussion, we decided to bid for some funding that would allow students, teachers and community members to become involved in the design and building of a new garden on the school grounds. The story of this project is told in some detail later in this book. The key point here is that as literacy researchers, we began to realize the gaps in our knowledge. We did not know how to think about space and place except as context. However, as we began to work with architects, we engaged with spatial theorists such as Lefebvre (1991) and Soja (1996) and social geographers like Massey. The parallels between critical literacy and the work of cultural geographers were engrossing.

The productive nature of both space and discourse in terms of subjectivity is critical for thinking about designing curriculum for social justice. Words matter. Places matter. Spaces matter. Young people could be invited and supported to imagine, and argue for, design and make material changes to their spaces and places—school buildings, structures, grounds, and the use of particular spaces by different groups. Young people can engage in *spatial practices*, in *representations of space*, and in thinking about *representational spaces*, when the school site is understood as material, relational and constructed, and as such, subject to reconstruction. Such an approach echoes Lefebvre's (1991) call for the possibility of working out of 'counter-plans' and 'counter-projects', in his view, 'a gauge of 'real' democracy' (pp. 419–420).

In the context of urban renewal, houses were boarded up and demolished, new local parks were designed and built. The combination of the old, the deteriorating and the new in the surrounding built environment was impacting children's lives and teachers' work. It was more than context. It was more than socio-economic background. Experienced teacher-researcher, Marg Wells, whose work we explore in detail later, already understood children's need to have a sense of belonging in the classroom, the school and the neighborhood. Her work as an early childhood teacher led to a discovery of the potential of making place the object of study and of children learning to understand, rather than fear, change.

It was the context of urban renewal in an area of high poverty and cultural diversity that pushed the team to look at the materiality of the local environment and the school with new eyes and to recognize the need to think beyond language. Our research team expanded to include an architecture colleague, Stephen Loo, and we, along with the teachers and students, had opportunities to explore the affordances of spatial literacies by undergoing the processes by which architects negotiate, design and plan a built environment—in this case, a school garden. And along with journalism colleague Jackie Cook, the team explored the potential of children documenting change in the built environment in a range of media.

Critical Literacy, Environmental Sustainability and the Food Bowl of Australia

The second element of our spatial turn came with the request to undertake collaborative research with the national association for primary English teaching. The association had already embarked on a partnership with the government department responsible for administering the river system, in a particular connected bio-region often referred to as the food bowl of Australia, that aimed to improve children's understandings about environmental sustainability. The department funded the publication of high quality annual anthologies of regional primary schools' writing and art about their 'special places' (see Comber, Nixon & Reid, 2007; Cormack, Green & Reid, 2007; Kerkham & Comber, 2013).

The association had invited the team to collaborate with them to research teachers' knowledge of environmental communication, including more critical approaches to studying the environment, and to design a program of teacher learning to build teachers' knowledge about environmental sustainability, critical literacy and the potential of various new digital media for learning, communication and representing knowledge. The research team then began by building their own knowledge, particularly in the area of place-conscious pedagogy.

The work of David Gruenewald (2003a; 2003b) was a useful starting point. Gruenewald had already identified the potential of critical pedagogy and place-based pedagogy learning from each other and blending to form a 'critical pedagogy of place' (2003a, p. 9) to 'ground place-based education in a pedagogy that is socially and ecologically critical'. He wants place-based education to take on sociological insights about the politics of people and places, and critical pedagogy to recognize that experience has a geographical dimension. He summarizes:

> A critical pedagogy of place aims to (a) identify, recover, and create material spaces and places that teach us how to live well in our total environments (reinhabitation); and (b) identify and change ways of thinking that injure and exploit other people and places (decolonization).
>
> (Gruenewald, 2003a, p. 9)

Importantly, Gruenewald (2008, p. 137) imagines ways of 'grounding culturally-responsive teaching in geographical diversity'. Putting these concepts together has been important to the teacher-researchers in the projects documented in later chapters because they teach particular groups of children, from many different places, a sense of cultural heritage and sometimes experiences in places in which they have lived or now live. Such children also learn within the built and social environs of schools that are situated in places that are also changing in complex ways.

Advocates of 'place-conscious education' argue that the education of citizens might have some direct bearing on the well-being of the social and ecological places people actually inhabit. Gruenewald (2008) suggests some key questions learners can explore with reference to their places:

> What is happening here? What happened here? What should happen here? What needs to be transformed, conserved, restored, or created in this place?
>
> *(p. 149)*

Critical approaches to place-conscious education explicitly position students to develop the skills and dispositions required to research issues that matter to the eco-social sustainability of local communities and built and natural environments. In terms of literacy education, more recent studies have begun to look at the ways in which such insights might play out in curriculum and pedagogy (Green & Corbett, 2013).

Putting Theory to Work: Enabling Pedagogies

Cochran-Smith and Lytle (2009) remind us of the necessarily 'local' nature of teaching:

> Even as teaching becomes more and more public, it remains at its heart, *radically local*—embedded in the immediate relationships of students and teachers, shaped by the cultures of schools and communities, and connected to the experiences and biographies of individuals and groups.
>
> *(p. 10)*

In these times of 'policy borrowing' (Lingard, 2010), where translocal discursive practices of standardization and performativity travel into the very hearts and minds of teachers (Ball, 2003), accounts of local accomplishments of critical pedagogies are urgently needed to nourish an increasingly fatigued and alienated profession and to retrieve an educational imagination. Infusing literacy and education research with understandings about place and space from other disciplines provides additional tools to support the fight for high quality free public education in schools serving poor communities. If teachers cannot imagine their pedagogy beyond the next high stakes literacy test, the education community becomes increasingly impoverished. It is time to mobilize teacher knowledge, developed and practiced locally though it may be, and recruit their expertise in the cause of curriculum design that is genuinely inclusive and simultaneously challenging. The rhetoric about ensuring 'excellence and equity' needs to be more than policy-speak.

Despite the force of globalization, educators and researchers need to resist storylines which take a deterministic stance and leave no hope. A number of educational theorists (Apple, 2010; Green, 2013) and social geographers (Massey, 2005) point to the importance of hope in imagining and taking action for justice. Soja (2010, p. 21) argues in the context of globalization that 'justice' is increasingly a 'mobilizing concept' for a widening range of organizations and groups with the escalation of economic and ecological disasters and imminent threats such as terrorism, war, poverty and genocide.

Young people can and should learn to work for justice from the outset of schooling and they can best begin this work by considering the everyday micro-politics of the classroom and the playground, the school and the neighborhood. This does not suggest that the local should be romanticized in any way (Nespor, 2008) or that young people be confined to the local in their inquiries. Rather, with an education infused with justice, where space and place are valued and explored, children can learn to be properly literate critical citizens.

In this book, the term *enabling pedagogies* is used to describe a family of approaches that position *all students as capable learners*, including critical literacy and place-conscious pedagogy. In literacy education, such approaches are based on the insights of researchers who have considered students' everyday and out-of-school local knowledges, and cultural and language practices, as having value in the context of their formal education. Such approaches stress that community 'funds of knowledge' (Moll et al., 1992) can be brought into academic learning spaces and that, indeed, these are resources that can be embedded in a 'permeable curriculum' (Dyson, 1993).

A distinctive feature of the work discussed in this book is the long-term scale of the collaborative inquiry between university researchers and classroom teachers working in culturally diverse and high poverty contexts. This ongoing collaboration has already continued for over three decades. While there is a core trio of teacher-researchers—Marg Wells, Helen Grant and Ruth Trimboli—many others have joined us along the way. The extent of the time means that we have been able to develop truly reciprocal research relationships, experiment and coproduce knowledge beyond the life of a single project. Mostly, the teachers have invited their students to join them as coresearchers.

Because they assume that all children are competent learners, their approaches are inclusive. Teachers who design and accomplish enabling pedagogies communicate high expectations for learning in the ways they design tasks, the way they speak to learners, the ways they speak about learners and the ways in which they go into the public domain with student performances and products. In their classrooms, children assemble complex repertoires of literate practices. These children become confident communicators, media-savvy multimodal text producers and engaged citizens. Understanding how places and spaces are designed to work is key to young people engaging with the community, connecting with the environment and becoming advocates and actors for the rights of people and places. Schools can become active sites of practice for student citizens.

The next chapter showcases the way one teacher, Marg Wells, designs her literacy curriculum to exploit the affordances of space and place and negotiates pedagogies of belonging.

References

Apple, M W 2010, *Global crises, social justice, and education*, Routledge, New York.

Ashton-Warner, S 1963, *Teacher*, Simon & Schuster, New York.

Ball, S 2003, 'The teacher's soul and the terrors of performativity', *Journal of Educational Policy*, vol. 18, no. 2, pp. 215–228.

Bowers, C 2005, *The false promise of constructivist theories of learning: A global and ecological critique*, Peter Lang, New York.

Burnett, C, Merchant, G, Pahl, K & Rowsell, J 2014, 'The (im)materiality of literacy: The significance of subjectivity to new literacies research', *Discourse: Studies in the Cultural Politics of Education*, vol. 35, no. 1, pp. 90–103.

Campano, G, Ghiso, M & Sanchez, L 2013, 'Nobody knows the . . . amount of a person: elementary students critiquing dehumanization through organic critical literacies', *Research in the Teaching of English*, vol. 48, no. 1, pp. 98–125.

Cochran-Smith, M & Lytle, S 2009, *Inquiry as stance: Practitioner research for the next generation*, Teachers College Press, New York & London.

Comber, B 1994, 'Critical literacy: An introduction to Australian debates and perspectives', *Journal of Curriculum Studies*, vol. 26, no. 6, pp. 655–668.

Comber, B 2001, 'Critical literacies and local action: Teacher knowledge and a 'new' research agenda', in B. Comber & A. Simpson (eds.), *Negotiating critical literacies in classrooms*, Lawrence Erlbaum, Mahwah, New Jersey, pp. 271–282.

Comber, B 2013, 'Critical literacy in the early years: emergence and sustenance in an age of accountability', in J. Larson & J. Marsh (eds.), *Handbook of research in early childhood literacy*, SAGE/Paul Chapman, London, pp. 587–601.

Comber, B & Nixon, H 2014, 'Critical literacy across the curriculum: Learning to read, question and re-write designs', in J. Zacher Pandya & J. Ávila (eds.), *Moving critical literacies forward: A new look at praxis across contexts*, Routledge, London & New York, pp. 83–97.

Comber, B, Nixon, H & Reid, J (eds.) 2007, *Literacies in place: Teaching environmental communications*, Primary English Teaching Association, Newtown, New South Wales.

Comber, B, Thomson, P with M. Wells 2001, 'Critical literacy finds a 'place': Writing and social action in a neighborhood school', *Elementary School Journal*, vol. 101, no. 4, pp. 451–464.

Connell, R W 1985, *Teachers' work*, Allen & Unwin, Sydney.

Connell, R W 1993, *Schools and social justice*, Our Schools/Our Selves Education Foundation, Toronto.

Connell, R W 1994, 'Poverty and education', *Harvard Educational Review*, vol. 64, no. 2, pp. 125–149.

Connell, R W, Ashenden, D J, Kessler, S & Dowsett, G W 1982, *Making the difference: Schools, families and social division*, Allen & Unwin, Sydney.

Cope, B & Kalantzis, M (eds.) 2000, *Multiliteracies: Literacy learning and the design of social futures*, Macmillan, Melbourne, Victoria.

Cormack, P, Green, B & Reid, J 2007, 'Children's understanding of place: Discursive constructions of the environment in children's writing and artwork about the Murray-Darling Basin', in F. Vanclay, M. Higgins & A. Blackshaw (eds.), *Senses of place: Exploring concepts and expressions of place through different senses and lenses*, National Museum of Australia Press, Canberra, pp. 57–75.

Cresswell, D 2004, *Place: A short introduction*, Blackwell, Oxford.

Davies, B 1993, *Shards of glass: Children reading and writing beyond gendered identities*, Hampton Press, Cresskill, New Jersey.

Durrant, C & Green, B 2000, 'Literacy and the new technologies in school education: Meeting the l(IT)eracy challenge?', *Australian Journal of Language and Literacy*, vol. 23, no. 2, pp. 89–108.

Dyson, A H 1993, *Social worlds of children learning to write in an urban primary school*, Teachers College Press, New York.

Fairclough, N (ed.) 1992, *Critical language awareness*, Longman, London.

Fenwick, T, Edwards, R & Sawchuk, P 2011, *Emerging approaches to educational research: Tracing the socio-material*, Routledge, London.

Foucault, M 1979, *Discipline and punish: The birth of the prison* (A. Sheridan, Trans.), Peregrine, London.

Foucault, M 1984, 'Of other spaces: Utopias and heterotopias' (J. Miskowiec, Trans.), *Architecture/Mouvement/Continuité*, October.

Fraser, N 1997, *Justice interruptus: Critical reflections on the 'postsocialist' condition*, Routledge, New York.

Fraser, N 2009, *Scales of justice: Reimagining political space in a globalising world*, Columbia University Press, New York.

Freebody, P 2013, 'Knowledge about language, literacy and literature in the teaching and learning of English', in A. Simpson & S. White with P. Freebody & B. Comber, *Language, literacy & literature*, Oxford University Press, South Melbourne, pp. 3–25.

Freire, P 1972, *Pedagogy of the oppressed*, Seabury, New York.

Freire, P & Macedo, D 1987, *Literacy: Reading the word and the world*, Bergin & Garvey, Westport, Connecticut.

Gilbert, P 1991, *Fashioning the feminine: Girls, popular culture, and schooling*, Allen & Unwin, Sydney, NSW.

Green, B 1988, 'Subject-specific literacy and school learning: A focus on writing', *Australian Journal of Education*, vol. 32, no. 2, pp. 156–179.

Green, B 2012a, 'Into the fourth dimension? Literacy, pedagogy and the future', in B. Green and C. Beavis (eds.), *Literacy in 3D: An integrated perspective in theory and practice,* ACER Press, Camberwell, Victoria, pp. 174–187.

Green, B 2012b, 'Subject-specific literacy and schooling: a revised account', in B. Green and C. Beavis (eds.), *Literacy in 3D: An integrated perspective in theory and practice*, ACER Press, Camberwell, Victoria, pp. 2–21.

Green, B 2013, 'Literacy, rurality, education: A partial mapping', in B. Green and M. Corbett (eds.), *Rethinking rural literacies: Transnational perspectives*, Palgrave McMillan, New York, pp. 17–34.

Green, B & Beavis, C 2012, 'Introduction', in B. Green and C. Beavis (eds.), *Literacy in 3D: An integrated perspective in theory and practice*, ACER Press, Camberwell, Victoria, pp. xv–xxiv.

Green, B & Corbett, M (eds.) 2013, *Rethinking rural literacies: Transnational perspectives*, Palgrave McMillan, New York.

Greene, M 1988, *The dialectic of freedom*, Teachers College Press, New York & London.

Gregory, E & Williams, A 2000, *City literacies: Learning to read across generations and cultures*, Routledge, London.

Gruenewald, D 2003a, 'The best of both worlds: A critical pedagogy of place', *Educational Researcher*, vol. 32, no. 4, pp. 3–12.

Gruenewald, D 2003b, 'Foundations of place: A multidisciplinary framework for place-conscious education', *American Educational Research Journal*, vol. 40, no. 3, pp. 619–654.

Gruenewald, D 2008, 'Place-based education: Grounding culturally responsive teaching in geographical diversity', in D. Gruenewald & D. Smith (eds.), *Place-based education in the global age: Local diversity*, Lawrence Erlbaum and Associates, New York & London, pp. 137–153.

Gulson, K & Symes, C (eds.) 2007, *Spatial theories of education: Policy and geography matters*, Routledge, New York & London.

Harvey, D 2009, *Social justice and the city*, University of Georgia Press, Georgia.

Janks, H 1993, *Language and identity*, Hodder & Stoughton/Wits University Press, Johannesburg.

Janks, H 2010, *Literacy and power*, Routledge, New York.

Janks, H 2014, 'Critical literacy's ongoing importance for education', *Journal of Adolescent and Adult Literacy*, vol. 57, no. 5, pp. 349–356.

Kalantzis, M & Cope, B 2008, *New learning: Elements of a science of learning*, Cambridge University Press, Cambridge.

Kamler, B 2001, *Relocating the personal: A critical writing pedagogy*, State University of New York Press, Albany, New York.

Kerkham, L & Comber, B 2013, 'Literacy, place-based pedagogies and social justice', in B. Green & M. Corbett (eds.), *Rethinking rural literacies: transnational perspectives*, Palgrave McMillan, New York, pp. 197–218.

Kress, G 2003, *Literacy in the new media age*, Routledge/Falmer, London & New York.

Leander, K & Sheehy, M 2004, *Spatializing literacy research*, Peter Lang, New York.

Lefebvre, H 1991, *The production of space* (D. Nicholson-Smith, Trans.), Blackwell, Oxford.

Lewis, C 2001, *Literacy practices as social acts: Power, status, and cultural norms in the classroom*, Lawrence Erlbaum, Mahwah, New Jersey.

Lingard, R 2010, 'Policy borrowing, policy learning: Testing times in Australian schooling', *Critical studies in education*, vol. 51, no. 2, pp. 129–147.

Lipman, P 2011, *The new political economy of urban education: Neoliberalism, race and the right to the city*, Routledge, New York & London.

Luke, A 2013, 'Regrounding critical literacy: representation, facts and reality', in M. Hawkins (ed.), *Framing languages and literacies: Socially situated views and perspectives*, Routledge, New York, pp. 136–148.

Luke, A 2014, 'Defining critical literacy', in J. Zacher Pandya & J. Ávila (eds.), *Moving critical literacies forward: A new look at praxis across contexts*, Routledge, London & New York, pp. 19–31.

Luke, A, Comber, B & O'Brien, J 1994, 'Making community texts objects of study', *Australian Journal of Language and Literacy*, vol. 17, no. 2, pp. 139–149.

Luke, A & Freebody, P 1997, 'The social practices of reading', in S. Muspratt, A. Luke & P. Freebody (eds.), *Constructing critical literacies: Teaching and learning textual practices*, Allen & Unwin, St Leonards, NSW, pp. 195–225.

Luke, C 1991, 'On reading the child: A feminist poststructuralist perspectives', *Australian Journal of Language and Literacy*, vol. 14, no. 2, pp. 109–116.

Lupton, R 2003, *Poverty Street: The dynamics of neighbourhood decline and renewal*, Policy Press, Bristol.

Lupton, R & Thrupp, M 2013, 'Headteachers' readings of and responses to disadvantaged contexts: Evidence from English primary schools', *British Educational Research Journal*, vol. 39, no. 4. pp. 769–788.

Massey, D 2005, *For space*, SAGE, London.

McNaughton, S 2002, *Meeting of minds*, Learning Media, Wellington, New Zealand.

Moje, E 2000, 'Critical issues: Circles of kinship, friendship, position, and power: Examining the community in community-based literacy research', *Journal of Literacy Research*, vol. 32, no. 1, pp. 77–112.

Moll, L C, Amanti, C, Neff, D & Gonzalez, N 1992, 'Funds of knowledge for teaching: Using a qualitative approach to connect homes and classrooms', *Theory and Practice*, vol. 31, no. 2, pp. 132–141.

Nespor, J 2008, 'Education and place: a review essay', *Educational Theory*, vol. 58, no. 4, pp. 475–489.

New London Group 1996, 'A pedagogy of multiliteracies: Designing social futures', *Harvard Educational Review*, vol. 66, no. 1, pp. 60–92.

Nichols, S, Rowsell, J, Nixon, H & Rainbird, S 2012, *Resourcing early learners: New networks, new actors*, Routledge, New York.

O'Brien, J 2001, 'Children reading critically: A local history', in B. Comber & A. Simpson (eds.), *Negotiating critical literacies in classrooms*, Lawrence Erlbaum Associates, Mahwah, New Jersey, pp. 37–54.

Pahl, K & Rowsell, J 2010, *Artifactual literacies: Every object tells a story*, Teachers College Press, New York.

Pahl, K & Rowsell, J 2011, 'Artifactual critical literacy: A new perspective for literacy education', *Berkeley Review of Education*, vol. 2, no. 2, pp. 129–151.

Piketty, T 2014, *Capital in the twenty-first century* (A. Goldhammer, Trans.), Belknap Press of Harvard University Press, Cambridge, Massachusetts.

Rappaport, J 2000, 'Community narratives: Tales of terror and joy', *American Journal of Community Psychology*, vol. 28, no. 1, pp. 1–24.

Sanchez, L 2011, 'Building on young children's cultural histories through placemaking in the classroom', *Contemporary Issues in Early Childhood*, vol. 12, no. 4, pp. 332–342.

Scollon, R & Scollon S W 2003, *Discourses in place: Language in the material world*, Routledge, London & New York.

Smith, D E 2005, *Institutional ethnography: A sociology for people*, AltaMira Press, Lanham.

Soja, E 1996, *Thirdspace: Journeys to Los Angeles and other real-and imagined places*, Blackwell, Oxford.

Soja, E 2010, 'Spatialising the urban, Part 1', *City analysis of urban trends, culture, theory, policy, action*, vol. 14, no. 6, pp. 629–635.

Somerville, M 2007, 'Place literacies', *Australian Journal of Language and Literacy*, vol. 30, no. 2, pp. 149–164.

Souto-Manning, M 2010, *Freire, teaching and learning*, Peter Lang, New York.

Thomson, P 2002, *Schooling the rustbelt kids: Making the difference in changing times*, Allen and Unwin, Sydney, Australia.

Vasquez, V 2004, *Negotiating critical literacies with young children*, Lawrence Erlbaum Associates, Mahwah, New Jersey & London.

Woods, A, Dooley, K, Luke, A & Exley, B 2014, 'School leadership, literacy and social justice: The place of local school curriculum planning and reform', in I. Bogotch & C. Shields (eds.), *International handbook of educational leadership and social (in)justice*, Springer, New York, pp. 509–520.

2

CRITICAL AND INCLUSIVE LITERACIES

Pedagogies of Belonging

Introduction

Classrooms are meeting places where children and teachers are 'thrown together' (Massey, 2005) and must negotiate spaces of learning. If we accept this view, then it is the teacher's role to design and enact pedagogies of belonging in order to include all children as active and equal participants. In order to support the development of learner identities, teachers may develop and draw on a range of pedagogies that not only create 'belonging' but also enable students to assemble complex literate repertoires in the process.

Making place, such as the classroom, home and neighborhood, the object of study can position all children as researchers. This can enable learning and allow access to rich resources for representation. When teachers focus on the social relationships of classroom spaces and help all learners to achieve a sense of belonging, children can work together to achieve the kind of justice that Connell (1993) imagined, where everyone is responsible for ensuring that everyone learns. The motivation in such classrooms is not based on competitive individualism but on collective responsibility.

Within this chapter, collaborative inquiries and ethnographies of teachers' work in high poverty contexts illustrate how the design of literacy curriculum and pedagogies can enable all children to engage in complex learning. Some of this collaboration with teachers has been sustained over several decades, and has enabled the documentation and dissemination of innovative and inclusive curriculum designs. When teachers are curriculum designers (Kress & van Leeuwen, 2001), rather than recipients of someone else's curriculum design, there is potential for them to work with the affordances of their own locales and communities.

As Pahl and Rowsell (2010) point out, children's literacy learning is done with artifacts and objects which come to have meaning and significance; teachers' work is similarly organized in, around and with material objects, frequently semiotic. Their semiotic work occurs across multiple modes and media: through verbal interactions (Cazden, 2001), written texts, embodied actions, classroom furniture arrangements, broadcast messages, semi-permanent signage and the more ephemeral posting of students' work. When this work is intentional, selective and designed by teachers, it gives a sense of teachers' inventiveness.

Pedagogy is discursive work (Comber, 2006), but it also involves the production of broader semiotic and socio-material relationships. Teachers use signs and symbols to teach students how to read all manner of texts. Teachers design and produce most of the signage on walls, blackboards and white boards, the hand-outs or worksheets they assign children, the books they choose, the oral and written feedback, and the orchestration of particular events and practices (Lewis, 2001). These all rely heavily on words and images. Its accomplishment is contingent on the extent to which teachers can communicate to students the intended tasks, activities and processes, which involves the use and invention of pedagogic texts and artifacts, the organization of people in space and time, and the employment of various tools and media.

To illustrate, we refer to a recent lesson with Grade 2 students. The teacher had made a series of illustrated and magnetized word cards to illustrate the different sounds that make 'er'; that is, 'ir' and 'ur' and even 'ear'. She had made enough so that each child could take a turn to identify a word and put it in the right list on the magnetic white board, words such as 'hung**er**' and 'laught**er**' in the 'er' column, 'return' in the 'ur' column and so on. The teacher had made these artifacts in her own time using her own resources. She gathered the students near her on the carpet to do the initial work together, and nominated individual children to select a word to read. She helped them to use picture and letter cues and sometimes gesture to hint at what the word might be. After all the words had been placed in the correct column and each child had taken a turn, she sent the students back to their groups with a list of all the words on a sheet of paper. They were to cut out the words, make their own columns and stick the words into their English scrapbook and illustrate them. They could help each other if needed, but a final product was to be put together by each child. Basically, they needed to replicate the task the teacher had just completed with them. When the children returned to their desks, she rehearsed with them again exactly what the task was, and what they would need—scissors, glue, scrapbook, word list and so on.

The task itself is ordinary enough, but in terms of teachers' work, this particular lesson begins to indicate at a surface level the complexity of orchestrating material objects, classroom discourse, teacher and child placement and movement in the room, as well as rules around participation for different stages of the lesson. Every literacy lesson involves more or less of these elements—focal texts (comprehension and production), teacher talk (often question and answer around the focal text and management of children's behaviors, bodies and work), children's talk, work and movements, the use of material objects, tools, technologies and furniture and so on. All of this must be done in a relatively small space and each child must be able to see and hear the key messages. Teachers' work needs to be understood as discursive, semiotic and requiring socio-material organization.

Something of the complexity and materiality of teachers' work is captured in the 8T's concept, coined by Comber and Cormack (1995) (see Table 2.1). Originally developed from Comber's early ethnographic research in a school in a high poverty locale, this heuristic summarized literacy teachers' work in terms of topics, techniques, tasks, talk, texts, tools, tests, territories. Later time and technologies were added. These are sites of practice in which the curriculum is negotiated.

TABLE 2.1 The Eight T's of Literacy Programming (Comber & Cormack, 1995)

Topics	What issues or content are selected to be studied/learned about from broad themes and units of work down to the detail of writing topics?
	Typical broad topics include: teddy bears, toys, natural disasters, zoo animals. Minor topics might be what gets talked about at 'morning news', what students write about.
Techniques	The teaching approaches used when working with individuals, groups and whole classes.
	Traditional, genre, whole language, critical approaches including shared book, activity time, reading aloud, direct instruction, text analysis; look-cover-write-check.
Tasks	What students have to do.
	Writing stories; answering teacher questions about shared text; reading aloud to parent or helper; drawing pictures about a book.
Talk	The sort of talk that occurs (directions, about texts, informal, formal), who gets to talk in what settings, who does most of the talking and who the least. What questions get asked about texts?
	Teacher talk about work, behavior, what is required, explanations of tasks, praise, discipline to individuals, groups, class. Student official and unofficial opportunities for talk, what they can talk about, the sort of analysis that gets conducted.
Texts	The sorts of texts that are available, in what quantities, when and where.
	The texts the teacher selects to use, read aloud or as examples, the texts students must produce. Texts that are most popular or least popular.
Tools	What students get to use when doing literacy related tasks.
	Tools range from basic technology of pencils, pens, scissors and staplers through to computers and lap tops. Who gets to use what, e.g. 'pen licenses'
Tests	What the teacher uses to make judgments about students' progress or ability or competence.
	Assessment strategies such as retellings, running records, spelling tests. The child's performance in talking to teacher or to the class.
Territories	Where students work on literacy, where they can go and under what conditions, where they cannot go; how they must behave in these places.
	Time spent on carpet close to the teacher, activities at desks; parts of the room, school, community that are used; directions given—'make a circle', 'form a line'.

In this book, teacher curriculum designs, and their associated artifacts that enable learner engagement, are explored and illustrated. In these accounts, depictions are provided of the context for the work and the kinds of tasks teachers put together. The teachers featured here have in various ways explored theory to inform their practice. This strength-based theoretical work offers alternatives to deficit discourses by evoking vocabularies of possibility. Concepts, such as those listed here, have proven to be generative:

- funds of knowledge (Moll, Amanti, Neff & Gonzalez, 1992)
- permeable curriculum (Dyson, 1993)
- culturally responsive pedagogy (Au, 2009; McNaughton, 2002)
- critical literacy (Janks, 1993; 2010; Luke & Freebody, 1997)
- multiliteracies (New London Group, 1996).

These theoretical frames engage teachers in thinking about the relationships between knowledge and power, language and identity, and family and schooling.

Ultimately, beyond these abstract concepts, teachers grapple with finding ways of enacting social justice in everyday classroom contexts. The challenge is to design activities that engage and enable meaningful learning over time, and allow particular students in particular places to develop durable learner dispositions and educational trajectories. Such activities are not simply about what 'works' in a generic sense, but rather are innovative and successful designs of curriculum and pedagogy. They are principled, responsive and customized to the specific needs of the students within particular contexts.

In this chapter, pedagogies of belonging, designed by one teacher to underpin classroom literacy learning activities, are described and discussed. Her approach is illustrated through a consideration of the artifacts produced by a student in her Grade 3/4 class. However, it is not only students who generate artifacts. Teachers also build a body of work over their careers, trialing, experimenting, exploring, watching and listening to their students, and we have learned with them and from them over several decades.

The temporal and organic nature of teacher expertise and practice, built over time and in different school communities, is illustrated here in the design of pedagogies of belonging through which children assemble complex repertoires of literate practices. Recently, the temporal nature of literacy teaching and learning has received increased attention as researchers consider time-scales as a key ingredient in educational practices (Compton-Lilly, 2013; Rowsell & Sefton-Green, 2015). Before exploring this complex, sustained and situated work of teachers over time, it is necessary to explore 'belonging', and how it relates to understandings of community and place.

Theories of Community, Place and Belonging

There is no need to romanticize place, or to privilege the local, or to assume that people automatically feel a sense of belonging where they live, or that communities are united or homogeneous. Massey's (2005) work makes it very clear that assumptions about particular people feeling a sense of belonging in specific places are often unfounded. Critiques of place-based pedagogy indicate that 'the local' (Ferrare & Apple, 2010; Nespor, 2008) needs to be understood relationally. Yet a sense of belonging is critical to children developing and sustaining a learner identity at school. Educators who understand that 'place' is culturally negotiated, embodied and material (Sánchez, 2011; Somerville, 2011), and that 'belonging spaces' cannot be taken for granted, have made important steps in negotiating pedagogies of belonging and designing curriculum that makes the relational nature of place and space the object of study.

For instance, Somerville (2011, p. 72) reports a long-term involvement of primary school children and teachers with a wetland in the Latrobe Valley in Victoria documenting children's learning in an 'enabling pedagogy of place'. She describes the children's bodily engagement in the place listening for, observing, photographing and audio-recording frogs, testing the water quality, and noting the weather and light conditions. The children post their moment-by-moment observations on a website which connects them with a partner school in Oregon. Their teachers invite local Indigenous elders to share their knowledge of the place with children in various forms; those stories and lessons are also recorded and posted. Reflecting on this learning, Somerville writes of the 'significance of that moment [where the student represents her experiences of observing and listening to the frog] being communicated globally on a website dispersed through time and space'. She concludes:

> The moment itself is so significant in a pedagogy of place because it is about knowing place in all its intimate detail as a place of inhabitation, a place where we dwell with other creatures. It is only knowing place in its ever changing forms through thousands of such intimate moments that we can read a place, that we can know how the place is going, how well it is. It is only through knowing a place in those thousands of intimate moments that we can learn to love a place and have knowledge to be able to take care of it.
>
> *(Somerville, 2011, pp. 74–75)*

It is this kind of bodily engagement in learning about a place that forms deep knowledge and deep connections with a place and its communities—human and nonhuman (see also Comber, Nixon & Reid, 2007). Somerville (2013) has also written extensively about what she has learned about place-conscious pedagogy through her ongoing shared inquiries and journeys with Aboriginal people. Clearly, there is much more to learn from Indigenous communities that have maintained a connection with learning through country.

In a very different place-making context, Lenny Sánchez (2011) describes his collaborative research with a teacher in Harlem in an area undergoing urban renewal. Working with second grade students, the teacher investigated the histories of previous occupants of this neighborhood—African American musicians, writers and intellectuals of the early 20th century—key people in the Harlem Renaissance. The teacher seized the opportunity presented by a mandated assignment to produce a biography of a famous American to engage in what Sánchez sees as a place-making project.

The teacher redefined the task as a shared inquiry about key actors in the Harlem Renaissance and engaged in research through viewing relevant films, listening to music, and learning from community members. Their research was frequently multimodal and embodied, as some children learned about opera singers, dancers and other performers (see also Kinloch, 2010). The class-wide project involved inquiry into the rich cultural histories of the people of the place where the school was situated. In one sense, the teacher and students reclaim the place of their heritage and its cultural legacies. When the investigations were completed, the collective results were presented to parents, peers and the wider school community—with children performing songs and dance routines, reading soliloquies, poems and so on.

These two brief examples illustrate how place-conscious pedagogies can help children to explore aspects of the dynamic histories and the ecologies of particular locales and to form a collective sense of understanding and connection. Rather than place as a static context or a backdrop, we can see how these embodied and situated inquiries, about the dynamics of people in places, enable learners to discover and belong.

Ultimately, young people are educated in particular places, by particular teachers, in specific classrooms, and with particular cohorts of peers, which may produce both constraints and affordances for learning. How they come to be in that classroom, in that school, in that area, and at that time is contingent upon family histories and needs in terms of education, work, housing, affiliations and so on. These also relate to regional, national and global economies and political conditions. While the term *community* conjures up a sense of belonging and neighborhood, it may mask significant diversity, and indeed conflict, within an area. It also obscures the fact that places are not limited to the local, but are always operating and constituting themselves in relation to others; they can be seen as 'glocal', as globalization impacts mobility, communications, work and leisure (Livingstone, 2008). Indeed, educators and school leaders, in particular, may need to think about their work as translocal or glocal (Brooks & Normore, 2010).

Moje's (2000) seminal discussion of the term 'community' in community-based literacy research highlights a series of problems. Moje (2000) asks:

> What does it mean to study community? . . . Am I entering a defined geographical space? A psychological space?
>
> *(p. 78)*

She reviewed her understandings of one student's potential memberships in various communities: gang, ethnic, neighborhood, adolescent, religious and so on. Finding them all wanting, Moje identifies slippage in the use of the term 'community'. She goes on to explain that neighborhoods and groups are heterogeneous, mobile and changing; hence, community can never be a stable category.

Her literature review indicates that community is not well defined, and is used interchangeably with terms such as neighborhood, culture, social-class groups, families, youth organizations, church, or intake area of a school. Further, she suggests that literacy researchers need to recognize transnational and mobile communities and ways in which people use new communication devices to sustain a sense of community across borders. Moje's work is relevant here because teachers often use the word 'community' to refer to the catchment area from which children come—that is, the places they live. The teachers whose work we draw upon in this book understood place as material, but also as social, dynamic and negotiated. It is material in the sense of its physicality—the dimensions of the classroom, the location of a hall, the absence or presence of a drama space, access to the editing suite, the number and size of the children in the room and so on. Recent innovative work in literacy studies has explored the ways in which new technologies complicate the relationships between the human, virtual and material worlds (Burnett, Merchant, Pahl & Rowsell, 2013). Here, we foreground the materiality of place—the changing built and natural environments and the 'stuff' (Miller, 2010) therein—as objects of study and representation.

Massey's (2003) problematization of static and nonrelational version of place is very helpful in this regard.

> We know we cannot understand the character of any place without setting it in the context of its relations with the world beyond. This is place as meeting place: different stories coming together and, to one degree or another, becoming entangled. This is the thrown-togetherness of physical proximity. And it is even more marked in an age of globalisation. 'A global sense of place.'
>
> *(Massey, 2003)*

Following Moje and Massey, schools can be understood as places in a sociospatial sense, as sites of opportunity for students who are simultaneously members of multiple communities. Indeed, schools and classrooms are meeting places, sometimes for children and teachers from many different communities, on a small but significant scale.

The appeal of Massey's approach is that her framings of place emphasize contingency, specificity, and the possibility of negotiating something new. This seems a productive way to think about schools in this globalizing era of increasingly mobile and culturally diverse populations. Clearly, this is an optimistic approach to thinking about globalization, especially in the face of research that indicates that the poor continue to receive the negative side effects of globalization (Katz, 2008; Lupton, 2003). The poor, for example, are less likely to be mobile by choice, and poor youth may be particularly constrained (Dillabough & Kennelly, 2010). Communities can 'fall apart' due to the lack of paid work in the area (Bauman, 1998). Yet, as educators, we need to work in a determined fashion against predetermined educational consequences of global crises (Apple, 2010). Going to school should be a learning experience for all children and all have a right to belong. With respect to designing critical and inclusive literacy curriculum, a multicultural, multilingual student population allows teachers and learners to use the resources of the remembered, the material here-and-now, and the imagined and projected to make and contest meanings.

> Place . . . does change us . . ., not through some visceral belonging . . . but through the *practising* of place, the negotiating of intersecting trajectories; place as an arena where negotiation is forced upon us.
>
> *(Massey, 2005, p. 154)*

Schooling in every sense forces the practicing of place, or the embodied negotiation of different people with different interests and histories in often crowded and nonpreferred spaces for extended periods of time (see Dixon, 2011). Nevertheless, it is crucial for children's learning that they do find ways of belonging at school.

Multiliteracies theorists Kalantzis and Cope (2008) argue that belonging strongly relates to learning:

> In order to learn, the learner has to feel that learning is for them. The learner has to feel a sense of belonging in the content, and that they belong to the community, or learning setting; they have to feel at home with that kind of learning, or way of getting to know the world. . . . The learning has to include them, and if they are learning in a formal educational setting such as a school, they also have to feel a sense of belonging in that social and institutional context. The more a learner 'belongs' in all these senses, the more they are likely to learn.
>
> *(p. 233)*

Increasingly, culturally diverse student cohorts are becoming the norm rather than the exception. Children may or may not know each other outside of the classroom, and they may or may not share cultural, linguistic or ethnic heritage.

Classrooms are sites of 'throwntogetherness' (Massey, 2005) par excellence, and it cannot be taken for granted that participants will simply get on. Belonging is fundamental to teachers' classroom management and students' learning and well-being. This chapter coins the phrase 'pedagogies of belonging' to draw attention to ways of designing and negotiating curriculum that are driven by the social goal (along with academic aims) of belonging.

Classroom Belonging: A Longitudinal Case Study of a Teacher's Enabling Pedagogy

Long-Term Collaborative Research Relationships

For over twenty years, teacher Marg Wells has worked in two elementary schools located in the western suburbs of Adelaide in an area referred to as 'Westwood' since it became the site of Australia's largest urban renewal project over ten years ago. Over that extended period, there has been close collaboration between Wells and academic researchers as critical friends, collaborative researchers and, in some ways, educational journalists, ready to capture projects and initiatives as they have evolved (see Table 2.2).

The table represents an extended and ongoing journey from studies of:

- student literacy development in schools situated in disadvantaged communities
- information technology, literacy and educational disadvantage
- critical literacy, social action and children's representations of place
- urban renewal from the inside-out and critical literacy
- redesigning school learning in high poverty communities
- conducting classroom design-based experiments on place-conscious pedagogy.

TABLE 2.2 Collaborative Research Projects Involving Marg Wells Since 1995

Years	Projects
2010–2012	*New Literacy Demands in the Middle Years*, Australian Research Council Linkage Project, B. Comber, P. Freebody, H. Nixon, V. Carrington and A. Morgan.
2009	*Investigating Literacy*, Department of Education and Children's Services SA, H. Nixon, B. Comber and R. Kerin.
2006	*Critical Literacy: Redesigning school learning in high poverty communities*, Australian Literacy Educators' Association, B. Comber and H. Nixon.
2003	*Urban Renewal from the Inside Out: Students and community involvement in redesigning and reconstructing school spaces in a poor neighbourhood*, Myer Foundation, B. Comber, H. Nixon, J. Cook and S. Loo.
2001	*Critical Literacy, Social Action and Children's Representation of 'Place'*, Divisional Research Grant, Education, Arts and Social Sciences, University of South Australia, B. Comber, P. Thomson and H. Janks.
1998–2000	*Socio-economically Disadvantaged Students and the Development of Literacies in School: A longitudinal study*, Strategic partnerships with Industry, Australian Research Council, B. Comber, L. Badger, J. Barnett and H. Nixon.
1997	*Socio-economically Disadvantaged Students and the Acquisition of School Literacies (Pilot No. 2)*, Department of Education, Employment and Training SA, B. Comber, L. Badger, J. Barnett and H. Nixon.
1995	*Literacy Acquisition and the Construction of Success and Failure in Disadvantaged Schools*, University of South Australia Research Development Grant, B. Comber, L. Badger, J. Barnett and H. Nixon.

In such projects, including those captured in this chapter, 'place' is a key resource in developing critical and inclusive literacies and enabling pedagogies. Collaborative projects such as these have often required funding and this is achieved most often in university and school partnerships. Such commitment between research partners within and beyond schools are propelled by a belief that more complex accounts of teachers' work are needed in order to avoid reductive minimalist versions of literacy pedagogy, which are becoming the norm or, worse still, mandated for teachers in poor communities (Comber, 2012; Ravitch, 2010; Sahlberg, 2011).

Wells and Her School Community

The school communities where Wells teaches are home to culturally diverse communities, including Aboriginal families, recently arrived immigrants and refugees, and first- and second-generation immigrant families. For example, Wells' current school includes Aboriginal, Sudanese, Chinese, Macedonian, Vietnamese, Cambodian and Anglo-Australian students. In 2012, 60% of students were classified as speaking English as an additional language (ACARA, 'My School', 2014). Wells generally teaches children in the first five years of schooling and her classroom includes children from linguistically and culturally diverse families.

Due to her reputation for engaging all children, she is often allocated students with behavioral difficulties. She works very hard at the beginning of every school year to establish a classroom in which respectful and harmonious social relationships are the norm, and there is a climate in which practices of inquiry and the challenges and joys of learning are foregrounded. To help her achieve this, Wells explicitly designs her first classroom program around the concept of 'belonging', believing in the importance of developing a sense of well-being and readiness to participate in the classroom as a collective learning community.

Wells aims to establish an ethos in which children negotiate shared ways of acting and interacting in class. Concepts such as bullying, justice, well-being, respect, goal-setting and friendship are explored through various activities which she describes as being 'all under the umbrella of belonging'. That is, Wells emphasizes the importance of establishing a classroom culture and space that makes children feel as though they 'belong'. She writes that for the first weeks of the school year:

> Setting up the room, labeling drawers, displaying artwork and presented work, playing get-to-know-you games, establishing routines and procedures, working together and making the room/space 'ours' is the main focus. Feeling like students 'belong' in the classroom is fundamental to being successful; to feel valued, accepted, part of a group (and yet an individual as well), comfortable, safe and able to take risks is necessary for learning to flourish.

Many of the learning activities Wells devises, such as completing simple sentences like 'I feel I belong when . . .' are unremarkable in themselves. What is significant, however, is what Wells does with children's responses to these provocations, and how she explicitly and cumulatively shares their ideas and feelings and builds on them. Her goal is to foster an ethos of collaboration and participation in a learning community. A similar approach has also been described by Edelsky (2006) as 'hookin' 'em in at the start of school', recognizing that there is a great deal of explicit work to be done by teachers and children at the beginning of a new school year to learn to belong to the classroom community. This work is not only about regulation of behaviors but also about the possibilities for something new as children get to know each other, play and learn together. Our long collaboration with Wells has demonstrated her consistent approach to high expectations, community-engaged and place-centered curriculum. The negotiation of classroom norms is not an end in itself, but done in the service of being able to look further afield, to move beyond the bounds of the classroom into the yard, the streets and the local area. The students need to come together as a reliable collective in order to be able to go out together to engage in research and community activities. Forming trusting and respectful relationships is necessary in order for Wells to take risks and push ahead with complex learning outside of the 'safety' of the classroom walls.

A central feature of Wells' pedagogical approach is that she explicitly positions her students as the bearers of rich cultural and linguistic resources that can become shared resources for learning. She also positions them as inquirers, as researchers who want to build deep knowledge about things that matter to them and to their communities and who wish to share with others. As a teacher, she believes that a focus on the places and environments that surround her classroom of learners in their daily lives provides a productive starting point for fostering knowledge of and respect for others and enhances their understanding of difference and sense of belonging.

Walking Together Through the Neighborhood

Where We Come From

Wells has found that conducting 'neighborhood walks' early in the year is a learning activity that reaps many rewards. Children prepare by poring over published maps that show local streets, parks and shopping areas. They plan which streets they will visit on their forays into the neighborhood on different days and the route they will take. They discuss who lives where, how they get to and from school, and other places they regularly visit. They also learn academically valued skills such as how to read and draw maps.

As they participate in the walks, each child becomes a lively and engaged expert as they approach the places they know and they talk animatedly about

FIGURE 2.1 Class-constructed map of the local neighborhood

things that matter to them about their neighborhood: their house, their family, their pets and so on. This activity, which foregrounds both differences and similarities among the children and houses and buildings in the area, is an inclusive practice that helps establish an ethos of understanding of and respect for social and cultural difference and, importantly, develops spatial literacies.

Over the years, Wells has explored a range of ways to document their neighborhood walks and to use this experience as a jumping off point to inquiry. One year, she and the class constructed a huge map (see Figure 2.1).

While out walking, children's houses and places of interest were photographed and attached to the map. This activity helped children to learn to relate their everyday places to the semiotic representations of places and introduced problems of scale and direction. Another time, children used KidPix software to make modifications to photographs of their houses and added cartoon characters. Another year, the walks were documented using PowerPoint and, another time, iMovie, and so on. On another occasion, the walks led to the production of a class authored and illustrated alphabet book titled *A Is for Arndale* (Comber & Nixon, 2008; Janks & Comber, 2006), and this text is featured in Chapter 4.

Wells is always alert to the affordances of different modes and media for different groups of children and is as equally at home with 'traditional school literacies' as she is with 'multiliteracies'. However, her pedagogical goal is to bring children's individual contributions and representations of people in places into a whole-class text to record the diversity of that experience. Whatever the medium used to record the neighborhood walks, Wells made one consistent observation: as children approached their own houses, they came to the front of the walking group and proudly pointed out their homes and features they loved—whether it was a pet, a tree, a swing, or something of personal value—and to which they wished to draw their teacher's and classmates' attention. Sometimes family members were at home and came outside to greet the class. The children began to situate themselves relationally to each other, to local institutions and businesses, and to consider their in-and-out-of-school lives and local knowledges, and those of their peers, as part of their shared resources for learning.

The embodied nature of the class walking together through the neighborhood around the school is important to Wells' approach and helps these children to locate themselves and their peers as members of the local communities living in specific material circumstances, as we discuss later. It also allows Wells to walk with children, to walk together their routes to school, to experience the local area from the children's perspective (see also Jones, 2006). However, sometimes it may not be feasible or safe for teachers and children to undertake such walks. Severe weather, crime rates, traffic and so on may mean that teachers are unable or reluctant to undertake neighborhood walks. Children may not live locally or may be bussed to school from various remote locales. Or, children may get to school by public transport or be ferried by parents and caregivers.

Nevertheless, such 'walks' can be undertaken in different ways. They can be done virtually using open sources, such as Google Earth or through the use of cameras and mobile devices to record significant neighborhood and home places and spaces, and students might then subsequently bringing these artifacts to the classroom. Where the school neighborhood is distributed, such as in rural or remote communities, the use of cameras can be pivotal as students and teachers bring in selected images and artifacts of their 'home places'. Teachers in rural communities have long known the power of bringing local/home inquiries into the collective space of the classroom (see Comber, Nixon & Reid, 2007; Green & Corbett, 2013).

Making the Neighborhood the Object of Study

Wells routinely integrates the use of pen-and-paper surveys to record items of interest such as what children like about certain environments, what they would like to see more of, or know more about. Even very young children have a clear idea of what they would like to see done differently in their local environments. For example, the following activity (see Figure 2.2) was completed after the students had made notes about matters of concern that arose during their walks, such as trees being removed. If we look at the way the teacher designed the task, we can see how she positions students as both critical and creative.

FIGURE 2.2 Three wishes: More trees, more ponds, more parks

Students were invited to say what worried them and what made them angry about their neighborhood as well as what they wished for.

Maxine Greene (1988) wrote many years ago about the importance of people being able to imagine something better. Arguing that imagination is politically significant, Greene explained that 'human freedom' involves 'the capacity to surpass the given and look at things as if they could be otherwise' (Greene, 1988, p. 3), and further that:

> When people cannot name alternatives, imagine a better state of things, share with others a project of change, they are likely to remain anchored or submerged.
>
> *(Greene, 1988, p. 9)*

She goes on to emphasize the importance of 'the ability to make present what is absent, to summon up a condition that is not yet' (Greene, 1988, p. 16). Wells' project allowed this kind of imagining. We see this creative design work and the associated visible material action over time as crucial to sustaining critical multiliteracies in schools (Janks, 2000; New London Group, 1996).

In the first example (see Figure 2.2), the Grade 2 student is able to convey her understandings about her local physical environment and her wishes for more trees, ponds and parks. She also conveys her fears, both in terms of the nonhuman world where big dogs jump the fence, and the school world where big kids

FIGURE 2.3 Three wishes: Two trees, more noise, more kids like me

tease. The task, which required both drawing and writing, allowed her to use her emerging semiotic repertoire to get her message across. Her writing in caption and speech bubble format is minimal but extremely effective. The writing of an older peer in the same class (see Figure 2.3) demonstrates that the task also allowed her to represent her views. The openness of the task is such that each child is able to make sense of it and respond to it in ways that reflect their capabilities and understandings. Such tasks are enabling not only because they are framed to support and challenge children's thinking and analysis, but also because they allow children to use their existing resources to make meaning.

It is complex and demanding pedagogical work to design tasks that afford all students the opportunity to represent complex ideas, no matter at what point they might be in terms of their literacy learning. In the student artifact, we can see the older student expresses complex understandings about race, age and socially appropriate behaviors both verbally and visually. At the same time, we see the 8-year-old grappling with questions about belonging in the neighborhood and her sense of self and her relationships to the social and physical world. Both children address questions of

- the natural environment or the nonhuman world (trees, ponds, dogs)
- the built environment (parks, rubbish, weeds)
- socio-spatial relationships (people who make a mess, older people who do not want noise, children like me).

When students display this work and read each other's material, there are still further opportunities for learning. Wells guides the children to identify common problems and then to think about what they might be able to do something about. In this case, the common problem, where they thought they might be able to take action, was the absence of healthy trees in the neighborhood.

Here, we want to draw attention to elements of the pedagogic principles that underpin this task design in order to demonstrate how this is enabling for learners. Key pedagogical elements visible in this learning activity include:

1. shared experience (walking the neighborhood)
2. critical inquiry (learning to observe the neighborhood as an environment)
3. framed representations (prompts and invitations to reflect on living in the neighborhood)
4. collective analysis (reading the class set of students' artifacts as data for analysis)
5. taking action to enhance a sense of belonging (weighing up the learning and planning change).

In terms of assembling literate repertoires, the task requires both creative and critical thinking. It allows the use of two modes: verbal and visual. It positions students to draw on personal experience and shared inquiry.

While the task is framed to assist students to think in different ways, it is also open enough to allow for different levels of complexity of response. The older student is able to show that she is aware of the politics of place in terms of age, gender and race (see Figure 2.3). She wishes for children like herself living nearby, the opportunity to make more noise where it will not disturb older people in a nursing home and neighbors who care for their property. These wishes make her astute observations about how people relate to each other in place very clear. Students have been prompted to notice and analyze what is going on and to represent their experiences and understandings as well as they can.

This one-page task, drawing and writing about one's sense of place and being in a place, motivates young children to represent their sense of belonging, their worries and their wishes. This information formed the basis of a unit of work on 'trees' discussed elsewhere (Comber, Thomson & Wells, 2001), however, here the purpose is to highlight the potential of place-conscious work even for children who are still learning to encode meaning.

Urban Renewal From the Inside Out: Belonging Through an Architectural Lens

Further Collaboration—Local and Global

After a number of collaborative literacy research studies during the 1990s, Wells' increasingly turned to the concepts of place and space. One such project allowed her to visit a school in South Africa that was working with critical literacy theorist and educational activist Hilary Janks. As part of the collaborative relationship, the principal and a teacher from Pretoria had visited Wells and her principal in the western suburbs of Adelaide and the visit was reciprocated, offering unique opportunities to both sets of visitors to expand the view from their own school sites.

Wells was inspired by the food garden program being developed at the Pretorian school (Janks, 2000; Janks & Comber, 2006), and so funding was sought to design and develop a connecting garden between the preschool and the school. It was envisaged as a place of shade and as a welcoming and inviting place for parents and children. Lacking sufficient knowledge in urban and landscape architecture, we invited Stephen Loo, an academic colleague and innovative architect with a strong commitment to community consultation, to join us in the bid. Further to this, communications academic and journalist Jackie Cook was invited to join in the project in order to assist teachers and students to document the change process in the school and the impact of the wider urban renewal project taking shape in the neighborhood and beyond the boundaries of the school.

Thus, the project assembled expertise not typically found in educational research. The cross-discipline study offered authentic and sophisticated learning experiences for this school community. The bid was successful and has been documented in a number of places (Comber, Nixon, Ashmore, Loo & Cook, 2006). Of particular focus here is how the architectural dimension enhanced understandings about belonging, space and place, and this became an extra discursive resource for teachers from that time onwards. Place and space were considered as more than a backdrop for children's learning, but understood as constitutive of learning and social relationships.

Architecture and Building Stories

To initiate the *Grove Gardens* project, as the teachers came to call it, architect Stephen Loo showed the children and teachers a PowerPoint presentation called *Building Stories*, which included images of contemporary buildings, spaces and structures, locally and from around the world. *Building Stories* was deliberately ambiguous to suggest both that buildings have stories and that people build stories. The images chosen were deliberately selected because they were likely to be unrecognizable buildings. Loo invited the children to build stories about the buildings by imagining what kinds of buildings they were, what might happen in them, who might use them, and who might belong to them. These examples, of sometimes bizarre and sometimes sublime buildings, offered what Loo described as 'unconventional semiotic footholds' (Comber et al., 2006) that allowed students to extrapolate from what they knew and imagine what they did not. Hence, children were encouraged to imagine beyond familiar everyday structures.

This lesson laid the foundations of the Grove Gardens project by introducing the language of architecture and the concept of belonging to spaces.

Loo spoke to the children about the concept of belonging in terms of the built environment.

> Let's think about something important here. Let's think about the people who use these buildings, and who the buildings belong to, and whether we can feel if we can actually belong to these buildings . . . When we design buildings, we want them to actually be very much a part of our lives. We don't want buildings that we cannot use, or feel uncomfortable in, or that make us unhappy.

The vocabulary that Loo introduced was readily appropriated by students and teachers, as well as the recognition that the process of design requires a sense of belonging and that spaces are in part made by their inhabitants. For example, when asked about who might use a particular building, one student replied:

CHILD: And the community.
LOO: Ah, the community! What do you think the community would do around this building? You're right. It's designed for this community that lives around the building.
CHILD: Just the design.
LOO: The design? Yeah! What do you think is special about the design? Look, let me tell you a story . . .

The children were assisted to understand that design processes need to consider the people who use a space, and how it is relevant to their lives, so that it becomes a place where they can actually belong.

Loo concluded the *Building Stories* event by emphasizing the agency of the community participants who take ownership of the spaces that architects design by devising their uses and meanings. Drawing upon the unconventional architectural images Loo had discussed, the children learned how to use what they knew, as well as the new languages they were learning, to build stories about these buildings. They identified materials, shapes and uses of buildings (*titanium, stone, deli, museum*) and aspects of the design process (*any shape, make anything, the spiral tower, the stacked building*). Where they struggled to access an appropriate descriptive repertoire to talk about some of the buildings, they referred to familiar objects with similar shapes (*looked like a telescope*). At this stage, they were using adjectives to describe buildings (*red, big, old, stone*), but were not describing buildings in terms of their constituent design elements, such as doorways, arches, decking, pathways, roofs, walls and windows.

Loo's practice as an architect and educator resonates with Soja's (2010) notion of spatial justice. Indeed, his classroom conversations with the children were intended to equip them with what Loo described as spatial literacies—understandings and practices about the design of built environments that would allow them to have a say in imagining and negotiating specific places and material objects in those spaces. Soja (1996), in discussing 'the space that difference makes', notes the importance to people of color in making spaces of belonging (see hooks, 1984). This is critical in working towards 'spatial justice' (Soja, 2010). Indeed, what was accomplished in this project was in part contingent on the interdisciplinary resources Loo brought on a practical, technical and aesthetic level as the participant expert architect. The teachers for their parts actively appropriated his discursive resources as parts of their pedagogical repertoire and were still attending to key concepts of the built environment with new classes many years later. This highlights the potential of teacher professional learning opportunities that go beyond the usual school domains.

A Belonging Space

The next theme explored by Loo was the notion of a *belonging space*. The goal was to assist children to conceptualize, articulate and design a belonging space that might eventually connect with the particular space that was to be redesigned and built in their schoolyard. A series of exercises invited children to rethink notions of space, shelter and structure. Teachers found that even young children have a strong sense of where they do and do not belong. Wells stated at the time:

> We were finding out, as young as 8 and 9, [children] have very clear ideas about where they belong and where they don't belong, and how they want things to be, and what should be there and what shouldn't be there. It's given them a chance to focus on that, and to have a voice to start talking about it.

Wells began by exploring belonging as a feeling and as an idea, then invited the children to nominate places they felt that they belonged, and finally to design a belonging space. She also allowed a number of iterations of these activities. For example, when they were first invited to talk about a belonging space, children focused on their bedrooms: how they were and how they would like them to be.

Wells encouraged students to explore their ideas further through writing poetry, drawing and making models, diorama and so forth. Because the children had initially focused on spaces that were indoors, she challenged them to extend their imagining into outdoor spaces by developing a belonging environment for a pet. This involved class discussion about general requirements such as food, water and shelter, and spaces for sleep, play and exercise, and moved to a consideration of the needs of a specific pet. Wells explained to us the belonging environment made as a diorama by a child who had always wanted a pony, clearly a very expensive pet!

> She doesn't have one, but she knew exactly what her pony would be like. It was going to have a fence that it couldn't jump over and get out, that

it was going to have access to water and food in this enclosure, and there was somewhere to lay down on some hay if it wanted to, and there was a little gate to get in and out of, so you could shut it in there if it needed. It had grass so it was nice and soft to run around on, and it also had a little pool over here because it liked to have a little swim, and its bed. It had a roof, a shade, and something nice and soft to sleep on, and it had a bit of protection there, and its name was written above so it knows that's where it sleeps. And just the way the horse was constructed . . . she thought of all the conditions, and it's just wonderful.

Pedagogies of belonging allow children to make bridges to academic learning, as they deal with the material here and now, and imagine what might be. By studying place and space, children were not stuck in the present or in the local. However, they were assembling ways of thinking, designing and conveying their ideas that could be applied to actual spaces and places in the school and, at the same time, feed their creativity and a sense of the possible. Artifacts produced over an extended period of time by one child show what this approach afforded for one student's developing literate identity, learning repertoires and resources for representation.

The Affordances of Exploring Place

Eight-Year-Old Tan and His Gallery of Belonging

Wells as curriculum designer is always on the lookout for ideas that allow children to express their views, knowledge, understandings and feelings in imaginative ways. Over time and across tasks, individual children need opportunities to develop style and explore preferred semiotic resources on multiple occasions. Here, we examine the work of one child, 8-year-old Tan, across a range of tasks associated with belonging, preferred and imagined spaces over the course of a school year.

After the *Building Stories* presentation, Wells designed a number of activities to invite students to think about belonging in various places and spaces. Initially, these activities were highly scaffolded with the teacher providing short prompts to which students responded. For example, Wells invited the children to choose an image of an amazing building and imagine that they lived in it—who they lived with, what it would be like inside the house and what they would do there (see Figure 2.4).

We can see Tan imagines his new abode as a home for his extended family. He imagines that it will be fitted out with a specific range of technology he desires to engage in: popular media and gaming. He also imagines 'a long red dragon' which comes alive and needs to be fed at a barbecue with friends, which Tan hosts. The potential of the unconventional images to open children's minds and provide semiotic footholds for imagining different ways of being is

1) I will live in my house with my mum, my dad, my uncles, my auntys and my half cousin.

2) Inside my house there is a black big screen TV, a brown sofa, a colourful fridge, some white beds, a grey P.S.2, a silver P.S.1,a blue Gamecube, Nintendo 64, a green X-Box, a blue Game-Boy, a black Game-boy-Advance, a silver Game-Boy-Advance S.P, a clean bathroom, a dusty closet, a long, red dragon.

3) One day I had a barbecue in my backyard with my friends. When the sausages were cooked, I had to feed my pet dragon and I had to cook chicken and oysters. All of my friends ate all the chicken and I ate all the oysters. After the barbecue was over, my friends went home and I had to pack up the barbecue by myself. After I finished packing up the barbecue, I went to sleep.

FIGURE 2.4 Tan's amazing building

in evidence here. Not only does Tan envisage the dwelling fitted out with the latest (at that time) technology he desires, but he also populates the building with friends and family and a Yugioh dragon. He runs with the invitation to imagine. As Wells continues to explore belonging in different ways, she often uses short questionnaires so that the class data can be pooled and discussed.

In a response to a short questionnaire about his current house, Tan wrote that he enjoyed living there 'because it has Foxtel and it has delicious food'. He reported that his favorite place was the lounge room because 'I like to watch Foxtel and play Yugioh cards'. When asked if he would prefer to stay in his current house or to move to a new house, such as those being built in the area, he replied: 'New house. Because there's not much rooms for everyone to sleep in'. Like many of his peers, Tan lives with extended family, including grandparents. In this short set of responses, his preferred activities and spaces are reiterated and they become themes as the year unfolds: his interest in popular media, including TV and associated cards.

This is a permeable curriculum (Dyson, 1993) at work in every sense. Tan can bring knowledge from his home and peer worlds to bear on classroom literacy assignments. The focus on place and belonging and the opportunity to imagine different spaces enable him to develop a set of semiotic resources that he can use in various learning contexts. Familiar images recur throughout Tan's work. In several texts, the dragon (which has origins in Yugioh cards and associated online games) is depicted in conjunction with other images and motifs familiar from quest adventure games, such as mazes, medieval weapons and keys.

An early illustration by Tan of his poem titled 'In my belonging space' depicted a room which contained not only the items that one might expect to find in such a space (bed, armchair, table), but also two sculptures or models of dragons hanging from the ceiling by chains as in a dungeon (top left Figure 2.5). Other sections of the room contain a table or storage board dedicated to weapons used in quest adventures (medieval weapons, shield, large dungeon key), and an extremely large media center containing several game consoles (labeled Gameboy, Playstation and Playstation 2), accurately drawn down to the minute details of accessories, wire connections and electricity plugs (top right Figure 2.5).

This text illustrates the productive potential, for this child at least, of encouraging children to produce visual texts alongside verbal texts, and allowing them to draw on their popular cultural resources and their embodied and imagined experiences in particular places and spaces. When this approach was combined with a focus on developing understandings of space, children in this project were able to work with and develop a range of spatial literacy concepts. These included abstract understandings about design and social space such as 'spaces of belonging', and more technical skills such as how to represent ratio and scale, and how to represent the relationships between objects in space.

FIGURE 2.5 Tan's belonging place

The Grove Gardens Consultation Phase

During the 'consultation' phase of the Grove Gardens project discussed earlier in the chapter, the children imagined, discussed, modeled and physically pegged out their possible designs in the school grounds; they visited several local community gardens; and explored the notion of 'spaces of belonging' in many iterations of curriculum work. As the culmination of many months of such work, Wells invited children to portray their views about how a garden might be imagined and designed. Pairs of students were responsible for producing texts that were later made into pages in what were collectively called 'consultation books'. The books were, in a sense, a purpose-made genre that fulfilled at least two purposes. First, they allowed children to represent on paper their key ideas about the garden by drawing from a repertoire of ideas that had been developed over a significant period of time, and as a result of working with various vocabularies, concepts and media. Second, the books constituted artifacts that documented the children's ideas in a form that could easily be shared with and commented on by others.

In the first written text, students addressed three questions:

- What would I like to see in the area?
- Why?
- What would it look like? Describe.

The second text was visual (some of which also included verbal labels as in architectural drawings) and was produced using their choice of medium, and represented their favored plan for the design of the area. Each visual text was produced on tabloid size paper but students were able to use a choice of paint, black ink pens, colored markers, collage, cellophane, leaves, popsicle sticks and so on to produce their images. When assembling the books, some blank space was deliberately left on the written text page to allow children and teachers in other classes, and parents, to provide feedback to the written ideas and visual images using marker pens. Here is the written text produced by Tan and writing partner Adrian:

> **What would I like to see in the area?**
>
> A big maze with some switches
>
> **Why?**
>
> So kids who are waiting can play in it while they are waiting for their mum and dad to pick them up and kids can get tricked because they won't know which is the beginning and which is the end.
>
> **What would it look like? Describe.**
>
> The walls around the maze are made of cement and are painted in gold. It will be 10 metres high and it will have traps inside it. You have to find a key to get out and you have to take a friend with you.

The boys summarize what they would like to see in the area using only six words: 'a big maze with some switches'. Here, they imagine the desolate schoolyard space transformed into a material representation of something that they are fascinated by in the worlds of electronics and electronic gaming—'a maze of switches'. Explaining *why* they would like to see the space designed like a maze of switches, they write:

> So kids who are waiting can play in it while they are waiting for their mum and dad to pick them up and kids can get tricked because they won't know which is the beginning and which is the end.

Tan and Adrian imagine the redesigned material space performing a dual social function: providing both a designated place for children to wait to be collected from school by their parents, and a place for children's pleasurable play that involves the complex and hidden spaces of a maze as well as other tricks and puzzles. When they describe how they would like the maze to *look*, we can see how the boys draw on their developing architectural design vocabulary and spatial literacies as they note specific details about the *height* of the walls (10 meters), the *material* used to make them (cement), and how they would be *decorated* (painted in gold). Two particular features they say they would like to see in the maze are that 'it will have traps inside it' and 'you have to find a key to get out'. They also stipulate that children would not enter the maze alone, but rather, 'you have to take a friend with you'.

The boys' written text therefore combines an awareness of the *social function* that the space designed as a maze will fulfill in the redesigned area (kids can play in it while they wait for their parents, and friends will enter the maze together) with aspects of their own specific and gendered interests in mazes and other games that include 'tricks', puzzles and quests ('you have to find a key to get out'). In other words, their writing moves between a description of Lefebvre's (1991) concept of *perceived space*—an acknowledgment of what the space is *actually* used for (waiting for parents, playing with friends)—and his concept of *lived* space—space that is lived or experienced but which the *imagination* also seeks to change. The boys are able to imagine spaces that connect the preschool and the school that do not simply support 'antiquated ideologies and representations' (Lefebvre, 1991, p. 417) of school structures.

The boys' writing shows that they are able to imagine how this newly designed space in the school yard could become a 'space of belonging' for members of the school community by improving the ways in which social relations are conducted within it. At the same time, they are beginning to imagine how, in design terms, the redesigned space could also replicate some of the features of electronic and fantasy games that they obviously enjoy: entering a maze; confronting switches, tricks and other obstacles; and searching for ways to successfully end adventures and quests. The fact that the boys want the high cement walls of the maze to be 'painted in gold' suggests that they are well aware that their design is intended to change the material and real-life world they inhabit, and is, in fact, being overlaid in their plan with elements of imagination, fantasy and desire associated with fantasy fiction and electronic game-playing. This is a mix of serious and playful writing and imagining.

As in their written text, Tan and Adrian's *visual* representation (see Figure 2.6) of what they would like to see in the area also combines elements of realism

FIGURE 2.6 Tan and Adrian's imagined garden

(grass, pathway, toilet blocks designed for 'big kids only' and some for 'little kids') and elements of fantasy (winged dragon, two kinds of maze). In relation to their developing spatial literacies, we can see aspects of the image resemble an architect's plan with its aerial view, a sense of scale, lines that depict a pathway linking one side of the area to the other, written labels indicating whether a structure is a toilet block or gate, and icons that represent design elements such as seating structures and shelters. Architectural vocabularies, as well as design and drawing conventions, have entered their semiotic repertoires. But, as in the writing, there are also other kinds of visual elements foregrounded in this image, elements not so obviously connected with the spatial. Most obviously different from an architect's plan is the vibrant red dragon with yellow wings that seems to be devouring one end of the pathway that links the school and preschool. As in many fantasy genres, the dragon is comparatively oversized in terms of scale, and its presence is further highlighted by the fact that, unlike other objects, it is depicted not from an aerial view but from a lateral view.

Thus, both their written and visual texts suggest the boys' desire for their playground space to be redesigned as a *social* place for play and adventure, but also as a space which specifically includes elements of popular culture and digital play with which they are familiar in their lifeworlds. This desire to include in school playgrounds aspects of play that are promoted to children by the leisure industries is common, not only to texts produced by Adrian and Tan, but also to many others students in Wells' class, and is also consistent with findings of the UK project *The School I'd Like* (Burke & Grosvenor, 2003).

The consultation book pages produced by Adrian and Tan illustrate what was made possible by Wells' emergent pedagogical approach, which brought together a focus on developing in children the capacity to take action about things that mattered to them with a focus on spatial literacies. This pedagogy allowed diverse children to draw on the range of cultural resources they had at their disposal, and to use these resources in order to connect not only with new concepts of spatial literacy, but also with more traditional school curriculum requirements. In the next chapter, there is evidence that Tan made sophisticated use of these semiotic resources in producing several pages of a class picture book, *Windows*, with a coauthor. There is also a range of other teachers building upon a place-conscious pedagogy to assist children to produce a range of genres (such as scientific report, poetry, auto-biography) and multimedia (film, photography, art work).

The Politics of Imagination: Producing Spatial and Social Worlds of One's Own

Exploring the spatial dimensions of lived experience can provide important inroads for young people into critical literacies that are material, imaginative and creative. Working with the discourses and practices of architecture to redesign part of the school grounds opened up opportunities for both children and their teachers to think in new ways. In the process, both children and teachers expanded their semiotic repertoires and engaged in imagining, negotiating and representing themselves in the spatialized world of the school and beyond. This chapter has provided only a snapshot of a complex project that ran over several years and impacted upon the teacher's long-term pedagogic repertoires.

Using space as a focus for learning and a frame for curriculum design is both generative and productive in the sense that it allows all children to contribute what they know about perceived and lived space. Further, it allows them to imagine how different people might populate different spaces, and how spaces might be reconfigured and why. In their artifacts, it is possible to see traces of their classroom pedagogical history:

- an architect's PowerPoint presentation about buildings and the stories that might surround them
- neighborhood walks
- discussions about local housing development issues
- workshops on belonging spaces
- visits to newly developed local parks
- visits to the university architecture studio, and to the CBD of the city of Adelaide, South Australia.

The project illustrated very clearly Jan Nespor's (1997, p. 12) argument that pedagogy is 'an ongoing collective accomplishment'. It involves 'real practices slowly accomplished over time and space, continuously modified to deal with change and contingency' (cited in McGregor, 2004, p. 366). Teachers involved in the project have been willing to expand the boundaries of what variously seems a shrinking normative space for literacy work and, at other times, an overloaded curriculum. The layered nature of the curriculum and pedagogical work they carried out with the children, and the ways that it drew on multiple traditions, allowed for and encouraged a simultaneous consideration of the aesthetic, the literary and studies of society, as well as the productive effects of working across multiple media of representation and communication. Their classes were sites of a rich and recursive pedagogy that was accomplished collectively over time and space.

A key affordance of making place, and belonging experiences in place, the object of study is that it provides rich material for all students. All students have experiences of places; all students have prior knowledge; therefore, all students are in a position of 'knowing', of having something to say. To ensure that children learn new things, the ways in which the teacher frames tasks is crucial. These enabling approaches are designed to build from what children already know, but are framed so that children also explore new insights. Rather than place-conscious pedagogy locking children into the here-and-now, these teachers use place as a jumping off point for imagining possible worlds and different futures. In the next chapter, key pedagogical principles of learning activities or tasks that are enabling are illustrated and discussed.

References

Apple, M (ed.) 2010, *Global crises, social justice and education*, Routledge, New York.

Au, K 2009, 'Isn't culturally responsive instruction just good teaching?' *Social Education*, vol. 73, no. 4, pp. 179–183.

Bauman, Z 1998, *Work, consumerism and the new poor*, Open University Press, Buckingham.

Brooks, J & Normore, A 2010, 'Educational leadership and globalization: Literacy for a glocal perspective', *Educational Policy*, vol. 24, no. 1, pp. 52–82.

Burke, C & Grosvenor, I 2003, *The school I'd like: Children and young people's reflections of an education for the 21st century*. Routledge/Falmer, London.

Burnett, C, Merchant, G, Pahl, K & Rowsell, J 2013, 'The (im)materiality of literacy: The significance of subjectivity to new literacies research', *Discourse*, vol. 35, no. 1, pp. 90–103.

Cazden, C 2001, *Classroom discourse: The language of teaching and learning*, Heinemann, Portsmouth, New Hampshire.

Comber, B 2006, 'Pedagogy as work: Educating the next generation of literacy teachers', *Pedagogies*, vol. 1, no.1, pp. 59–67.

Comber, B 2012, 'Mandated literacy assessment and the reorganisation of teachers' work: Federal policy and local effects', *Critical Studies in Education*, vol. 53, no. 2, pp. 119–136.

Comber, B & Cormack, P 1995, *Cornerstones*, Module 1 Socio-cultural issues in early literacy learning and Module 4, Frameworks for critical analysis of teaching, Department for Education and Children's Services, Adelaide.

Comber, B & Nixon, H 2008, 'Spatial literacies, design texts and emergent pedagogies in purposeful literacy curriculum', *Pedagogies*, vol. 3, no. 2, pp. 221–240.

Comber, B, Nixon, H, Ashmore, L, Loo, S & Cook, J 2006, 'Urban renewal from the inside out: Spatial and critical literacies in a low socioeconomic school community', *Mind, Culture and Activity*, vol. 13, no. 3, pp. 228–246.

Comber, B, Nixon, H & Reid, J (eds.) 2007, *Literacies in place: Teaching environmental communications*, Primary English Teaching Association, Newtown, New South Wales.

Compton-Lilly, C 2013, 'Temporality, trajectory, and early literacy learning', in K. Hall, T Cremin, B. Comber & L. Moll (eds.), *International handbook of research on children's literacy, learning, and culture*, Wiley-Blackwell, Oxford, pp. 83–95.

Connell, R W 1993, *Schools and social justice*, Pluto Press, Toronto and Our Schools/Our Selves Education Foundation & Leichhardt, NSW.

Dillabough, J & Kennelly, J 2010, *Lost youth in the global city: Class, culture, and the urban imaginary*, Routledge, New York.

Dixon, K 2011, *Literacy, power, and the schooled body: Learning in time and space*, Routledge, New York & London.

Dyson, A 1993, *Social worlds of children learning to write in an urban primary school*, Teachers College Press, New York.

Edelsky, C 2006, *With literacy and justice for all: Rethinking the social in language and education*, Lawrence Erlbaum, Mahwah, New Jersey.

Ferrare, J & Apple, M 2010, 'Spatializing critical education: Progress and cautions', *Critical Studies in Education*, vol. 51, no. 2, pp. 209–221.

Green, B & Corbett, M (eds.) 2013, *Rethinking rural literacies: Transnational perspectives*, Palgrave McMillan, New York.

Greene, M 1988, *The dialectic of freedom*, Teachers College Press, New York & London.

hooks, b 1984, *Feminist theory: From margin to centre*, South End Press, Boston.

Janks, H 1993, *Language and identity*, Hodder & Stoughton/Wits University Press, Johannesburg.

Janks, H 2000, 'Domination, access, diversity and design: A synthesis for critical literacy education', *Educational Review*, vol. 52, no. 2, pp. 175–186.

Janks, H 2010, *Literacy and power*, Routledge, New York.

Janks, H & Comber, B 2006, 'Critical literacy across continents', in K. Pahl & J. Rowsell (eds.), *Travel notes from the new literacy studies: Instances of practice*, Multilingual Matters, Clevedon, pp. 95–117, reprinted in M. Mackey (ed.) 2007, *Media literacies: Major themes in education*, Routledge, New York.

Jones, S 2006, *Girls, social class & literacy: What teachers can do to make a difference*, Heinemann, Portsmouth, New Hampshire.

Kalantzis, M & Cope, B 2008, *New learning: Elements of a science of learning*, Cambridge University Press, Cambridge.

Katz, C 2008, 'Bad elements: Katrina and the soured landscape of social reproduction', *Gender, Place and Culture*, vol. 15, no. 1, pp. 15–29.

Kinloch, V 2010, *Harlem on our minds: Place, race, and the literacies of urban youth*, Teachers College Press, New York.

Kress, G & van Leeuwen, T 2001, *Multimodal discourse: The modes and media of contemporary communication*, Arnold, Hodder Headline Group, London.

Lefebvre, H 1991, *The production of space* (D. Nicholson-Smith, Trans.), Blackwell, Oxford.

Lewis, C 2001, *Literacy practices as social acts: Power, status, and cultural norms in the classroom*, Lawrence Erlbaum, Mahwah, New Jersey.

Livingstone, S 2008, 'Engaging with media—a matter of literacy?', *Communication, culture & critique*, vol. 1, no. 1, pp. 51–62.

Luke, A & Freebody, P 1997, 'The social practices of reading', in S. Muspratt, A. Luke & P. Freebody (eds.), *Constructing critical literacies: Teaching and learning textual practices*, Allen & Unwin, St Leonards, NSW, pp. 195–225.

Lupton, R 2003, *Poverty street: The dynamics of neighbourhood decline and renewal*, The Policy Press, Bristol.

Massey, D 2003, 'Globalisation: What does it mean for geography?', Keynote Lecture presented at the Geographical Association Annual Conference, UMIST, April 2002, accessed February 10, 2011, www.geography.org.uk

Massey, D 2005, *For space*, SAGE, London.

McGregor, J 2004, 'Spatiality and the place of the material in schools', *Pedagogy, Culture and Society*, vol. 12, no. 3, pp. 347–372.

McNaughton, S 2002, *Meeting of minds*. Learning Media, Wellington.

Miller, D 2010, *Stuff*, Polity, Cambridge.

Moje, E B 2000, 'Circles of kinship, friendship, position, and power: Examining the community in community-based literacy research', *Journal of Literacy Research*, vol. 32, no. 1, pp. 77–112.

Moll, L C, Amanti, C, Neff, D & Gonzalez, N 1992, 'Funds of knowledge for teaching: Using a qualitative approach to connect homes and classrooms', *Theory and Practice*, vol. 31, no. 2, pp. 132–141.

My School website 2014, Australian Curriculum, Assessment and Reporting Authority (ACARA), Pitt Street, Sydney, accessed March 26, 2014, http://www.myschool.edu.au/

New London Group 1996, 'A pedagogy of multiliteracies: Designing social futures', *Harvard Educational Review*, vol. 66, no. 1, pp. 60–92.

Nespor, J 1997, *Tangled up in school: Politics, space, bodies, and signs in the educational process*, Lawrence Erlbaum, Mahwah, New Jersey.

Nespor, J 2008, 'Education and place: A review essay', *Educational Theory*, vol. 58, no. 4, pp. 475–489.

Pahl, K & Rowsell, J 2010, *Artifactual literacies: Every object tells a story*, Teachers College Press, New York.

Ravitch, D 2010, *The death and life of the great American school system: How testing and choice are undermining education*, Basic Books, Philadelphia.

Rowsell, J & Sefton-Green, J (eds.) 2015, *Revisiting learning lives—longitudinal perspectives on researching learning and literacy*, Routledge, London & New York.

Sahlberg, P 2011, *Finnish lessons: What can the world learn from educational change in Finland?* Teachers College Press, New York.

Sanchez, L 2011, 'Building on young children's cultural histories through placemaking in the classroom', *Contemporary Issues in Early Childhood*, vol. 12, no. 4, pp. 332–342.

Soja, E 1996, *Thirdspace: Journeys to Los Angeles and other real-and-imagined places*, Blackwell, Malden, Massachusetts.

Soja, E 2010, *Seeking spatial justice*, University of Minnesota Press, Minneapolis.

Somerville, M 2011, 'Becoming-frog: Learning place in primary school', in M. Somerville, B. Davies, K. Power, S. Gannon & P. de Carteret, *Place pedagogy change*, Sense, Rotterdam, pp. 65–79.

Somerville, M 2013, *Water in a dry land: Place-learning through art and story*, Routledge, New York & London.

3
ASSEMBLING ACADEMIC LITERACIES THROUGH LEARNING ABOUT PLACE

Introduction

In the previous chapter, it was argued that the study of *belonging places* allows teachers to build on young people's local knowledge and experiences in critical and inclusive ways. All students can learn to participate, negotiate and work together as they undertake research and imaginings about places and spaces. The study of place also opens possibilities for students to assemble a range of academic literacies associated with different ways of knowing. As Moje and colleagues (Moje, McIntosh, Kramer, Ellis, Carrillo & Collazo, 2004, p. 41) argue, the sheer diversity of what children bring to school requires 'strategic integration of various knowledges, Discourses and literacies that youth bring to school and experience in school'. Even in the elementary school classroom, teachers can begin to explore how various phenomena, such as urban renewal or conservation of an indigenous plant, can be known through specific disciplinary, professional, vernacular and cultural knowledges and how those ways of knowing are captured in particular discursive and semiotic practices.

In previous work, for example, we explored how children came to represent their knowledges and experiences of the Murray-Darling Basin region in Australia through a discourse analysis of their artifacts (Cormack & Comber, 2007). In assembling knowledge of aspects of place and a range of semiotic and discursive resources for representing that knowledge, children also expand their tools for imagining how things might be different. When the classroom becomes a meeting place or belonging space—what other literacy scholars have seen as a 'third space' (Gutierrez, Baquedano-Lopez, Alvarez & Chiu, 1999; Gutierrez, Rymes & Larson, 1995; Moje et al., 2004), following Bhabha and Soja—possibilities for negotiating something new become apparent.

Various disciplinary lenses and their literate practices, such as geography, history, literature, ecology, design and technology, can be applied to the study of places (see Figure 3.1), and students can demonstrate what they learn through various forms of multimodal text production and the arts more broadly. For instance, Hull and Katz (2006, p. 43) document the ongoing work at the Oakland Centre storytelling center for local youth known as DUSTY, arguing for the potential of digital technologies for youth 'to articulate pivotal moments and reflect on life trajectories'. Part of that storytelling involved young people thinking about where they live and their relationships with everyday local practices. They write about the area as a 'dangerous place' and recognize the 'pull of the streets' (Hull & Katz, 2006, p. 53) and the need to consciously explore different possibilities to avoid a destiny of violence, drugs and other risks. Young adults at DUSTY were able to do significant positive—indeed, life-changing—identity work at DUSTY, and in the process assembled new repertoires of literate practices.

Literacy and media education researchers working with new technologies in elementary schools have also noted the affordances of new technologies for children to produce multimodal texts to represent themselves or their knowledge about particular subjects, including specific places. In these contexts, the importance of building knowledge of both relevant content and media are seen as important (Dezuanni, 2015; Luke, Dooley & Woods, 2011). Dezuanni

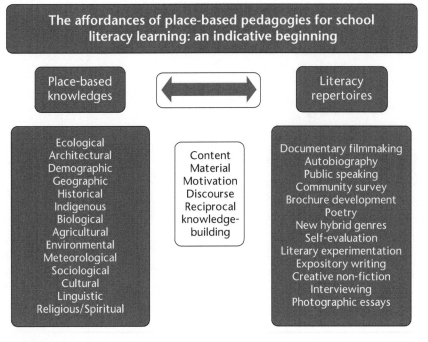

FIGURE 3.1 The affordances of place-based pedagogies

(2015, p. 15) argues that 'abstract concepts can provide substantive experiences for students because they can challenge and expand their existing knowledge base'. This chapter explores how teachers have worked with students to produce a range of texts, featuring material and social place, through film, reports, autobiography and so on.

Literacy has never been a content-free, nor ideologically neutral, practice, yet so much of schooling tends to proceed as though it was process without substance. Policy often treats literacy as though it was a generic skill. However, literacy is always a goal-driven social practice (Street, 2001); we are always reading or writing or viewing or producing texts *about something*, and the focus of our communication is never neutral. It is always about the representation or understanding of phenomena from various points of view. However, sometimes in school we ask children to produce texts without giving them sufficient time or reason to develop their knowledge. Sometimes we ask them for more detail and to expand on their ideas. Those of us who write know that expanding and providing detail requires a serious engagement with the ideas in question. The study of place allows for an extensive selection of substantive and meaningful content. Such inquiries are not only motivational, but also come with rich possibilities for new academic learning. Making place the object of study provides multiple avenues for young people to assemble appropriate vocabularies, genres and discourses associated with different discipline areas.

When students are positioned as researchers of place, they are able to learn within and across curriculum areas. Participating as student researchers significantly alters student subjectivity (Bautista, Bertrand, Morrell, Scorza & Matthews, 2013). They are part of a collective learning community actively investigating how things work and working towards change (Fielding, 2001). In this chapter, we show how teachers build on students' personal experiences and cultural resources as a bridge for introducing more abstract ideas and conceptual knowledge. For example, one teacher took her students walking through nearby hills to first learn to identify the weeds, and then the nonindigenous plants, and then specifically the 'verbascum' plant. At each stage, this teacher worked explicitly to expand students' conceptual and linguistic repertoires (Gascoyne, 2007).

Immigrant students in another class learned to write autobiographies after researching with their families, and through locating and examining library resources about their home countries (Comber & Nixon, 2013). As discussed later in this chapter, students in another class learned about the strength of various structures in the built environment by starting with a study of chicken's eggs in the natural world, then gradually moving to the arch as a sophisticated structure used in architecture and design. In these instances, teachers work across the curriculum, through literature, design and technology, and science, to build student conceptual knowledge on a particular subject. They show students how to research by drawing on both the local and expert knowledge of appropriate people to learn about place in situ.

In place-conscious curriculum, teachers build complex knowledge of topics of interest that address local challenges while also tackling broader conceptual thinking (Cormack & Green, 2007; Green & Corbett, 2013). Their often ambitious projects capitalize on the affordances of planned or actual change in the natural world or built environment, rather than depending on simulations or already recontextualized school material.

Hence, teachers might invite Indigenous elders, botanists, bird watchers, architects, town-planners, project managers and engineers into their classrooms. In the case of architecture, as described in Chapter 2, real-world texts and significant documents such as actual drawings and plans and specifications of machines, professional architecture magazines, and architectural models were brought into classrooms. Professionals, such as architects or project managers, explained how to make sense of such texts and to use them for their own purposes. Students were then involved in this actual practice, working with architects as the latters' clients. The built environment was treated with acknowledgment of the complex material processes and issues of cost, sustainability and future functionality, and these were explored in relation to the potential impact on student places and lives.

This chapter begins with a brief discussion regarding academic discourse, identity and place, and the argument that place-conscious pedagogies have particular affordances that allow children to assemble new and unfamiliar academic discourses. We then turn to examples of practice where teachers have explored place with children and, in the processes, inducted them into specific ways of thinking and knowing and representing that knowledge. The teachers develop pedagogies for building children's academic literate repertoires while simultaneously building their specific field knowledge (in various traditions). These pedagogies are explored as teachers conduct research with children about problems and questions emerging from the study of 'place'.

Academic Discourse, Identity and Place

Many literacy theorists have noted that learning to produce texts involves identity work (Ivanic, 2004; Kamler, 2001; Lewis, Enciso & Moje, 2007). It is not only a matter of being able to use particular vocabulary, encode words recognizably or produce meaningful clauses. While children have to learn all of this, they also need to learn disciplinary ways of knowing and ways of speaking. They need to be able to read the social context to make judgments about appropriateness. James Gee (1990, p. 142) famously wrote some time ago of 'Discourse as a sort of identity kit'. One has to feel like, speak like and act like a member of community to take up the discourse. Children are grappling with multiple layers of semiotic work as they represent their meanings. Place-conscious pedagogy is an excellent and accessible way for children to build field knowledge simultaneously with assembling specific discursive resources. In other words, building field knowledge and building literate repertoires can go hand in hand. Students can build a positive sense of their academic identities as they engage with and inquire into the everyday world.

For example, if children are studying the removal of weeds in a particular area in order to allow native flora to flourish, it makes sense that they learn the scientific names for the plants, how to draw them accurately and how to produce an information pamphlet for other visitors to the area about fostering its eradication. If they are learning about how to rebuild the habitat of particular birds, it makes sense that they are inducted into the discursive practices of ornithologists, such as how to read an atlas of bird migration, and learn the botanical names for the specific plants and the layers of flora required for different birds. It makes sense to learn the bird sounds and their specific colorings. It makes sense to keep records of sightings.

As Gee (2004) has pointed out, the discursive practices of everyday vernacular science with respect to a 'hornworm' differ from the discursive practices of those who study and write about insect physiology or insect biochemistry. Drawing upon the work of Halliday, he notes the very different use of language to convey meanings employed by the scientists, pointing to the use of nominalizations, specialist sentences, precise terms of measurement and so on. Students will not just naturally appropriate such language from everyday, popular or commonsense discussions on the topic. These disciplinary literacies are the result of being apprenticed into specialized discursive practices over time. Our work with teachers who invite experts to work in the classroom suggests that while school students may not acquire all aspects of such practices, they do appropriate elements of the vocabulary and appear to enjoy having more precise terms to identify and explain material objects that previously they may have not even noticed or been aware of. For example, students became really interested in 'insulation' after the project manager explained how this material functioned in terms of heating and cooling a building. We have found that young people who may not have access to the linguistic practices of various professions in their daily life may be particularly interested in hearing the experts talk and playing with the ideas and words that appeal to them.

These two incomplete examples indicate the vast semiotic material associated with learning about place and the nonhuman world. This material is rich with possibility for children learning to make meaning in various modes and media and in the process to assemble emergent discursive practices of the disciplines, or at least to begin to see themselves in that light. As we go on to demonstrate, they may imagine themselves as botanists, architects and filmmakers: people who know, and represent, places in various ways. This is not as a result of explicit teaching of subject-specific genres out of context or deconstructing how disciplinary literacies work as an isolated academic exercise, but by engaging young people in complex ideas and projects with people who are expert in the topic at hand. This is not to suggest that students do not need to assemble specific disciplinary literacies or particular genres; unquestionably, they do (Freebody, Chan

& Barton, 2013; Gillis, 2014; Moje et al., 2004)! As Freebody and colleagues point out, we need to better understand:

> how each domain of school knowledge uses a diverse array of commu-
> nicational and knowledge-accessing technologies to put semiotic systems
> to work in its own way.
>
> *(Freebody et al., 2013, p. 315)*

They argue that keeping literacy apart from broader curriculum concerns has had negative consequences in the past. Understanding the real demands of learning in various curriculum areas and learning to produce evidence of that learning needs more research and policy attention to build further upon the ground-breaking body of work conducted by scholars working with systemic functional linguistics (Christie & Derewianka, 2008; Christie & Maton, 2011; Halliday, 1978). Studying and becoming knowledgeable about particular aspects of places may provide just one approach to the motivation and the 'real content' for the challenging and complex work of understanding and producing the required semiotic and discursive organization of disciplinary texts.

We have known for some time that the ways in which teachers interact with children—through classroom discourse—are key to the opportunities that are pro-vided to them to learn (Cazden, 2001). We agree with this emphasis. We also believe that understanding the ways in which they design wall-charts, activities, tasks, discussions, guides for students to produce texts, and worksheets are a part of classroom discourse and that their use of various discourses, keywords and images is key in negotiating positive pedagogies. In other words, the semiotics of assignments and all classroom products are integral to the messages children receive and a key element of the resources on offer.

Educators who are committed to social justice recognize the significance of teachers having high expectations for their students, making this evident in the scope of their curriculum and being able to communicate this to students. The operationalization of high expectations curricula (Dudley-Marling & Michaels, 2012) is contingent upon teachers being able to bring these elements together. When children do not feel as though they belong at school, or feel themselves to be different from their peers, acquiring English literacy at school can be an alienating experience. Yet if a classroom is a welcoming space for all students, it can become a meeting place (following Massey, 2005) inherent with possibility for negotiating something new. In Janks' (2010) synthesis model of critical literacy, diversity becomes a productive resource for the classroom community. That is, students' multilingualism, multiculturalism and discourses, and their different life histories become shared resources for learning and problem-solving when they are recognized and operationalized in the classroom space.

In what follows, we explore how different teachers build curriculum in various ways to exploit both student diversity and the specific affordances of place. In doing so, they induct students into new discursive practices that allow them to add to their current knowledges and experiences, without denying their linguistic, cultural and geographical histories and sense of identity. The new discursive practices are made available in the context of real-world highly motivating and meaningful projects. Students are adding to existing repertoires—ways of knowing, ways of talking and ways of representing by becoming involved in a bigger project.

Politics, People and Places: Children as Filmmakers

For almost three decades, we have followed and documented the innovative pedagogical practices of Helen Grant, who is a primary school teacher-researcher in Adelaide, South Australia (Comber, 2006; Nixon & Comber, 2005; Nixon, Comber, Grant & Wells, 2012), and she has also written about her work (Grant, 1999; Grant, 2014). Grant teaches children who are learning the English language as a second (or third) language or dialect, and she also teaches media studies to mainstream classes across the school.

Across her career, Grant has actively developed professional knowledge about systemic functional linguistics (Halliday, 1978); critical literacy (Janks, 1993; 2010; Luke & Freebody, 1997); multiculturalism (Lo Bianco, 2003); multiliteracies (Kalantzis & Cope, 2008; New London Group, 1996); and visual literacies (Callow, 2013). Personally, she has also developed her knowledge of world music, youth cultures, languages, travel, the arts and film, in particular. She brings this particular repertoire of knowledge and dispositions towards social justice to her inventiveness as a teacher (Comber, 2006).

Here, the focus is on how Grant designs language and literacy learning activities through jointly constructing films with her diverse student groups. Highlighting the titles and topics of her films, we see how a sense of place infuses her work. After discussing her broad corpus of work as a teacher-filmmaker, we examine one film in some detail, as it illustrates key principles of her enabling pedagogies and what they afford for students developing academic literacies in English.

The Archive: A Teacher's Corpus of Work

Returning to the idea of the school as a meeting place, Grant's pedagogy epitomizes how to work with the diverse cultural and linguistic resources and histories of children, and what they bring to school, while enabling all to engage in new learning together. One of the ways she achieves this is through her filmmaking, which she does in a range of learning contexts: a lunchtime film club; collaborative projects with mainstream classroom teachers and their students; and with new arrival students who are also often refugee children who have recently come to Australia.

Grant's archive of films includes titles such as *Cooking Afghani Style*, *Hidden Treasures of Adelaide*, *Sudan* and *Waves of Culture*. These titles suggest a focus on place and culture and, indeed, that is the case. Grant invites students to use what they know from their own places, as well as present and past home cultures, and the local area. While Grant is informed by Moll's and colleagues' work on 'funds of knowledge' (Moll, Amanti, Neff & Gonzalez, 1992) and encourages her students to conduct research on family expertise, her community is less homogenous, in the sense that children come from many different cultures and places. Hence, Thomson's idea of the 'virtual schoolbag' (Thomson, 2002, p. 1) is helpful here. Thomson's metaphor conceives that each child brings a bag to school full of things they have already learned at home, from friends and from the world in which they live. The extent to which they can make use of that knowledge, have it recognized, exchange it and build on it affects their belonging and ongoing educational trajectory.

Importantly, Grant uses their existing languages as resources as well as introducing ways of representing their messages in English. She uses their everyday knowledge and interest in popular culture, but introduces them to the meta-language of multiliteracies. Grant starts with children's existing knowledge of a place (for example, Adelaide, Sudan, Afghanistan) and guides them to conduct further research, assemble new knowledge and represent their accumulated understandings in film. While her pedagogy starts from where children are, it does not remain there. Her teaching context is very much reflective of 'superdiversity', where it is no longer obvious 'Who is the Other? And who are We?'(Blommaert, 2013, p. 5).

Even young children can participate in such a process. For instance, in *Waves of Culture*, 5-year-old children simply give a 'hello' greeting in their first language accompanied by an appropriate movement, such as a bow or a wave. *Cooking Afghani Style* resembles the very popular western television cooking show genre, hosted by renowned chefs such as Jamie Oliver, Kylie Kwong and others. Producing the film as a counter-text to those who would choose to demonize Afghani culture, Grant gave recently arrived immigrant Afghani heritage children an opportunity to represent what was important to them about their culture.

Within Grant's group, a selection of boys and girls decided on the menu, shopped for the ingredients at the market, prepared the dishes and filmed the whole process. They also selected images and symbols from the surrounding city of Adelaide and from the library. For example, the grave of an Afghani person is discovered in the cemetery and a young female student revelled in being able to read the Arabic inscription on the head stone. The children storyboarded the film, wrote the script, rehearsed, demonstrated and filmed the cooking, and spoke the voiceover instructions. As they did so, they also (re)claimed, or at least made familiar, some local landmarks as cultural touchstones.

Filmmaking, Multiliteracies and High Expectations

In terms of enabling academic literacies (Lea & Street, 2006), Grant explicitly teaches the students about text design and production using the meta-language

FIGURE 3.2 Photograph of students looking at street art

of multiliteracies. Together, they viewed and deconstructed how such programs are produced, and designed and produced their own films, drawing on their experience and their new knowledge of English and visual literacies.

The film *Hidden Treasures of Adelaide*, partly funded by a local council, shows how children worked with local artists to revisit parts of the city, especially those streets and lanes decorated by 'street artists' (Figure 3.2).

In making this film, children explored how to 'market' the city of Adelaide as a tourist destination, considering how images and verbal texts might persuade viewers. Through looking at Adelaide, in part through the lens of street art, they also learned about ways filmmakers take an angle on the familiar, and in this case, 'graffiti', to question assumptions. Hence, it is in the process of making a film that students learn about the politics of literacy. They learn about not only who can write (or draw) about what, but also, where and when.

In the next chapter, student filmmakers demonstrate how lived experiences in Sudan and Afghanistan might be used as resources in making classroom films. At the same time, these students also learned about their homelands through family, peers, community, library and Internet research, and ways in which they might interweave such information into their accounts.

Cooking Afghani Style, for example, as a primary school film text, is in the cooking-show tradition. The children studied and deconstructed a range of TV cooking shows before designing their film for an audience of peers and the wider community. *Sudan* follows a different format, and is a documentary about the country Sudan itself and children's experiences of leaving Sudan and coming to Australia. It is produced for a school student audience. In terms of the needs of recently arrived refugees' children, producing these films allowed them to learn how to write a script, produce storyboards, prepare subtitles where needed, cast the film, rehearse the voice-over, gather the props, select the music, and all of the other tasks that producing a high quality short film for publication requires. In terms of learning English, these tasks required students to use English for specific purposes.

Because the films were to be publicly launched, they were *high stakes* products and required a great deal of drafting, rehearsing and editing. Students had to think about audience expectations. Making a film provided a motivational reason for these young students to engage in high-level multiliteracies to meet their goals, while Grant explicitly introduced the language of multiliteracies and filmmaking.

The Politics of Literacy and the Literacy of Politics

Australia has a liberal democratic system of government at both national and state levels (http://www.dfat.gov.au/facts/sys_gov.html: accessed November 20, 2014). In common with Britain and the United States of America, its core values are religious tolerance, freedom of speech and association, and the rule of law. The federation of states (hence, the Commonwealth of Australia) was formed in 1901. Federal elections are held every three years and it is compulsory for all citizens over 18 years of age to vote. The media actively engages with both state and national elections.

In Australia, most schools have a 'student representative council' (SRC)—a student elected group representing the views of students in discussions with the school council, school leaders and the teaching body. Each year, Grant is actively engaged in mentoring student representative council members as part of her broader commitment to understanding the school as a social place, a meeting place, and a place where everyone needs to learn to work together and where everyone's interests need to be considered. Student representatives at Grant's school are elected by their peers from across the school in a secret ballot and, for a year while in office, they meet regularly about a number of issues including:

- ways the school could be improved, in terms of facilities, sports offerings, and events
- suggestions for changing school rules, uniforms and so on
- nominating social problems, such as bullying or racist behavior, for further action or consideration by school leadership.

SRCs have a two-fold purpose: first, to provide young people with opportunities to have a voice on issues and ideas for the improvement of their school;

and second, to support young people to learn how a democratic system works through participating in practice.

Grant has always taken an active role in supporting the SRC in the schools where she has worked. She saw an opportunity to produce a film that could be useful in her school context to educate newcomers to the school about democratic elections. She decided to work with film club students to make a satire of the whole election process, and this inspired the title, *Kissing Babies and Pressing the Flesh.*

At the time the movie was produced, a national election was imminent. In Australia, schools are often used as polling sites for elections and the booths are often left in the school following election day. Grant, as resourceful as ever, used this material as sets for parts of the film. What follows is a description of this fourteen-minute film.

Kissing Babies and Pressing the Flesh

The film opens with two political reporters, a boy and a girl from Year 6, introducing themselves and the topic of their program and that they will be joined by their 'on location reporter' who is 'on the campaign trail'.

All three reporters are dressed for the part, while the studio-based jour-nalists sit behind the desk with their papers, reminiscent of evening news. The on-location reporter has a large boom microphone and a camera crew as he interviews children in the school playground. They articulate that they will be exploring 'candidate speeches', 'what the voters think', 'televised debates', 'playground walks', and what the voters should consider in choos-ing their representatives.

The camera then pans to the school playground where the roving reporter asks individual children:

Why do you think people join the SRC?
What qualities do you think an SRC representative needs?

In vox pop style, a number of answers are rapidly included before going back to the 'news desk' for some commentary and analysis.

The two key presenters each take a different view on the playground interviews. The male presenter parrots 'my research shows' but ultimately opts for the argument that he will vote on the basis of the candidate's popu-larity, the promises they make, and the incentives they offer (including lol-lipops). The female presenter very properly advocates for candidates who offer proper policies to improve the school.

In making the film, the students (with Grant as teacher and producer) use humor and satirize the worst features of election campaigns in order to expose how they work. The male presenter, duped by both enticements and fear, becomes a foil in the face of the female journalist's more sophisticated understanding of democracy.

A number of other techniques are employed by Grant to make the contrast quite stark, including still images and captions to show two candidates at opposite poles of the continuum between altruism and self-interest. When the camera returns to further vox pops in the school playground, we hear some very insightful comments from prospective candidates, including the importance of being able to 'convey other people's opinions', making 'realistic decisions' and being 'responsible and trustworthy'.

Voters reiterate the need to 'have a voice' to make the school 'a better place' and to elect 'someone who represents all of us'. Children from a range of cultural and linguistic heritages are included among the speakers.

We can imagine how much the student participants learned about language in the production of this film. They were engaged in producing the script, conducting the research, filming, editing and, finally, launching the film. An incredibly useful and humorous resource was produced for viewing and discussion by children and teachers within the school, and sometimes beyond the school among families, teachers and researchers.

In the process of making this film, Grant was able to teach the children about the literacy of politics: that is, the ways in which language is used to persuade, distort, exaggerate, lobby and so on. Keywords such as 'representation', 'voting', 'candidate', 'policies' and 'campaign' all required discussion and understanding. Research was needed to investigate how television journalists go about their work and how they construct news bulletins. As a result, students and the teacher became critical viewers and analysts of 'the news'. It is not simply a matter of the aesthetics of design.

This work involved students learning about the ideological and rhetorical choices involved in producing texts for advertising and journalism (see also Rowsell, 2013).

If we consider this work in terms of the affordances of community-based and place-conscious pedagogy to foster academic literacies, we can see a number of key principles at work:

- making use of local material resources (polling booths and election paraphernalia)
- making a socio-cultural process the object of study (the SRC election and purpose)
- starting with children's interest in and knowledge of television and media
- deconstructing how specific media texts work, and their political discourse
- analyzing the risks and possibilities of the practice
- representing complex and opposing points of view.

In the next chapter, Grant's work is further explored in relation to literacy learning as a collaborative process. The focus then will be on the particular affordances of filmmaking about place and identity for recently arrived refugee students from Sudan learning English as an additional language. However, in this next section, the attention shifts from an urban context to explore the potential of place-conscious pedagogies for students learning academic literacies within rural and regional communities.

River Literacies: Building Environmental Knowledge and Communication

The three-year study explored here involved coresearchers located in New South Wales and South Australia, an educator from the Primary English Teaching Association (PETA) of Australia, and teachers from around a large region of Australia known as the Murray-Darling Basin, which spans four different Australian states. The focus of the project was on how teachers could develop children's environmental communication repertoires.

The research built on an existing project managed by PETA called *Special Forever*, where children in the Murray-Darling Basin geographical region were invited to submit their writing and art for consideration for publication in an annual anthology of children's work that portrayed places that were special to them. The project was sponsored by the Murray-Darling Basin Commission[1], which was keen to enhance young people's understandings about conservation of the environment and sustainability, especially considering the careful use of water and care of indigenous flora and fauna.

The publication of children's work in *Special Forever* had been running for over a decade, and the sponsoring organization and the educator from PETA were concerned that the children's work was mostly celebratory and a little formulaic. Despite the realities of drought, pollution and overuse of resources within the region, children's writing and art rarely showed critical engagement with these serious environmental issues. Consequently, the *River Literacies* project was developed. The first stage involved over twenty teachers working collaboratively with academic researchers to:

- build teacher knowledge of the environment
- explore critical perspectives on literacy and the environment
- experiment with new technologies for communicating children's knowledge.

In the second year, more teachers were invited to join as collaborative researchers. Eventually, eight teachers from these groups went on to conduct extensive classroom research (see Comber, Nixon & Reid, 2007). In this chapter, the work of two experienced teachers illustrates how a focus on an aspect of the local natural environment enabled teachers to build students' deep field knowledge of the topic, and develop the appropriate academic literate repertoires to communicate their learning.

Detox Schooling: Reanimating Literacy for the Environment

One of the teacher-researchers, Wendy Renshaw from Beechworth School, had been teaching for over twenty-five years and had grown up in the region and expressed deep, life-long embodied connections with the Murray River.

> The river is—you're going to talk about special places and that—well I had my special place on the river, and that's mine, that's my time out, that's my safe . . ., that's my gum tree, and that's my part of the world. I love it.

Her stated professional interests at the beginning of the study included environmental education, multiliteracies, ICT and visual arts. Renshaw's pedagogical repertoire, with respect to environmental communications, was considerable and multidiscursive. Built cumulatively across her career, it allowed her to approach topics in complex and creative ways, with different points of connection and publication possibilities for students. Further to this, her work on environmental communications was part of a whole-school plan towards making her school environmentally sustainable and reducing its ecological footprint, a plan that was developed in connection with an initiative known as *Learnscapes* (http://www.learnscapes.org/).

The Beechworth School's *Learnscapes* plan was visible in the foyer, and highlighted a living environmental education for sustainability, including the development and management of school grounds and buildings designed specifically to:

- enhance the physical surrounds
- provide educational and environmental experiences for the students
- promote sustainable management of the grounds, including such things as habitat creation to attract indigenous birdlife
- minimize resource use, including water, energy, products and materials
- forge strong connections between the school, community groups and organizations such as *Landcare*, *WaterWatch* and the local Indigo Shire Council
- enhance conservation and the protection of heritage values in the school and its grounds
- develop and maintain curriculum, teaching and learning in support of environmental sustainability.

The environmental sustainability curriculum at Beechworth started with the materiality of school: its spaces and practices became the object of study and renewal (see Renshaw, 2007). In 'improving the school', the principal and her colleagues initiated a broad reculturing, reinvigorating, renovation and replanting project. For Renshaw, a whole-school shared vision and a deliberate plan was important in order to go beyond *isolated* experiences or pockets of good practice on particular environmental issues.

During the period of the research, Renshaw reported a range of curriculum and pedagogical projects that saw young people apply for classroom roles as gardeners, selling organic liquid worm-castings, looking after the school's chickens and so on. She aimed for depth of knowledge and for students to be able to articulate clearly what they had learned from their inquiry processes.

CALLIE: Well, *Learnscapes* would be like just looking after our school, like planting some vegetables in our garden and stuff, and picking up the pine cones and picking up some rubbish, and yeah, and weeding the gardens and everything.

SOFIA: And there's this wet . . . there's an underground spring down the back of our school, and we're trying to make the spring come up again, and we're trying to make the water rise, so we keep putting things in there and stuff.

CALLIE: Yeah, put it back to its natural, how it was.

LAURA: In *Learnscapes*, we're cleaning up the school, and down at the basketball court there's a whole lot of weeds, bracken, that is supposed to be a little garden, and five/sixes are going to fix that garden up, and even perhaps help with *Learnscapes* and they're going around carrying wheelbarrows and pick up leaves and plant little trees.

The children were clearly aware of the plans for regenerating the school environment, and Renshaw's pedagogical repertoire enabled children to produce academic literacies, develop a strong sense of responsibility for the environment and acquire sophisticated understandings of the issues about sustaining and regenerating local flora.

During the year in which Renshaw conducted her research, her Grade 5/6 class of thirty-one mixed-ability students was engaged in projects relating to the local district's 'natives': the indigenous plants and birds of the local area. This included investigations of the micro-ecology of the school grounds and their surrounds. Renshaw spent considerable time demonstrating to young people how to source reliable information from local experts, written resources, and materials available on the Internet. She strongly believed that giving students extended time to build their knowledge base was crucial in enabling the communication and action that would follow. She indicated to students the kinds of websites that were likely to be helpful. Together, they built a class rubric for evaluating science reports. They compared various reports and the scores they awarded to such reports based on their specified criteria.

Students chose one species of indigenous plant or bird to research more closely, with the initial goal of preparing a report to present to their peers. Later, their edited illustrated reports were mounted for other students to read on the walls of the outdoor classroom. This had already involved Renshaw informing them, along with community experts such as a local botanist and environmental worker, the kinds of plants and birds that were indigenous to the area and that might be listed as rare or under threat. In this way, their research would guide the regeneration of a habitat within the school's own grounds in order to build and sustain the original flora and fauna.

This kind of authentic environmental work, including building frameworks for understanding and action, required a serious investment of time. It is also challenging work for students, indicating the teacher's high expectations. Whether such academic challenges are concerned with science or political processes or history, there is an intrinsic motivation when the focus connects with children's lived experiences in places, but this does not consign their learning to the local or leave them with existing knowledge alone. Indeed, the opposite is true. When students are able to build in-depth field knowledge and the discursive practices of the subject area, they become knowledge producers, rather than simply passive readers. Also, the level of student investment that comes from connecting with the more-than-human world, as noted by place-conscious pedagogy scholars (Smith & Sobel, 2010; Somerville, 2011), is evident here.

Renshaw helped young people to write to learn, as well as to inform the wider school community. She also encouraged them to submit their writing for publication in the *Special Forever* anthologies, and her students' publications often tackled hot political topics such as the rights of farmers to graze their cattle in the Snowy River area. At the same time, she designed new multimedia assignments that required young people to display their scientific understandings through engagement with and use of radio, animation and film. The following assignment for Renshaw's Grade 5/6 class—to produce an animated film, a filmed community announcement, or a talk-back radio program—provided students with the opportunity to demonstrate what they had learned about the district's native plants or birds and threats to their well-being.

Animated Film Assignment

Act now!
Theme: Reducing our environmental impact.
Brief: Design and create a short animated film with a clear message that demonstrates and encourages behaviors that reduce environmental impact to ensure the survival of your researched Indigo Shire bird or plant species. Evaluate using an animated film rubric.
Group: As an individual, partner or traditional group.
Audience: Children, parents and teachers.

Getting started: Some ideas to consider include: planting, the removal of invasive plants, developing a wetland.

Use a template to storyboard your animation or write a script.

OR

Film a community service announcement (up to 3 minutes in length).

OR

Produce a radio-talk back segment.

This task was ambitious and involved ongoing decision-making, false starts and multiple attempts before students or Renshaw were satisfied with their efforts. Many students wanted to improvise on the basis of their affinity with media discourses and genres, but Renshaw kept on insisting on scripts, rehearsal and incorporation of what they had learned from their research. It is important to note that Renshaw keeps extending the expectations for what her students will produce. There is a sense in which they just want to get on and have fun with the technology and the possibilities of various media and modes, but she keeps on demanding that they make use of what they have learned about either the indigenous flora or fauna, and to embed this into their products. For example, it is not enough for them just to demonstrate their knowledge of talk-back radio alone, however entertaining that might be.

There was a complex interplay between newly assembled scientific knowledge and specific associated vocabularies and the everyday, often colloquial, language and style of the media. The tensions between Renshaw's expectations and students' initial interpretations of the task were ultimately very productive. Her critical feedback was fundamental to upping the ante on student performance through her insistence on them incorporating the specialized conceptual understandings they had developed through their inquiries. This kind of enacted curriculum clearly needs more classroom research to examine closely the ways in which environmental knowledge, disciplinary literacy and the affordances of new digital technologies are brought into the pedagogical and discursive space of the classroom.

The environmental communications curriculum and pedagogy at Beechworth Primary School was underpinned with long-term commitments to critical literacy and social justice. In attending to place and also nonhuman inhabitants and phenomena, potentially it addressed a missing element in the field of critical pedagogy (Gruenewald, 2003a; 2003b; Martusewicz & Edmundson, 2005). What did these goals and aspirations mean for young people's understandings of the environment, their emerging dispositions with respect to water, flora and fauna, their capacities to communicate, *and* their literacy repertoires? Interviews with the principal, teachers, community volunteers and, most importantly, the young people in Renshaw's Grade 5/6 classroom were carried out and it became clear that students had appropriated the discourses of sustainability and understood their responsibilities to take action for the environment.

L: Well, if we didn't learn about this, later on, if no one learnt and no one did anything about it, the Earth could like be destroyed like in 100 years.
G: It's sort of good because then you learn, then you go back and tell your parents, and then they'll tell somebody else, and they'll tell somebody else. Not everybody will do something, but . . .
L: But the great majority probably will . . .
M: Yeah, because if we start polluting here, then it will go into Lake Sambell, into the . . . into the Murray, and that will go all the way up to Adelaide.

This was a school explicitly conscious of its history, its situatedness within a micro-environment and the larger regional ecology, and a sense of its responsibilities for future lives and landscapes. Children were genuinely being educated about these matters, not going through the motions of reading and writing politically correct texts about conservation, evident when schools, and institutions more generally, often pay lip-service to topics such as global warming or pollution as though they were abstract subjects or problems occurring elsewhere.

Bird Watching: Learning to 'See' and Represent the Nonhuman World

Rosemary Clifton had been dedicated to the *Special Forever* project for over a decade before her involvement in this project. Each year, she encouraged students from her school to submit artwork and writing to the publication, and many were successful in having their products published in the anthologies. She taught a Grade 5/6 class, known as an *opportunity class*, for students identified as having high intellectual potential, which may or may not have been evident in their actual school achievements thus far. Hence, she saw her role as extending them academically in whatever ways she could. She actively looked for opportunities to engage students in learning to read different perspectives, values and standpoints. She emphasized the importance of students learning to research and argue a case, and she actively recruited and prepared a debating team for regional competitions each year. Clifton was a farmer and a 'greenie, but not a radical greenie', and was committed to teaching for eco-social justice and readily addressed the politics of place within the curriculum. She explained:

> I can't see the point in learning about, you know, Antarctica or the rain forests in Brazil, when they don't even know that there's going to be a coal mine under their backyard. I mean it doesn't make sense.

It was not that Clifton was not interested in global questions about the environment. Indeed she was, and such topics were often on the debating agenda, but she believed that it was foolish to overlook what was happening in the local area and to miss opportunities to research the likely impacts of various proposals for change. Whether it was removing significant trees to expand a sporting club's facilities or a major development such as coal mining, she was alert to the potential of her students engaging with such issues. She aimed for her students to become place-conscious and eco-ethical citizens who could weight up the costs of certain actions that might appear, at first, unproblematic (see also Kerkham & Comber, 2013). As Clifton encouraged her class to think about the environment, and as she shared her passion for protecting trees, children began to point out things they noticed, including various birds in the schoolyard.

During the research project meetings with teachers, team members suggested that Clifton might want to take advantage of her students' interest in birds, their talent for art and the school's location in easy walking distance of a botanic gardens to study birds more systematically. The project had also provided Clifton with new opportunities to learn about various technologies, including ways of weaving sound and photography into texts. Clifton ran with these ideas and independently took classes to the point where she became an accomplished photographer.

Working with these expanded resources, she negotiated with her students to undertake an extended study of birds, including those they saw at home, those at school and those in the nearby gardens. To supplement what they could from books, such as specially purchased illustrated field guides, and the Internet, she began to look to the community for people who might add to students' knowledge of birds. These included Indigenous elders; local Twitchers (or bird watchers), including a radio personality; and family members with particular expertise and interest, such as a grandparent who had an egg collection. Looking out to the wider community in this way, with expectations of potential community assets, is a key feature of place-conscious pedagogy and one of the synergies it shares with inclusive or community-based pedagogy (Gruenewald, 2003a; Smith & Sobel, 2010). Importantly, it also offers possibilities for children to see that learning is social and available in the 'real' and 'local' world. It fosters reciprocal relationships between groups who might not otherwise have opportunities to communicate and learn from each other.

To illustrate how this worked for students, we show how Clifton's pedagogy was enabling academically, particularly for one Aboriginal student in her classroom. Jackson was placed in Clifton's class because he was more capable than his current academic performance suggested; however, his motivation for academic work had not been high. Along with his peers, he became enthused about the class study of 'birds in the backyard'. Jackson's writing explained how their study proceeded:

> During our visits to the Botanic Gardens we took photographs, wrote poems, drew pictures, sketched trees and even painted a few paintings. While we

were there, we learnt about how different bushes and shrubs can attract different types of birds. Would you believe the Wattlebird doesn't eat wattle, well believe it, it is true; in fact they eat nectar of eucalypts and other trees and shrubs. If we planted more of these flowering eucalypts then we would attract more Wattlebirds and maybe some other different kinds of Honeyeater.

This kind of audience-aware report writing did not just happen because Jackson liked birds. Clifton had carefully planned their visits to the botanic gardens, as the task sheet below illustrates.

The Task

Work by yourself or in pairs. You must remain very quiet. Find a comfortable spot to sit so you will not have to move because sudden movements and noises scare birds away. Wear dull, bush colored clothes so that you blend with the surroundings. Write down your observations straight away.

Location: _____

Date: _____   **Time:** _____

Like Wells, who worked with her students as researchers of the local community (see Chapter 2), Clifton actively taught students how to notice, how to observe, and how to make field notes. The bodily and discursive practices of bird watching were thus taken seriously and undertaken together, and students were given time to practice and opportunities to engage in these activities regularly. Having practiced in the schoolyard and the botanic gardens, they were then encouraged to keep watch and notes at home. To further add to the experience, Clifton invited a local bird watcher and national radio commentator to visit the classroom and speak to students about birds in the region and their migration paths and seasons. He provided bird watchers' checklists so that students could officially record their observations and contribute to a regional bird watchers' data archive.

It is important to note that working 'in the local' does not confine students to the local. Indeed, their growing interest in birds resulted in them thinking beyond the local as they began to study the flight paths of migratory birds. They began to understand concepts such as of 'migration' and 'flight paths' and 'seasons' in different ways. The tangible connection to the birds enabled the study of spatial and temporal concepts in a connected fashion, rather than as abstract notions without context. The specialist vocabulary is learned in the process of engagement. Students were introduced to the idea of identifying birds by sound, and after practicing with guidance in the school and local parks, they also downloaded others from the Internet to accompany their illustrated reports. Clifton adapted observation sheets from environmental education sites into classroom assignments that were designed to capture student bird watching practices.

Location:	
Date: _____ Time: _____	
Habitat: ground, bushes, tree trunks, treetops, river swamp, etc.	What was it doing? (Feeding, building a nest, etc.)
	Feeding: insects on plants, in the air, in the water, seeds, nectar, etc.
	Movement on the ground: hops, walks, stands on one leg, etc.
	Flight: fast, slow, straight, gliding, hovering, aerobatics, etc.
	Call: describe in words
How many types of bird did you see while observing?	
Other special observations	

FIGURE 3.3 Observation sheet for bird watching

Clifton consistently included Aboriginal perspectives in her curriculum offerings and invited local Aboriginal elders into the classroom to talk to the children about local flora and fauna. They shared books, written in Aboriginal languages, with the children and also told stories about birds and animals. This inspired Jackson, who wrote a reflection afterwards:

> One of these dreamtime stories was of the gugurrgaagaa (kookaburra). They said its call was a sign for Aboriginal skypeople to light the big fire up in the sky to light and warm up the land.

Jackson continued and explained that in Aboriginal culture, the willie wagtail is 'a spiritual messenger bird who brings news of unfortunate events, of earthquakes, floods, deaths and fires'. The class's serious engagement later led to Clifton's application for a grant with the Aboriginal elders to fund the recording and publishing of such stories as told to children.

Clifton asked a local finch-breeder to show his bird collection to the class and to point out specific features of their markings, shapes of feathers and so on. Jackson was also excited by this field trip and wrote in detail about the range of finches (see Figure 3.4).

Students practiced making close sketches of the finches and also referred to their illustrated field guides. Clifton and students jointly constructed a scientific report on the pelican so that students could learn how such reports were structured linguistically. They developed multimodal PowerPoints and Photo Stories about birds they had studied independently, picture books for younger students in their school, poetry for a regional competition, and class galleries of their varied artworks about local birds. Jackson's engagement continued and was evident in his writing:

We found out the gardens are a birdwatchers' paradise. Our visits to the Botanic Gardens have shown us a huge variety of birds that live in or visit Tamworth. We saw birds like the Jenny-wren hopping along the ground searching for food, the Fantail darting from tree to tree collecting insects in its beak, and the Double Barred Finch waiting for predators to leave the area before taking a drink of water from the pond. It made us realise that birds are living in many different kinds of habitats.

In this piece, Jackson demonstrated his natural confidence with scientific words, like 'habitat' and 'predator'. He also employed literary flourishes, informed by careful observations, to make his report more engaging for readers: the 'Jenny-ren hops' and the 'Fantail darts'.

~~Birds in our backyard~~

Have you ever wondered what birds visit your backyard?

Our class has been involved in a project called 'What bird is that?' which has opened our eyes to the world around us.

I didn't know our school had so many different kinds of birds, until now. Before this project, I had only noticed two kinds of birds; the Magpie and the Pigeon. I now know that there are may kinds of birds, and the Pigeon is actually named the Crested Pigeon and the Black-backed Magpie lives in our area and the White-backed Magpie lives in South Australia.

In our school playground we not only have Magpies and Crested Pigeons but we also have Grey-crowned Babblers, Mistletoe Birds, Rainbow Lorikeets, Wattel Birds, Blue-Cheeked Honeyeaters, Dollarbirds, Rainbow Bee eaters, Noisy Miners, Estern Rosellas, King Parrots, Magpie Larks, the attention seeking Australian Raven and even the tiny Yellow-rumped Thornbill.

When our class went out into the schoolyard to study birds we were amazed to see Blue-cheeked Honeyeater bashing a dragonflies head on the edge of a tree branch before devouring it.

Now I can even tell the difference between male and female birds by their colouring and size. The distinctive brilliant scarlet markings on the male King Parrot set it apart from the dull green colouring of the females head. The male Superb Fairy-wren has brilliant blue head colourings with a pale blue hood and deep blue throat as the Jenny-wren (female) is just a dull, light grey-brown.

As a class we went on an excursion to Mr. M's house to see his amazing finch collection. He showed us his finch collection and told us about the colour patterns on finches and how they're used to identify the different breeds of finches. After seeing his finch collection we studied the Zebra Finch. They are my favourite type of Finch and they live in the hills around our district. The male Zebra Finch is grey with white near its beak black tear drops and chestnut cheeks near the white. He also has a black chest, yellow belly an orange stripe and a black and white striped tail. On the other hand the female is just grey with a yellow belly and striped tail. Mr. M also had an Asian Finch; it was bronze with a black face. I also found out that if you breed two different breeds of finches, you get a mule; (that means you can't breed from it) which unfortunately means that our strange, wonderful colourful patterns on our finches are limited.

The Council bird routes opened in March and we walked to the ceremony. We found out the gardens are a birdwatchers paradise. Our visits to the Botanic Gardens have shown us a huge variety of birds that live in or visit our town. We saw birds like the Jenny-wren hopping along the ground searching for food, the Fantail darting from tree to tree collecting insects in its beak, and the Double Barred Finch waiting for predators to leave the area before taking a drink of water from the pond. It made us realise that birds are living in many different kinds of habitats.

During our visits to the Botanic Gardens we took photographs, wrote poems, drew pictures, sketched trees and even painted a few paintings. While we were there, we learnt about how different bushes and shrubs can attract different types of birds. Would you believe the Wattlebird doesn't eat wattle, well believe it, it is true; in fact they eat nectar of eucalypts and other trees and shrubs. If we planted more of these flowering eucalypts then we would attract more Wattlebirds and maybe some other different kinds of Honeyeater.

This project has opened up a whole new world by allowing me to see the large diversity of birds around me, and it will encourage all of us to plant more trees and have a bird safe environment.

FIGURE 3.4 Jackson's writing about finches

Writing such as Jackson's did not just happen. Jackson and his peers appro-priated the discursive practices of the bird watchers over time and as a result of being there in an embodied sense. In Figure 3.5, we see another map Clifton provided to assist students to record sounds on their field trips or in their back-yards. Often, teachers despair at the lack of detail in students' writing, yet in order to produce rich writing, students need to assemble in-depth knowledge over time and on different occasions in a range of learning activities. Clifton did not shy away from any of the complex elements of ornithology, for to do so would be to reduce opportunities for learning. The motivation to express learning arose from students' embodied experiences connected to the pleasure in, and appreciation of, the more-than-human world. Jackson concluded his report with the following:

> This project has opened up a whole new world by allowing me to see the large diversity of birds around me, and it will encourage all of us to plant more trees and have a bird safe environment.

When Clifton reflected on Jackson's writing, she added that earlier in the year, he 'couldn't write a paragraph, would not put two words on a page'. Jackson is able to develop his identity as an academic writer because he has

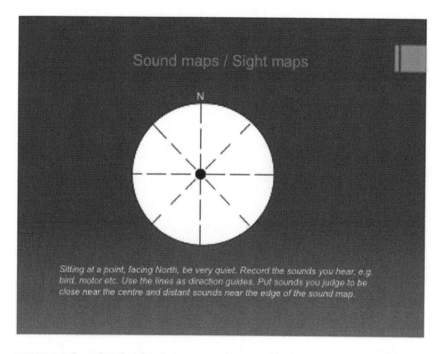

FIGURE 3.5 Sound and sight maps

experienced enabling pedagogies. Clifton's teaching provides time and space for young people to assemble new knowledge about specific topics within their reach and develop researcher dispositions. These accomplishments underpin what they are then able to produce as writers, or more broadly as multimodal text producers and designers. These young people are learning about the semiotics of place in a range of ways and then learning how to communicate their knowledge in a range of media and genre. There is coherence to their study, 'birds in the backyard', that provides a sense of continuity and possibility. For Jackson, it opened up a whole new world. With his new-found expertise, Jackson went on to participate with his teacher and peers to write research proposals seeking funding and to present at conferences for other young people and their teachers around the Murray-Darling Basin region. This is the kind of knowledge creation that David Hargreaves (1998) envisaged in which schools might participate and even lead the way.

The Built Environment: Developing Spatial Concepts and Language

Place, Space and Architectural Knowledge

We return now to the work of Marg Wells and her colleagues, this time drawing on their work in a project entitled *Investigating Literacy 4–9* (see Acknowledgments). This project was concerned with developing inquiry approaches to curriculum design and literacy pedagogy with middle school teachers. At this time, Wells was teaching Grade 3/4 children and was joined by two teaching colleagues: Ruth Trimboli, a Grade 5/6 teacher and long-term collaborator, and Linda Longin, a media studies teacher.

At that time, planning was well underway for a new *superschool* to be built on the existing school grounds. The concept of a superschool has been debated and can mean different things in different places. In this context, three old small neighborhood primary schools, of two to three hundred students each, were to be closed and demolished and one large school of approximately six hundred students was to be built with modern facilities and new technologies. Naturally, this impending change became the subject of teachers' inquiries. As you saw in Chapter 2, each year, Wells conducted a complex long-term program with her classes to develop their sense of belonging through their understandings of place. Neighborhood walks early in the year with this particular cohort of children had revealed a lack of spatial language for conveying directions. Wells therefore began working closely with the children on expanding their linguistic capacities for producing and following directions. This was important in developing children's meta-language and the ability to write and understand the abstract language of instructions.

The children examined their current school built environment and photographed places where they felt they belonged. Influenced by her earlier work with architect Stephen Loo, Wells introduced them to the features of buildings and helped them to construct a range of experiments to test the strength of various building designs using a variety of material, including egg shells, match-sticks and so on. Simultaneously, Wells introduced a range of images via websites and architecture magazines to expand their imaginations in preparation for thinking about how the new school might look. This program developed the children's understandings of science, the arts and technology, and embedded literacy and numeracy in meaningful activities. The guiding question for their curriculum work was: *Does a building look the way it does because of what it is for and who is using it?*

This pivotal inquiry question was surrounded by numerous related investigations and associated activities and participation in a range of events and production of artifacts. Wells designed many sub-inquiries and tasks to explore the relationships between people and place that also helped students to assemble new and expanded literacy repertoires. In planning this work, Wells was explicitly informed by the state curriculum framework in terms of Essential Learnings (Futures, Identity, Interdependence and Thinking) and key learning areas (Design and Technology, English, Health and Physical Development, Science, Society and Environment, and Mathematics). Her design allowed students to develop understandings of complex concepts at the same time as they acquired the linguistic and semiotic resources to represent what they were learning.

While Wells worked in this fashion, embedding literacy across the curriculum, her class was also part of the whole school's 'literacy block' program for three days a week between 8:50 am and 10:50 am. At this time, students were grouped for activities including guided reading and a range of other reading, grammar and punctuation and writing activities, such as writing narratives to practice for national tests of literacy and numeracy. Students also read for about twenty minutes at the start of every day, illustrating how the mandated literacy curriculum was never compromised, but rather was applied and extended across the curriculum.

Wells invited children to think about the actual physical spaces of the school: 'where they feel good, what they enjoy doing and to begin to see that different activities in different spaces impact on this . . . and that they are different for everyone'. Activities included taking photos, making a Photo Story (My Belonging Spaces) and writing (such as school history and recounts of individual's first days at school). After negotiating with her colleagues—Ruth Trimboli, the Grade 5/6 teacher, and Linda Longin, the media studies teacher—Wells decided to focus on the physical changes that were due to occur within the school grounds: the building of the new school and then the scheduled demolition of the old school.

> With the old buildings earmarked for demolition and a totally new school planned to be built, I wanted my students to be involved in thinking and planning what the new school should look like.

Wells had a strong commitment to children being able to contribute to decision-making and looked for opportunities to advocate on their behalf in order to make spaces for this to happen whenever possible. Her approach evokes strong connections with Soja's (2010) 'spatial justice', as she is not prepared to accept that her students should not have a say in the design and the subsequent spatial practices of their new school. Informed by Lefebvre and Foucault, Soja (2010) argues:

> The starting point remains the same: human spatiality in all its forms and expressions is socially produced. We make our geographies for good or bad, just or unjust, in much the same way that it can be said we make our histories, under conditions not of our choosing but in real-world contexts already shaped by socio-spatial processes in the past and the enveloping historically and socially constituted geographies of the present. This profoundly displaces the idea of space merely as an external environment or container, a naturalized or neutral stage for life's seemingly time-driven social drama.
>
> *(p. 103)*

The socially and politically constructed nature of spaces is akin to the socially and politically constructed nature of texts: both can be questioned, redesigned and remade. The synergies between critical and spatial literacies are evident here. Wells' dedication towards spatial justice was deeply ingrained in her pedagogical disposition and was frequently her starting point in imagining curriculum. She reported that she wanted her students to become 'architects' in the sense that they would orient to spaces like architects; this would allow them also to know that places and structures could be made differently. If as Soja (2010, p. 103) observes, 'space is filled with politics and privileges, ideologies and cultural collisions, utopian ideals and dystopian oppression, oppressive power and the possibility for emancipation', what better place to begin to learn about how space works than in the institution of schooling, especially at a time of building a new school as part of the wider urban renewal of the suburb. What better context than this for learning about their rights to the school. In order to develop students' spatial understandings, she realized they would need knowledge and information. She began by having students think about eggs (as a home and as a shape) and invited them to collect egg shapes in everyday life (see also Comber, Nixon, Ashmore, Loo & Cook, 2006, on Wells' earlier work around the egg shape). She thus began with a concept that students knew about from their own experience. She moved on from there to consider 'the dome' and the 'arch', both architectural terms, which relate to the egg. She designed experiments for the students to conduct, examining the strength of the egg shape. She printed and laminated color copies of various items that incorporated a dome shape, such as an army helmet, igloo, chair, lantern, toilet bowl, and domes in various parts of different buildings. Collectively, these illustrated the characteristics of domes and provided a basis for a study of domes as a design feature.

Using online images of large buildings and hard copies of architectural magazines, Wells introduced students to a range of designs that included domes and arches. They carried out a range of experiments (using cardboard and toy cars) to determine how much weight an arch could carry before it would collapse. Wells helped students connect their prior everyday knowledge with new academic forms of knowing and to learn the discourses (vocabulary, genres, media) associated with formal knowledge. Table 3.1 lists a range of tasks and activities Wells designed and employed to build her students' knowledge of place and space across the learning areas.

Wherever she could, Wells planned social outcomes for the work students had undertaken. For example, the work on directions was summarized in an insert for the school newsletter, and was formally presented at the whole school assembly. During their neighborhood walks, students took photographs of buildings they regarded as significant in some way, and focused on various features, such as pillars or verandahs. They also photographed key signage in the local area, including street names, warnings, business names and so on. These images contributed to individual and class Photo Stories entitled *The Walk*. Simply, Photo Stories are a visual way of telling a story or recounting a journey through a sequence of photos. Microsoft developed a software application to support such a process, but of course it can be done through PowerPoint or any other program that allows images to appear in turn. Some applications allow verbal narration and a range of other multimodal effects.

TABLE 3.1 Building Knowledge of Place Across Learning Areas

Learning Area	Task or Activity
Design & Technology	Build cardboard arches and test weight supported
English	Write formal addresses
Society & Environment	Locate where people live on map and plan a neighborhood walk
Resource-Based Learning	Search for books and sites about buildings, building features and materials
	Use Google Earth to find their house and the school
English	Give directions (oral and written) in classroom, around the school and home to school
Society & Environment & English	Participate in neighborhood walk using maps and recording information about buildings
English & Drama	Organize and present assembly
English	Write a descriptive text about a chosen building
Maths & Technology	Draw a floor plan of own house

This work demonstrates the affordances of place-based pedagogy, and in this case, the built environment provides the context for students' literacy learning in the middle years. The archive of student work included examples of young people:

- conducting surveys
- writing recounts (of their first day at school)
- writing descriptions (of a house design)
- providing directions (of getting to school)
- producing Photo Stories (of the neighborhood walk)
- undertaking and documenting experiments (the strength of dome structures)
- learning how to produce storyboards (preferred places in the school)
- planning a whole school assembly and so on.

Learning about new genres and media was done in the context of representing their experiences of places. Because they built up their knowledge and information before writing, students had the vocabulary and the conceptual resources available to weave into their productions, allowing for more detail and accuracy.

In order to produce complex and thoughtful products, it is necessary for students to first build up their conceptual knowledge and linguistic resources. Rushing to prepare products, even with the incentive of new media and software, can result in poor outcomes. Building up students' field knowledge and mobilizing understandings developed from experience places them in a powerful position to design texts that accurately represent their learning. In-depth and rich learning underpins their representations. Multiple opportunities to discuss related concepts and questions allow students to consider different angles and perspectives on an issue.

Belonging Places Across Time

We turn now to the related curriculum and pedagogical work of Ruth Trimboli, the Grade 5/6 teacher. Within her classroom, Trimboli had a focus on Australia, including its history and geography, and immigration and Indigenous Australia. *Belonging*, as a concept, was introduced through students reflecting on their own experiences, with many as refugees and immigrants, and also through formally studying Aboriginal culture and history.

This broader work on the significance of place and belonging in Australian history underpinned and linked to an interview-based documentary film students produced about their own school and a sense of belonging. They focused on the kind of school they wanted to see built in the context of the superschool development, and how that might engender a sense of belonging in the future. In part, this new work was inspired by her earlier collaboration with Wells in the Grove Gardens project (see Chapter 2).

As part of the theme of *belonging*, Trimboli worked with students to produce a book about their histories of belonging in different places across their lives. Her documented learning objectives were to:

- motivate students to improve their writing skills through writing about themselves and their world
- give them opportunities to find out more about their family background, culture and reasons for being in Australia. Also, to give them a sense of pride in acknowledging that their world is important and that other people would find their stories interesting to read
- increase their skills and abilities in writing, reading and comprehension. Increase their confidence when speaking in front of an audience
- increase students' knowledge about Australia
- develop students' skills in working cooperatively in group situations using Cooperative Learning Strategies
- improve their questioning techniques
- develop higher order thinking skills.

At the beginning of the year, Trimboli spent considerable time building the students' capabilities with narrative structures in preparation for the national tests, and she hoped that this would prepare them well for writing extended texts around the theme of 'belonging'. She introduced students to a range of books about place including:

- *My Place* (Wheatley, 1987)
- *A School Like Mine* (DK Publishing, 2007)
- *Children Just Like Me* (Kindersley, 1995).

In addition, her class undertook a PMI (Plus, Minus, Interesting) analysis of their Ridley Grove School grounds. Trimboli emphasized social skills and used the Placemats Collaborative Learning Strategy to discuss: *What do you think generally about the school?* Trimboli also used her approach to critical thinking to support students to brainstorm questions they might want to ask people in interviews about the history and future of the school. Once again, the teacher had ambitious plans for students to understand the big picture within which their classroom work is located.

> Australia and *A School Like Ours* is . . . my major thing for the year and that all ties in with one another anyway, because it's all about Australia. . . . They're going to be looking at their country of origin, their neighborhood, things that have been talked about in those books . . ., their family, their school, . . . what they think that other kids would be interested in reading later on. Then with Australia . . . I'm going to be looking at . . .

Aboriginal settlement, migration, some history. Then we're going on to landscapes and rocks, which is the Science part of it, and we're also doing some mapping work, and we've been looking at Google Earth, looking at some of the landmarks in Australia.

The focus on place did not restrict Trimboli's scope to the local, but rather allowed her to draw explicitly on cultural, historical and geographical dimensions when considering Australia as a nation. Importantly, her work was informed by research conducted elsewhere, such as the UK project *The School I'd Like* (Burke & Grosvenor, 2003), and her knowledge of her colleague Marg Wells' collaboration with a South African school. When she discovered that her initial attempts to get the depth of thinking she wanted from the students about their school did not measure up, she tried other alternatives.

In Term 1, I introduced the Six Hats and explored the concept of belonging, and we brainstormed words related to belonging. . . . In term 2 we used a Place Mat to analyse the school and using the Six Thinking Hats, but I found that that didn't quite get to what I wanted to get to. So then I ended up doing a brainstorm . . . of all the major things that . . . have happened in the school. . . . This is leading up to . . . what they did in the UK, *A School I'd Like*. So some focus on the things that we've had here and what we really liked, and they actually went around to all the other classes, and they were quite keen about doing that, and eventually I'd like to get them to do it up in a graph on Excel.

Trimboli continuously reflected on what she had already done, recognizing here that generic approaches to so-called critical thinking did not deliver the more sociological and spatial analysis she was hoping for. This is interesting because such 'leveled' or stylistic approaches to thinking typically ignore questions of power. In order to get beyond bland descriptions, she was going to have to go further. Preexisting frames simply organize what is known without interrogating how and why particular places become preferred. She imagined where she might go next. A range of activities underpinned her approach: brainstorming, collaborative learning, critical thinking, and engaging students as researchers. A rich and diverse range of strategies and activity structures are evident here, with no single or simple way of approaching the topic. Significantly, the project moved across different disciplines, including Science, History and Geography, and provided opportunities for the construction of different kinds of texts, from report writing to personal narratives and filmmaking. Trimboli's sheer persistence was clear: she did not give up on her goal to support students to develop a deep and critical level of understanding of the concept of 'belonging'.

Consequently, putting together their book, *A School Like Ours*, was a much longer project than anticipated and was not completed until later in the year.

Trimboli's 'belonging project', like that of Wells, was extended over time and included a number of different assignments. Some of these were individual tasks, but many were undertaken in pairs, small groups or as a whole class. Thinking about their own experiences of different places and studying Australia culturally and in terms of landforms provided students with rich material for the production of complex texts.

Linda Longin, the media studies teacher at Ridley Grove School, supported both her colleagues and their students to experiment with new ways of documenting and representing their learning about the school as a *belonging* place in the context of the new school development. In addition, she provided valuable perspectives on the teachers' focus students in her weekly diary from her observations of their approaches to working in her lessons. With Wells' Grade 3/4 class, she began by brainstorming places in the school which they valued and how those places were used by students and teachers. She helped students to organize their groups to select their preferred places, and then to make a storyboard on how they would like to represent their nominated place. Finally, Longin supported students to use photography to represent their places and produce a Photo Story. She and Wells worked together to ensure their lessons complemented each other:

> Yes, because we talk together, so she's talking about the outside of the buildings, I'm talking about the inside, yes, and part of this film is to ask people—it might be their fellow classmates, or I think someone was going to ask the librarian—what do you want in this area for the new school, and so it's looking at what we've got now, how we value what we've got now, and what we'd like for the future.

Longin assisted Trimboli's Grade 5/6 class to make documentary films based on interviews about the school: past, present and future. She began by critically reviewing some films made by former students.

> Yes, and I purposely chose a really good one, and a not very good one, and they could see the difference . . . the types of questions that were asked, the types of answers that were given, the filming process itself, and the editing process as well, so they could really see the difference there, and it gave them an idea of what I was expecting.

With her guidance, Trimboli's students could see what made some filmed interview sequences work well, and what got in the way in those interviews that seemed less successful. This gave them an idea of what Longin's expectations were for their films.

> They came up with a list of counsellor, school chaplain, principal, canteen workers, SSO, and a few teachers . . . a librarian, students. . . . The purpose of the interview is to find out what connections these people have with

the school, their feelings about the school now and in the past, and their thoughts on the new school, so it's just a personal point of view.

She explained how she worked over time to develop the students' interview questions and to help them make the transition from their questions into storyboarding their film shoot.

> Then we talked about open-ended questions. We brainstormed *why do we ask open-ended questions?* And we brainstormed that, and came up with these ideas, and then we talked about sentence starters. . . . They had copies of that and went away in their groups—and again I go through the whole process of making groups—and using those ideas, wrote questions, and I said that they had to write maybe ten questions. . . . And they create their storyboard from those questions, so their storyboard has to tell me who's doing what and how, basically, *who, what, how* . . . And each person that they were interviewing gets a photocopy of the storyboard beforehand, so they've had time to think of interesting answers, yeah. Now after they film they download onto the computer, and then they spend a week or two editing.

The media studies teacher's detailed account of her process of working with Trimboli's and Wells' classes makes it clear that serious planning and high standards are integral to the way she operates. Hence, students get a consistent message from all their teachers. While media studies is highly motivational for many students, it is never presented as a soft option, but rather as a learning area where they learn new skills about organizing their learning in teams and representing that learning in a variety of media. Longin played a key role in helping all children to investigate how they felt about the school and their experiences of a range of cultures, and to document the change process as it unfolded. Her approach contributed to a positive school ethos and the sense of a shared project.

The alignment between Wells, Trimboli and Longin, and their work on place-based pedagogies, is clear. Each of them exploited the opportunities associated with the *superschool* development to have the students reflect and talk with school community members about the school as a place. Of course, such work could be done in any school at any time. However, in this case, the extra motivation was provided by the wider context of urban renewal and the development of the new school.

Conclusion

During the middle years of primary school, children face a number of developmental and learning challenges that relate to their literacies and identities. They need to:

- read and write to learn
- produce extended and complex texts

- become part of a peer group
- develop their own sense of identity
- operate at an increasingly independent level in terms of the everyday academic, personal and social demands on them.

These challenges may sometimes seem discrete to educators, but from the perspective of young people, it involves a lot of complex work in terms of learning how they relate to others (in and out of school); how they manage themselves and others; and how they relate to the world around them as they begin to imagine possible futures. From a student's point of view, these separate developmental challenges must be integrated to provide a sense of well-being and to help them forge an academic identity. Given these challenges, place-based education is an ideal starting point for expansion of children's literate and social repertoires.

In addition to the affordances of space and place for children's literacy learning, the study of place also fosters children forming relationships with places, both in terms of belonging and responsibility. There's a positive productive reciprocity here. Children learn *about* spaces and places, *from* spaces and places, *in* spaces and places, and in the process learn about their obligations for the care of spaces and places. Massey's (2005) notion of throwntogetherness provides a dynamic way of conceptualizing classroom spaces—spaces that must be negotiated, that are always under development, always about the meeting of people on their various trajectories: teachers, students, parents and communities. If space and place become the focus of learning, rather than seen as background, the school can become a genuine meeting place, where teachers and students work together to learn more about its populations, history, ecology, architecture and so on. These inquiries are not just feel-good activities, though they may contribute to positive relationships and community building, they begin to demonstrate to children who has a say in the organization, design and management of particular places and that how things work is always in the interests of particular groups. A 'critical spatial perspective (Soja, 2010, p. 200) can allow children to work, with their teachers, to imagine and argue for their rights to occupy fairer, safer, healthier and enhanced shared places.

At the same time, as discussed further in Chapter 4, the spatial literacies that teachers and children assemble emerge in the context of their purposeful learning. They do begin to appropriate aspects of the discourses of architecture or botany, for example, and they learn about questions of representation and voice through making texts in various modes and media to present to a range of audiences (see Figure 3.6). This involves teachers inducting students into traditional school literacies associated with subject-specific knowledges, such as reports and narratives, but they do not stop there. These teachers develop what Grant (2014) has described as hybrid genres—that is, a range of purpose-built and collaboratively constructed semiotic artifacts that have real-world goals (see Figure 3.6).

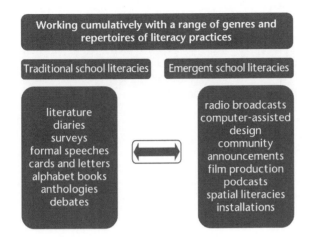

FIGURE 3.6 Traditional and emergent literacy practices

In the next chapter, several 'hybrid' texts are collaboratively produced in a range of classrooms that allow children to learn about communication and place in ways that have durable and positive effects for their learning, both in and out of school.

Note

1. The Murray-Darling Basin Commission (since 2007, the Murray-Darling Basin Authority) is responsible for the management of water across the region. The Murray and Darling rivers flow across four states of Australia; hence, the need for a representational body. See http://www.mdba.gov.au/about-mdba.

References

Bautista, M, Bertrand, M, Morrell, E, Scorza, D & Matthews, C 2013, 'participatory action research and city youth: Methodological insights from the council of youth research', *Teachers College Record*, vol. 115, no. 10, pp. 1–23.

Blommaert, J 2013, *Ethnography, superdiversity and linguistic landscapes*, Multilingual Matters, Bristol.

Burke, C & Grosvenor, I 2003, *The school I'd like: Children and young people's reflections of an education for the 21st century*, Routledge/Falmer, London.

Callow, J 2013, *The shape of text to come: How image and text work*, Primary English Teaching Association, Newtown, Sydney.

Cazden, C 2001, *Classroom discourse: The language of teaching and learning*, Heinemann, Portsmouth, New Hampshire.

Christie, F & Derewianka, B 2008, *School discourse*, Continuum, London.

Christie, F & Maton, K 2011, *Disciplinarity: Functional linguistic and sociological perspectives*, Continuum, New York.

Comber, B 2006, 'Critical literacy educators at work: Examining their dispositions, discursive resources and repertoires of practice', in R. White & K. Cooper (eds.), *Practical critical educator: Integrating literacy, learning and leadership*, Springer, Dordrecht, pp. 51–65.

Comber, B & Nixon, H 2013, 'Urban renewal, migration and memories: The affordances of place-based pedagogies for developing immigrant students' literate repertoires', *Multidisciplinary Journal of Educational Research*, vol. 3, no. 1, pp. 42–68.

Comber, B, Nixon, H, Ashmore, L, Loo, S & Cook, J 2006, 'Urban renewal from the inside out: Spatial and critical literacies in a low socioeconomic school community', *Mind, Culture and Activity*, vol. 13, no. 3, pp. 228–246.

Comber, B, Nixon, H & Reid, J (eds.) 2007, *Literacies in place: Teaching environmental communications*, Primary English Teaching Association, Newtown.

Cormack, P & Comber, B 2007, 'Doing justice: Young people's representations of the Murray-Darling Basin', in E. Potter, A. Mackinnon, S. McKenzie & J. McKay (eds.), *Fresh Water: New perspectives on water in Australia*, Melbourne University Press, Carlton, Victoria, pp. 134–152.

Cormack, P & Green, B 2007, 'Writing in English: How a school subject constitutes students' relationships to the environment', *Australian Journal of Language and Literacy*, vol. 30, no. 2, pp. 85–101.

Dezuanni, M 2015, 'The building blocks of digital media literacy: Socio-material participation and the production of media knowledge', *Journal of Curriculum Studies*, vol. 47, no. 3, pp. 416–439, accessed November 20, 2014, http://www.tandfonline.com/doi/abs/10.1080/00220272.2014.966152#.VG0v6SgVrzJ

DK Publishing 2007, *A school like mine*, DK Publishing/UNICEF, New York.

Dudley-Marling, C & Michaels, S 2012, *High-expectation curricula: Helping all students succeed with powerful learning*, Teachers College Press, New York.

Fielding, M 2001, 'Students as radical agents of change', *Journal of Educational Change*, vol. 2, no. 2, pp. 123–141.

Freebody, P, Chan, E & Barton, G 2013, 'Literacy and curriculum: Language and knowledge in the classroom', in K. Hall, T. Cremin, B. Comber & L. Moll (eds.), *International handbook of research in children's literacy, learning and culture*, Wiley-Blackwell, Oxford, pp. 304–318.

Gascoyne, G 2007, 'Weeding verbascum: Dealing with problem behaviour through environmental action', in B. Comber, H. Nixon & J. Reid (eds.), *Literacies in Place: Teaching environmental communications*, Primary English Teaching Association, Newton, pp. 112–127.

Gee, J 1990, *Social linguistics and literacies: Ideology in discourses*, Falmer Press, London.

Gee, J 2004, *Situated language and learning: A critique of traditional schooling*, Routledge, New York.

Gillis, V 2014, 'Disciplinary literacy: Adapt not adopt', *Journal of Adolescent & Adult Literacy*, vol. 57, no. 8, pp. 614–623.

Grant, H 1999, 'Topdogs and underdogs', in *Practically Primary*, vol. 4, no. 3, pp. 40–44.

Grant, H 2014, 'English as an additional language learners and multimedia pedagogies', in A. Morgan, B. Comber, P. Freebody & H. Nixon (eds.), *Literacy in the middle years: Learning from collaborative classroom research*, Primary English Teaching Association Australia, Newton, pp. 35–50.

Green, B & Corbett, M (eds.) 2013, *Rethinking rural literacies: Transnational perspectives*, Palgrave McMillan, New York.

Gruenewald, D 2003a, 'The best of both worlds: A critical pedagogy of place', *Educational Researcher*, vol. 32, no. 4, pp. 3–12.

Gruenewald, D 2003b, 'Foundations of place: A multidisciplinary framework for place-conscious education', *American Educational Research Journal*, vol. 40, no. 3, pp. 619–654.

Gutierrez, K, Baquedano-Lopez, P, Alvarez, H & Chiu, M 1999, 'Building a culture of collaboration through hybrid language practices', *Theory Into Practice*, vol. 38, no. 2, pp. 87–93.

Gutierrez, K, Rymes, B & Larson, J 1995, 'Script, counterscript, and underlife in the classroom: James Brown versus *Brown v. Board of Education*', *Harvard Educational Review*, vol. 65, no. 3, pp. 445–471.

Halliday, M A K 1978, *Language as social semiotic: The social interpretation of language and meaning*, Edward Arnold, London.

Hargreaves, D 1998, *Creative professionalism: The role of teachers in the knowledge society*, Demos, London.

Hull, G & Katz, M 2006, 'Crafting an agentive self: Case studies of digital storytelling', *Research in the Teaching of English*, vol. 41, no. 1, pp. 43–81.

Ivanic, R 2004, 'Discourses of writing and learning to write', *Language and education*, vol. 18, no. 30, pp. 220–245.

Janks, H 1993, *Language and identity*, Hodder & Stoughton/Wits University Press, Johannesburg.

Janks, H 2010, *Literacy and power*, Routledge, New York.

Kalantzis, M & Cope, B 2008, *New learning: Elements of a science of learning*, Cambridge University Press, Cambridge.

Kamler, B 2001, *Relocating the personal: A critical writing pedagogy*, State University of New York Press, Albany, New York.

Kerkham, L & Comber, B 2013, 'Literacy, place-based pedagogies and social justice', in B. Green & M. Corbett (eds.), *Rethinking rural literacies: Transnational perspectives*, Palgrave McMillan, New York, pp. 197–218.

Kindersley, B 1995, *Children just like me*, Moondrake, Melbourne, Australia.

Lea, M & Street, B 2006, 'The 'academic literacies' model: Theory and applications', *Theory Into Practice*, vol. 45, no. 4, pp. 368–377.

Lewis, C, Enciso, P & Moje, E B (eds.) 2007, *Reframing sociocultural research on literacy*, Routledge, New York & London.

Lo Bianco, J 2003, *A site for debate, negotiation and contest of national identity: Language policy in Australia*, Language Policy Division, Council of Europe, Strasbourg.

Luke, A, Dooley, K & Woods, A 2011, 'Comprehension and content: Planning literacy in low socioeconomic and culturally diverse schools', *Australian Educational Researcher*, vol. 38, no. 2, pp. 149–166.

Luke, A & Freebody, P 1997, 'The social practices of reading', in S. Muspratt, A. Luke & P. Freebody (eds.), *Constructing critical literacies: Teaching and learning textual practices*, Allen & Unwin, St Leonards, NSW, pp. 195–225.

Martusewicz, R & Edmundson, J 2005, 'Social foundations as pedagogies of responsibility and eco-ethical commitment', in D. W. Butin (ed.), *Teaching Social foundations of education: Contexts, theories and issues*, Lawrence Erlbaum Associates, Mahwah, New Jersey, pp. 71–91.

Massey, D 2005, *For space*, SAGE, London.

Moje, E B, McIntosh, K C, Kramer, K, Ellis, I, Carrillo, R & Collazo, T 2004, 'Working towards third space in content area literacy: An examination of everyday funds of knowledge and Discourse', *Reading Research Quarterly*, vol. 39, no. 1, pp. 38–70.

Moll, L C, Amanti, C, Neff, D & Gonzalez, N 1992, 'Funds of knowledge for teaching: Using a qualitative approach to connect homes and classrooms', *Theory and Practice*, vol. 31, no. 2, pp. 132–141.

New London Group 1996, 'A pedagogy of multiliteracies: Designing social futures', *Harvard Educational Review*, vol. 66, no. 1, pp. 60–92.

Nixon, H & Comber, B 2005, 'Behind the scenes: Making movies in early years class-rooms', in J. Marsh (ed.), *Popular culture, media and digital literacies in early childhood*, Routledge/Falmer, London, pp. 219–236.

Nixon, H, Comber, B with H. Grant & M. Wells 2012, 'Collaborative inquiries into literacy, place and identity in changing policy contexts: Implications for teacher development', in C. Day (ed.), *International handbook on teacher and school development*, Routledge, London, pp. 175–184.

Renshaw, W 2007, 'Shaping the learning landscape', in B. Comber, H. Nixon & J. Reid (eds.), *Literacies in place: Teaching environmental communications*, Primary English Teaching Association, Newtown, pp. 128–145.

Rowsell, J 2013, *Working with multimodality: Rethinking literacy in a digital age.* Routledge, London & New York.

Smith, G & Sobel, D (eds.) 2010, *Place- and community-based education in schools*, Routledge, New York & London.

Soja, E 2010, *Seeking spatial justice*, University of Minnesota Press, Minneapolis.

Somerville, M 2011, 'Becoming-frog: Learning place in primary school', in M. Somerville, B. Davies, K. Power, S. Gannon & P. de Carteret, *Place pedagogy change*, Sense, Rotterdam, pp. 65–79.

Street, B (ed.) 2001, *Literacy and development: Ethnographic perspectives*, Routledge, London.

Thomson, P 2002, *Schooling the rustbelt kids: Making the difference in changing times*, Allen & Unwin, Sydney, Australia.

Wheatley, N 1987, *My place*, Ashton Scholastic, Sydney.

4

LITERACY LEARNING AS COLLECTIVE AND SPATIAL PRACTICE

Introduction

In this period of escalating standardization with respect to literacy, students are typically positioned as competitive individuals, yet the contemporary moment actually requires young people who can collaborate and communicate, who can work together as designers, as problem-solvers, as media-makers. The demands of climate change and an overcrowded planet require the design of spaces for collective ownership and living. The 21st-century citizen will need to be more than a self-serving consumer. Their literate repertoires will increasingly involve collective meaning-making. How can teachers support and teach young people to work collaboratively to become researchers; to ask significant questions; find out and share the answers; and then disseminate their ideas in ways that influence and shape their local places and environments? The focus of that work needs to have substantive material that will capture children's imaginations and sustain them for complex academic learning.

The purpose of this chapter is to demonstrate how the study of place affords complex opportunities for collective meaning-making practices. Instead of literacy lessons being an individual pursuit only, making place the object of study can foster collaboration. This in turn means that children need to negotiate about what they have observed, what they understand, what they wish to represent. The politics of literacy are foregrounded as they grapple to produce texts with a partner or group or the whole class.

Because the experience and study of place can readily be organized as a shared focus, it offers great potential for collaborative learning. For instance, young people can consider the ways in which places are portrayed and construct alternatives. They can examine the representations of different people in place and contest those. They can consider the ways spaces are organized and suggest changes. They can design new spaces—both real and imagined. This chapter includes a range of strategies and processes that have been used by teachers to build students' confidence and competence in the analysis and production of complex texts, particularly representations of people and places, in multiple modes and media.

Dudley-Marling and Michaels (2012) recently put together a collection of classroom studies documenting 'high expectations' curriculum. The teachers, working in culturally and socio-economically diverse classroom contexts, designed and enacted complex academic learning in English, mathematics, science and other subject areas. They show that when given opportunities to engage deeply with rich ideas over time and work together to discuss their thinking, students were able to accomplish sophisticated learning that met their teachers' high expectations. This move, being able to enact high expectations curriculum, is key in turning around deficit discourses that circulate in schools in poor communities. Similarly, in place-conscious curriculum, students address ambitious academic challenges that arise from local material and demographic change (Smith & Sobel, 2010). Through working with everyday local realities, teachers seek to foster a sense of purpose, cultivate resilience, broaden the capacity to negotiate and imagine possibilities, and foster a sense of what might be accomplished to improve the way things are. Examples of teacher-designed collaborative literacy tasks, through which students work in pairs and groups to research, imagine and report on aspects of place, are the basis of this chapter.

Inspired by Vygotsky's (1978) insights about what people are able to accomplish with help from more expert others, many researchers have considered literacy learning as a socio-cultural practice (Dyson, 1989; 1993; 1997; 2013; Gutierrez, 2008), foregrounding the ways in which children learn how language works in the context of use with adults and peers. Correspondingly, interactions of children are not innocent (Gilbert, 1991). Children's actions are motivated sometimes in their own interests, resulting in the exclusion and to the detriment of others (Comber, in press, 2015). Earlier work in critical literacy (Comber & Kamler, 1997) reveals that even in contexts where the teacher's explicit intention was to foreground the dangers of relations of power and promote understandings of justice, existing racial tensions between students sometimes overrode the pedagogical agenda. However, if we return once again to the idea following Massey (2005) of the classroom as a meeting place, which must necessarily be negotiated, then this situation should not deter teachers from opening up conversations about people, politics and place. Indeed, when such matters cannot be talked about in a safe environment, exclusionary practices can go underground, with serious consequences for children.

When teachers design curriculum underpinned by a theory of literacy as a socio-cultural practice, the affordances of peer learning can be built into the activity and participation structures. It is then possible to move beyond the competitive individualism so dominant in an era of standardization, and for the student cohort and teacher to become a learning community. Collaborative text production in classrooms can be a positive site for identity work, community building and the development of literate repertoires.

Place-Conscious Pedagogy and Academic Literacies: Working Collectively in School Spaces

In the classrooms described below, pairs or teams of students, in collaboration and over time, design and construct a range of texts, beginning with a class-made alphabet book focusing on the changing local area and concluding with films coproduced by a teacher and her ESL and film club students. The examples are taken from two different school communities. Marg Wells and Ruth Trimboli work together in a poor inner western suburb school, often collaborating on extended curriculum projects. Helen Grant works in a city school, also highly multicultural, but with children from a range of socioeconomic circumstances. In both contexts, the teachers engage children in working collaboratively to produce and publish multimodal texts that represent their learning about place and spaces.

Reclaiming the Alphabet Book: De-Colonializing Literacy Learning

When the urban redevelopment project known as Westwood in the western suburbs of Adelaide, South Australia, began in 1999, Marg Wells took every opportunity she could to become involved in the consultation process and to involve her students. She engaged them in research about the indigenous flora and fauna, consulted on the design of new public playgrounds, and got involved with artists in residence and streetscape projects. She was an initiator in the Grove Gardens project and actively exploited the building of the new *superschool* as discussed in Chapter 2. Through all of this, Wells searched for the most inspirational children's literature to assist her in exploring the themes of belonging, change and people's histories in places. For example, she used wordless picture books such as Jeannie Baker's *Belonging* (2004) and *Window* (1990), and Aboriginal artist and author Elaine Russell's *A Is for Aunty* (2000) and *The Shack That Dad Built* (2011). Wells used these texts as models for students of other ways of knowing and representation and contested the frequent approach in books for children that infantilize them or present an openly ideological mainstream middle-class white view of the world.

Historically, alphabet books often portray their subjects in very stereotyped ways. For example, consider the following pages from a 1940s alphabet book. The cover presents a quintessential image of a drover moving cattle through the Australian bush. The skin color of the male rider is not possible to see as he is clothed and facing the bush. A working dog is by his side. A huge

FIGURE 4.1 Cover of *Australian ABC* (194–)

eucalypt frames the page. He looks relaxed and the cattle well fed. This is colonial Australia, where space is no problem, where the adventurous farmer can do well. There is no sense of the invasion of Aboriginal country by white·settlers.

The first page of the actual book addresses both the letter A and the letter B. This entire page, in the same outback hues, is replete with a white map of Australia in the center of the blue sky. The text reads:

A IS FOR AUSTRALIA,
LAND OF THE FREE.
THAT'S WHERE I WAS BORN,
LUCKY, LUCKY ME.

FIGURE 4.2 A is for Australia, B is for Boomerang from *Australian ABC*

This rhyming text appears on the top of the page in the center. This 'lucky country' ideology has always ignored the impact of white invasion on Aboriginal people and, indeed, on their country. The following text appears:

B IS FOR BOOMERANG,
USED BY OUR NATIVE BLACK.
WHEN THROWN PROPERLY,
IT ALWAYS COMES BACK.

On the left side of this text is a back view image of a naked Aboriginal man with paint visible on his arms and legs and holding two spears. On the right side of the text, a very large boomerang is suspended in mid-air, presumably on its way back to its owner. The man is there to represent the 'native black' who use boomerangs. These kinds of colonizing discourses are not uncommon in books produced for children. More broadly, Aboriginal people in Australia still suffer greatly from ignorance and racism, both of which frequently impact negatively on their success in education (Luke et al., 2013).

With respect to literacy education, as Allan Luke (1991) showed over two decades ago, children's literature and, indeed, school readers frequently provide problematic representations of race, gender, age, class and so on. Children are inducted into normative ways of thinking at the same time as they learn to read. However, increasingly, children's authors are producing counter-texts: texts that trouble unitary limited accounts of history and contemporary life (Vasquez, 2010). As well as searching for children's literature that presents complex and diverse viewpoints, teachers can also produce texts with children for classroom use that present alternative ways of viewing the world. Wells does both. Having reviewed a great number of alphabet books, Wells was delighted to find *A Is for Aunty* (Russell, 2000). Russell is an Aboriginal artist and storyteller who grew up on an Aboriginal mission called Murrin Bridge in the Lake Cargelligo area of New South Wales. Each letter of the alphabet illustrates a different memory of a significant place in her childhood in the 1940s and 50s during a period where some Aboriginal children were taken from their homes and placed in foster families or in institutions. Coincidentally, this was the same era in which the *Australian ABC* book, discussed earlier, was published.

This practice of removing children has been reported in *Bringing Them Home: The Stolen Children* (Commonwealth of Australia, 1997) and remains a destructive legacy that, like Aboriginal land rights, has not been reconciled in Australian contemporary life. Nevertheless, Russell's stunning artwork depicts people happily engaged in activities such as billycart races, picking quandongs and yabby fishing: pleasurable practices that featured in her childhood. She describes her art as naïve because it portrays everyday objects, people and features of place in bold colors. Russell explains that she did not want to use Aboriginal dot paintings to tell her stories, as that was not part of her story and it did not feel right to copy it (Art Gallery of New South Wales, 2011). She wanted a style that all children would be able to understand, with easily recognized objects and scenes, such as the river, presented in a straightforward manner.

Russell also recalls that as a child going to the mission school, she won an art competition in which they had been asked to portray an island, sandy beaches and little canoes. She had previously lived on the coast before her family relocated to the mission, and she recalls that because her peers had never seen a beach, they were not able to draw it as well she could. As part of her prize, she had the opportunity to go to the Philippines with the visiting teacher who had organized the competition. However, her mother would not let her go, perhaps fearing that she would be taken from the family permanently, as had happened to so many other Aboriginal children.

The Production of a Local Alphabet Book: A Is for Arndale

Wells studied *A Is for Aunty* with the children, reading it on many occasions and looking closely at the artwork. She invited the children to think about places in the local area that were significant to them and to think about what was important about that place. She explained that they were going to produce an alphabet book themselves, like Elaine Russell's, and that the readers of their book would be other children at the school, but also children at a school in South Africa Wells was planning to visit. The authentic audience of children in another country was significant in what the students eventually produced (Janks & Comber, 2006). In the book and discussion, the focus is on the places the South Australian children chose as significant and how they depicted those places in their written and visual texts.

Russell's entries include:

> A is for aunty, B is for billycarts, C is for canoe, D is for ducks, E is for emus, F is for fence, G is for games, H is for humpy, I is for inspection day, J is for joey, K is for Kangaroo, L is for lagoon, M is for mission, N is for Nessy, O is for owl, P is for possum, Q is for quandong, R is for river, S is for suppertime, T is for teacher, U is for uncle, V is for valley, W is for witchetty grubs, X is for railway crossing, Y is for yabbies and Z is for zinc ointment.

Without being didactic, Russell's alphabet book provides a historical retelling that contests the ways in which Aboriginal peoples are often depicted in books

FIGURE 4.3 *A Is for Arndale*

for children. Hence, it provides an important model for Wells' class in terms of its perspective (Indigenous), its selection of content (everyday, outside activities), and the aesthetic (bold and vibrant).

The children's entries include:

> A is for Arndale, B is for bike-track, C is for catchment, D is for deli, E is for eating McDonalds, F is for fishing, G is for Gameboy, I is for icecream van, J is for judo, K is for kindy, K is for karate, L is for library, M is for movie land, N is for netball, O is for football oval, P is for pets, Q is for quiet, R is for rugby, R is for royal show, S is for school, T is for TV, U is for Greater Union, V is for Vietnamese restaurant, W is for Westwood, X is for school crossing, Y is for yabbies and Z is for busy roads.

In places, students were creative about their choices in order to 'cover' the letters with their preferred places. The range of places and activities extend from sites of entertainment (movie theater), a shopping mall (Arndale) and the outdoors (catchment, bike-track, yabbies), to problems and solutions with the built environment (busy roads, noisy neighbors), to the redevelopment of their suburb (Westwood).

The quality of the writing and the illustrations indicate that the children had been inspired by Russell's work. The class alphabet book shares a number

FIGURE 4.4 Pages from *A Is for Arndale*

of aspects of Russell's aesthetic: the stark bold colors and clear outlines, and the relationships between objects and places. It is important to note that the production of this text was a collective class achievement. This includes so many aspects and decisions negotiated in putting it together, including the selection of writers and artists for different letters of the alphabet and the key word and content for the various pages. All of this required significant talk and brainstorming as a whole class and then further discussion between pairs.

This kind of negotiation of textual production means that students get to see and hear what is at stake as decisions are made. Often, such processes are not visible when children write or draw alone. In this case, individuals and pairs of children worked on the visuals and the verbal texts, drafting and redrafting together until their entry was of a standard that the class and the teacher considered good enough for their book. At the end of the process, individual children's work was published as part of a class collection, contributing to the sense of belonging and a collective disposition towards capability. It is an exemplary case of curricular justice, where the collective is responsible for the learning and achievement of the whole group, with the teacher setting a standard that is based on genuine purpose and audience.

As a consequence, this class built a collective memory about what they have shared and accomplished over time (Gregory & Williams, 2001). Following Doreen Massey's (2005) work, the classroom is constituted as a meeting place with the potential for something new to be negotiated and produced. It becomes the site of collective book-making about the local area, which is undergoing change; student representations are inspired by those of an Aboriginal artist and author representing her own dynamic histories in place. The pedagogy associated with the text production allows for the affordances of student diversity (in terms of talents, resources, interests, and histories in and relationships with places) to be properly exploited. The collaborative multimodal text production is an ideal way to work positively with the unavoidable fact that classrooms are sites of 'throwntogetherness' (Massey, 2005, p. 151), as children's life trajectories find them sharing a classroom together. Wells designs tasks that capitalize on their diversity and lead to the production of inspiring artifacts. The children's pages contribute to an alphabet book that tells many stories of Arndale and its spaces and places.

The pedagogical appeal of the alphabet book is that it seems a manageable project for any classroom teacher anywhere, in terms of scale, teacher knowledge of English literacy and the resources required. Though we have written about the production of *A Is for Arndale* previously, we have revisited it here in this era of superdiversity (Blommaert, 2013) with Massey's understandings about the relational aspects of place and time in mind and with the hope that it may inspire the next generation of teacher-researchers as it has inspired others in the past (Comber & Nixon, 2005; Janks & Comber, 2006). The work of these theorists foregrounds the dynamic nature of culturally diverse population mobility across places and times.

Windows: Being Able to Imagine Alternatives

Jeannie Baker is an award-winning author of wordless picture books, who focuses on depicting changes in places over time (http://www.jeanniebaker.com/). She has published a number of books that have become crucial assets to Wells and her colleagues, including *Belonging* (2004), *Window* (1990) and *Mirror* (2010). Baker's art involves breath-taking color collage images of scapes of various kinds—streetscapes, homes, and changing views through a window across decades. Key themes include the environment, family and sustainability. Her work explores visually many of the concepts that are central to a place-conscious pedagogy. Her representations include both critique (see *Window*) with items such a billboards with clichéd slogans and clearing of land for urban sprawl, and celebration of place (see *Belonging*)—for example, in a streetscape being reclaimed in minuscule incremental ways by a community through planting and sharing pot plants. These books have triggered a range of creative ideas for Wells and her colleagues, and discussion below focuses on two class-produced books in the tradition of Baker's work, *Windows* and *Memories*, but not in terms of the medium, but rather in the concepts and the gradual aggregation and accumulation of text.

Throughout the period of the urban regeneration from 1999 until the present, these books were key texts in generating conversations about the representation of people in place during environmental change for the better and for the worse. *Window* shows a changing view from the same window. In the first image, a woman holding a baby is looking through that window onto a richly wooded area. As the little boy grows up, the view out the window changes, as the bush is replaced by buildings and infrastructure, including roads, supermarkets and dwellings. A birthday card for the boy on the windowsill each year indicates another year has passed. Jeannie Baker has conveyed the story completely through her detailed collage that is then photographed to form the pages of the book. Educational theorist Maxine Greene (1988) emphasizes the arts as a particularly key site for children's learning. She writes of:

> the relation between freedom and the consciousness of possibility, between freedom and the imagination—the ability to make present what is absent, to summon up a condition that is not yet.
>
> *(Greene, 1988, p. 16)*

In Wells' highly multicultural, multilingual classroom, a wordless picture book holds much promise. As was the case with Elaine Russell's images, all children can read and make meaning from Jeannie Baker's art. They are rich with details and different children may notice different things but, together with the teacher, they can build a story of the people in the place as constituted by the artist. Greene (1988) sees this kind of coconstruction of meaning as the main benefit of education:

It is through and by means of education . . . that individuals can be pro-
voked to reach beyond themselves in their inter-subjective space.

(p. 12)

In Wells' classroom, children receive such invitations consistently as she challenges them to observe, to see objects and people both in the actual material
world of the school and beyond, and in the produced world of the arts and
popular culture. This is one of the key affordances of place-conscious education.
It offers children continual invitations to see, to notice, to make meaning, to
make connections. In response to the book *Window*, Wells pursues similar goals.
Importantly, reading the book together on multiple occasions provokes the kind
of 'intersubjective space' of collective meaning-making that Greene envisages:

There are few places where individuals are impelled to come together in
speech and action, few arenas where freedom can 'sit down'.

(p. 19)

Coming from a completely different theoretical location to Greene (1988),
Michele Foucault (1988) has also argued that wherever there is power, there is
resistance, and that there are always 'spaces of freedom' even when disciplinary power reaches in a capillary-like fashion into all our institutions, including
homes and schools. Working with children to explicitly investigate how places
are constructed and how places are experienced by different people may offer
approaches to negotiating positive and productive spaces for ongoing identity
work. The collaborative production of a class-made book, entitled *Windows*, is a
case in point. The plural title 'Windows' signals that the children were invited
to look through a range of windows in order to construct their texts and to
imagine places within and beyond the building where the window was situated.

Wells' takes an optimistic line in working with children in two ways. First,
she helps them to see how they can make a material difference to their spaces
by showing them how to take social action through writing letters, lobbying,
speaking out and so on. Second, she allows them to play with space to design
and construct possible worlds. Her overriding message in her curriculum offerings
and task framings is that place is open to interpretation, open to change, open
to reconstruction. The tasks Wells assigned to students, enabling the collective
production of the class *Windows* text, included:

1. Search through books, magazines and newspapers to select and copy a picture
    of a window (taken from the outside looking in)
2. Imagine yourself inside that window looking out
3. Write about being inside the window (the space on the inside, what you are
    doing) and what you can see out of the window
4. Draw the inside of the window and then the outside without the frame.

Here again, we can see that Wells' semiotic consciousness is attuned to opportunities for students to create complex multimodal texts. Working in pairs, students chose windows that ranged from port-holes to windows in castles, skyscrapers, lighthouses and aeroplanes.

Tan and Emmanuel's Window to a Belonging Place

This discussion now centers of the texts jointly produced by Tan, whose work we discussed in Chapter 3, and Emmanuel. Tan is of Vietnamese heritage and Emmanuel of Sudanese descent. The boys wrote together, and chose the title *My Window*. Not only did they write together, but they also chose to write as one person, beginning with the sentence: 'In my room I can see the clothes that my mum bought me, my bag and closet that I put my clothes in'.

The writers go on to describe a cozy room with a cat sitting by the fire, a poster and the boy sitting by the fire with his father who is telling about 'when he was young'. Their text carries the traces of conversations the class had about Jeannie Baker's *Window*, in the sense that they introduce the father and his reminiscing about the past and also noted the toys he had been given for his birthday.

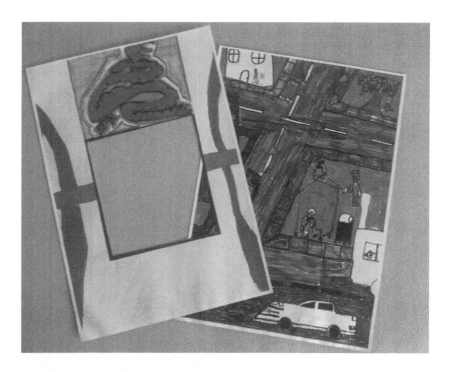

FIGURE 4.5 Tan and Emmanuel's window

The second paragraph turns to what can be seen outside the window, including vehicles such as cars and a 'bus carrying children', who might be 'going swimming because they got their bathers'. The boys' text is rich in detail and the places are alive and populated with people moving through the spaces visible from inside. The paragraph is written as though the author is standing at the window and adding to the description as they watch. In quick succession, we are told that they can see:

- His mother waiting for the bus
- An old rubbish bin
- A new pathway
- A new traffic light
- The Optus building
- New neighbors
- An autumn tree.

These observations are embellished with details about the place mentioned and sometimes a commentary about what the writers hope for, such as the mother not having to wait for long, friendly new neighbors with kids to play with, and that the squirrels are not too cold. They report new neighbors moving in, and the writer recollects playing in his favorite tree with his friends who have moved away. The place is layered with invested emotions of care and change. It is a belonging place the boys portray. It is also a place that is being refurbished. They write with the knowledge acquired from studying the urban renewal occurring locally and with the graciousness appropriated from authors such as Jeannie Baker and Elaine Russell. The writing demonstrates a genuine interest in the everyday relations of people in places, whether in built environments or the nonhuman world. It is important to remember that the boys have also produced a visual text on two separate pages. The first page is the window frame. The second page is what can be seen through that window.

In Figure 4.5, the curtains on either side of the window are a bold yellow and red, like a coat of arms. Immediately above the window is a poster featuring the red dragon familiar in Tan's other work discussed earlier. We discovered Tan's repeated use of the red dragon after looking through the archive of his work over several school terms. We think it is significant that the tasks are open-ended enough for Tan to weave this emblematic character into his schoolwork. Anne Haas Dyson (1993) first introduced the idea of a permeable curriculum. In such a curriculum, children use knowledge from their homes, peer and school worlds as they assemble new repertoires of practice. Tan and Emmanuel worked together to produce their visual and verbal text, drawing on what they learned from school in terms of urban renewal, what they enjoy from popular culture in terms of Yugioh cards replete with a red dragon, and what they know from their everyday lives, lived in the neighborhood and beyond.

FIGURE 4.6 View through the window

Through the window, we see a blond haired mother waiting at the bus stop, the traffic lights, the rubbish bin, a person moving in, and a person walking a dog. When we turn the page, we see the full scene depicted in the writing, including a moving car, a bus, a truck, the Optus building and a squirrel swinging in a tree devoid of leaves. Neither of the boys' mothers were blond haired and there are no squirrels in Australia. Here, we see the boys playing with the task, embellishing their pages of the book linguistically, culturally and with imagination. The result is an impressive text in every sense. Visually, it is interesting on numerous levels, offering a view from above to some degree, yet a closeness that takes the reader into the scene. The roads are dominant in the wider view. They even dwarf the Optus building, one of the tallest in their city.

This combination of strategies works incredibly well for the English literacy development of culturally diverse students. Children thrive as learners in these contexts and the quality of their work, whether verbal or visual texts, is very impressive. They learn a great deal from composing together and the artifacts they produce are often more ambitious than they might accomplish alone. In this context, students become both independently literate but also interdependently literate. Reimagining the English literacy curriculum to fully take account of the possibilities of cooperative multimodal coauthoring is an exciting prospect in contrast to minimalist individualist approaches to literacy achievement.

Multimodal text production and communication in the wider world is increasingly common (Jewitt, 2009; Kress, 2010; Kress & van Leeuwen, 2006; Rowsell, 2013), given the affordances of digital technologies for bringing together a range of semiotic tools into easy reach. Using mobile phones, young children can, for example, Skype, take photographs, record movies, play games, read stories, listen to songs, email, search on Google maps, use the telephone and so on. Tablet communication technologies have, it seems, created endless possibilities for meaning-making. These devices, as Kress (2010, p. 194) points out, allow, among other things, 'flexibility of sensory engagement with the environment'; 'adaptation of previous knowledge';'real-time mobility';'learning *how to* processes'; and 'individual optimization of resources'. Such technologies can be considered 'cultural resources' (Kress, 2010, p. 195) and, as we will demonstrate, fundamental to children becoming literate in a second or third language.

The potential of multimodality is explored further in relation to children who are still developing their spoken and written English in the next section, when we discuss how Marg Wells and Ruth Trimboli researched with their classes and produced two books of *Memories*, and the ways in which Helen Grant produced films with her recently arrived refugee students and children in a lunchtime film club.

School Memories: Students as Researchers and Publishing as a Classroom Collective

From 2010–2013, a project titled *New Literacy Demands in the Middle Years*[1] saw teachers of students in Grades 4–9 conduct classroom design experiments (Cobb, Confrey, di Sessa, Lehrer & Schauble, 2003) to investigate whether explicit interventions made a difference to their students' literacy learning.

The project included teachers from three primary and three high schools. In the tradition of participatory methods in literacy education for social justice (Bautista, Bertrand, Morrell, Scorza & Matthews, 2013; Cochran-Smith & Lytle, 2009), the teachers were supported by the research team to undertake theoretically informed classroom projects and assess the effects on student learning in a range of ways. Classroom design experiments have much in common with other approaches to teacher research with the addition of a carefully designed intervention and the collection of baseline and postintervention data. Here, we report only on the work of Wells, Trimboli and Grant, teachers already featured in this book (see also Morgan, 2013; Morgan, Comber, Freebody & Nixon, 2014; Wells & Trimboli, 2014).

Wells and Trimboli's work in this project was informed in part by the book *Place and Community-Based Education in Schools* (Smith & Sobel, 2010). Trimboli explained:

> Place-based education is learning that is rooted in what is local—the unique history, environment, culture and so on . . . of a particular place. I think the histories of people in a place are important to that place and are really a part of that place. . . . investigations of the lives of people in their own communities and their histories become a cultural aspect of that place where they are now living and learning.
>
> I think it is important that kids still value their culture even though they are now living somewhere else. It's important that they don't forget their past, and that they see that their past history is as important as anyone else's, and that history is not just about the people who went to war, governed a country, or discovered something, and that other people will be interested to read it. I wanted them to develop and maintain a pride in who they are.

Educational researchers have noted the ways in which elite private schools build on tradition, intergenerational family networks and the production of artifacts in the school and beyond, which further promote its distinction (Kenway & Koh, 2013). Frequently, the resources for such work are not available in schools serving poor populations. However, the production of collective memories through yearbooks, photographs and other memorabilia is now more readily accessible with the advent of new technologies which allow for easier self-publication. In the context of the impending school demolition and opening of a new school on the premises, Wells and Trimboli decided to involve their students in conducting oral history interviews with current and previous staff and students to record, edit and publish a record of the school in a number of formats, including two color, hardcover books.

Wells' goal in the project was to enhance the children's capacities for and confidence with oral communication, given that many of her students were

FIGURE 4.7 Memories books

learning English as a second language. Her literacy program included many opportunities for drama—for speaking and performing in front of the class and the school—readers' theater and activities which required them to rehearse for speaking informally and formally in public. Wells explains:

> [Trimboli and I] shared a similar goal: to develop competent, confident communicators who can understand and embrace change. To do this I positioned my students as 'researchers'. Over the course of the year the literacy skills needed to research and document the new development were taught, practised, developed and built on. By researching what was happening I wanted my students to not only gain knowledge, experience, literacy skills and confidence but I also wanted them to be more prepared for the move to the new school next year and to cope with the change. . . . I developed these skills . . . in a topic I called 'Talking Walls'. The children conducted interviews to collect and record 'memories' from the staff and students at Ridley Grove School in 2010 and make them into a book.

Drawing on the popular song title 'If walls could talk', and inspired in part by Nadia Wheatley's *My Place*, Wells prepared her Grade 4/5 students to interview current teachers and students about their memories of Ridley Grove Primary

School. This positioning of students as researchers is a key move in critical literacy (Comber, 1994) and orients students to question what is going on and why things are the way they are. Part way through this work, children from Wells' class outlined what they were doing at a school assembly:

> This term our topic is interviews. We are becoming journalists. This topic helps us with our speaking skills, confidence, listening skills and note-taking skills. We are interviewing all staff members, all teachers and some students. Room 15 has to be very organized by setting their interview times with staff and teachers. We work in pairs . . . and use an interview checklist. . . . We are doing this because it is the last year of Ridley Grove and we want to keep the memories alive.

The children's report to the school assembly made it clear that they actively took up their roles as researchers and journalists and they fully understood the context for their work as memory gatherers in the school's last year. At a local South Australian Education Union project conference for middle years teachers in November 2012, Wells presented the details of her approach:

- All current staff and a selection of students from reception to Grade 7 were interviewed (48 staff and 58 students).
- Students formulated the questions for a general questionnaire that was given to all people before their interview so they had time to think and write down some notes. During the interview, students asked questions and took notes for clarification.
- The data collection process was long, involved and demanding. Students worked with a buddy to carry out these tasks. They had to make appointments, keep a timetable, carry out interviews, take photos and/or recordings, write the information into a text, save it in a 'Memories' file on the computer, check their work and show it to the person they interviewed for approval, complete a checklist of tasks, complete a self-assessment sheet and get feedback from the staff members they interviewed.
- The number of interviews carried out by each group, and the person chosen to be interviewed, varied depending on the literacy level of the student.
- All interviews and photos have been put together in the 'Memories' book, a 'feel good' book that captures everyone's thoughts and memories. This book is finished and is now an available resource within the new school.

(Wells later published on this work with her colleague, Trimboli; see Wells & Trimboli, 2014)

There is not space here to do justice to the complexity of the design of Wells' curriculum and pedagogy. Throughout the year, students also observed the physical changes occurring on their school grounds and interviewed the project manager regularly about what was occurring within the newly built walls which they were unable to see from outside. With guidance from him and their teacher, through PowerPoint displays including photographs and designs, they were introduced to the discourses and practices of architects, planners, project managers and so on. Importantly, they were encouraged to question all aspects of the design and the use of space, and even successfully challenged the lack of a space for drama and performance (Comber & Nixon, 2011). While collecting the memories of others about the old school, they were simultaneously witnessing the building of the new school and hearing about its design features. Students learned about and prepared for change through in-depth engagement in the school's history, its changing dimensions and imagining themselves into its future.

The resulting published book, *Memories*, is fifty pages in length. Most pages have several photographs of staff and/or students and quotations from the interviews recorded by Wells' students. Wells produced the book based on the students' written summaries of interviews they conducted, drawn from field notes and audio-recordings. From the point of view of Wells' original goals for students' language and literacy development, becoming researchers and journalists positioned them as powerful observers and listeners who needed to attend to their speaking and listening in order to guarantee the quality of the memories recorded. Below, we refer briefly to just two pages from the book, which indicate

FIGURE 4.8 Memories, including the counselor's

how the multicultural make-up of the school was the object of comment for a number of respondents.

On one page of the book, the school counselor is reported as telling students that she has enjoyed the cultural diversity at the school, noting that over the years, there have been 'new cultural groups appearing. We have more cultural groups represented now than ever before. Indian and African students have only been here in the last few years'. Several other pages are specifically devoted to this aspect of the school. For example, on a page dedicated to ESL teaching and learning, the ESL teacher is reported as having 'enjoyed working with children from all around the world and watching them become good English speakers'. On the same page, the memories of two ESL tutors are also included:

> [They] have lots of fond memories of Ridley Grove. They have spent time with students from a variety of backgrounds and have learnt many things from them. They enjoyed the reconciliation events and loved watching Blessing dancing on the basketball court and walking to the rhythm of African drumming.

Finally, the memories of Blessing—the dancing African boy mentioned by the tutors—are featured on this page. For him, a strong memory of the school has been working with the ESL teacher and making progress with learning to read and write standard Australian English: 'she helps me with my literacy. I am getting better at adjectives and pronouns.'

FIGURE 4.9 Blessing's memories

Other pages, featuring a range of languages other than English, and language and bilingual teachers, testify not only to the linguistic and cultural diversity of the school but also to the significant impact on teachers and learners of collective experiences such as drama productions, 'culturally colorful end-of-year celebrations' and Christmas concerts. For example, the bilingual support officer reports that she:

> will always remember the first Cultural Festival she organized. The Vietnamese dance was hard work but she had a great time. She also enjoyed the play 'Shrek' and a lot of other performances.

The Chinese language teacher also highlights the importance of embodied and collective performance in her happy memories of the school:

> Her memory of Ridley Grove is the time she spends with her students and when they work together to do singing practice. She also enjoyed the Christmas concert and Melbourne Cup [annual national horse racing event] celebrations.

Wells was the overarching editor of the book with her class of coresearchers and journalists. The entire process ensured multiple opportunities for exploring the affordances of teaching and learning in a culturally diverse school. When teachers become involved as editors and publishers of the children's work, the investment in an excellent product is heightened. Their combined work was visible for the whole school community and remains so into the future. Once again, we note the semiotic work of the teacher here in designing the book and bringing it into fruition. The teacher had entered into a collective writing relationship with the students.

Researchers and Journalists of the Local Historic Setting

Wells' fellow teacher, Ruth Trimboli, embarked on a similar project with the Grade 5/6 class. Over the course of the year, she developed students' understanding of history through literature, Aboriginal studies and Australian history, not shying away from the politics of invasion versus settlement. For instance, she studied the work of author and illustrator Nadia Wheatley's (1987) account of the first fleet's arrival in Australia in *My Place*. The themes in Wheatley's work explore the impact of the invasion of Australia on Aboriginal people and the environment, and the challenges faced by immigrants to Australia. Her work is very generative for fostering conversations between children about the different relationships different people have with place and how those relationships change over time.

Trimboli shared other literature as well, including auto-biographies written by Aboriginal authors such as Olympic runner and gold medal winner Cathy

Freeman (2007) and Aboriginal artist Sally Morgan (1987). Gradually Trimboli built the students knowledge of the history of place and of autobiography and how people write about their own histories, especially in connection with places or journeys to places. Many of Trimboli's students were the children of immigrants and refugees or themselves recently arrived in Australia. On a number of occasions, Trimboli assisted students to research, write and present their autobiographies. On this occasion, she introduced students to the concept of oral history, also a key component of place-conscious pedagogy. She supported students to interview previous students and staff from the school, which was to be demolished, and to write reports that were to be self-published in an anthology titled *Memories of Ridley Grove R-7 School, 1946–2010*. Trimboli writes in the front pages of the book:

> Students were involved from the very beginning. They created the questions, made phone calls to organize times for interviews, took photographs and video recordings.

Trimboli and her class researched the origin of the school. The first page documents its beginnings:

> A new school in Woodville Gardens was first suggested in 1943, due to the overcrowding of existing schools in the area. The population was expanding rapidly due to building programmes of both the South Australian Housing trust and the Commonwealth War Workers Housing Trust to cater for the nearby munitions factory.

One of the key goals of place-conscious education, as mentioned earlier, is to make young people aware that places have been constructed and that they could have been made differently. Understanding that schools are part of wider public policy and that they are subject to change and review was important for these young people witnessing urban renewal and the demolition of their school and construction of the new *superschool*. Learning historically about population, local industry and housing offers these students new discursive resources for grappling with the changes that surround them. We can see here strong synergies between critical literacy's focus on language practices and power relations, and place-conscious pedagogies' recognition of the politics of people, places and spaces. Places, including school spaces and the buildings themselves, should not be simply taken for granted as the way things are.

Students asked their informants a range of questions, transcribed the responses, and edited their text to make it suitable for publication. The questions varied depending on the interviewee's relationship with the school. One of the first students to attend the school in 1946 was asked the following questions, among others:

- When you left this school how did you feel?
- Did you like the students and the things that were here then?
- How old were you when you left and what year was it and what year were you in?
- What were the teachers like?
- Did other children respect you?
- Did you have a best friend and what was their name? What was he or she like?
- What was your favorite subject?
- Why did you choose to come to this school?
- How did you feel when you were at the school?

Of interest here is the interviewer's focus on feelings and relationships. There are traces here of the work Trimboli has done on 'belonging' (see Chapter 3). In answer to another question about whether there were 'any nice children when you were here', the respondent explains:

> Yes to me they were nearly all nice. It was a new suburb and the children were all about the same age. Our fathers worked at the ammunitions factory in Finsbury. We had freedom to play on the street, to walk to the pictures, open paddocks to fly kites in, a dam to find tadpoles and we could go mushrooming.

This perspective on the neighborhood at this time could not have been accessed except through oral history. It all tells a very positive story of a working-class community at a particular time, an area that later became one of the poorest in Australia, and was most recently subjected to 'urban renewal'. In this context, the urban renewal involved a consortium of public and private interests working together. The Westwood Consortium consisted of Urban Pacific, City of Charles Sturt Council, City of Port Adelaide Enfield Council, and the Government of South Australia. At this time, it is the largest housing redevelopment project in Australia. Since 2006, it has changed the face of five suburbs. Another pair of students interviewed a former student who attended the school in its first decade and later became a teacher and returned to the school in that role. The boys' questions were quite different:

- What was the landscape like when you were at Ridley Grove?
- Were there any major changes to the buildings from the time you were here?
- Were there any buildings that were here before and are not here now?
- Is there something at this school that you really miss?
- What are your best memories of the school?
- What was your favorite type of technology or things you used to teach the students?

These boys have clearly used the opportunity to focus mostly on the materiality of the school and classrooms as a built environment. This kind of work allowed space for different students to pursue a range of interests and as part of a classroom research collective to elicit different histories of the school. Each individual or pair of students was responsible for only one developed entry. Together, the anthology is much more than the sum of its parts, as collections of memories are put together with different insights into the school, its neighborhood and its people.

Schools as Meeting Places: Literacy as a Joint Enterprise

Social geographer Doreen Massey's (2005) notion of *meeting* places provides a lens for examining contemporary globalizing societies and how people are *thrown together* in places and need to negotiate ways of relating with each other, and, indeed, with places. Massey writes:

> Place . . . does change us . . ., not through some visceral belonging . . . but through the *practising* of place, the negotiating of intersecting trajectories; place as an arena where negotiation is forced upon us.
>
> *(Massey, 2005, p. 154)*

Culturally diverse school communities certainly require negotiation, but they also hold within their walls the potential for significant learning, especially when teachers make place and the changing and relational nature of place the object of study, as was the case reported here with the work of Wells and Trimboli. In reflecting on her design-based experiment, Wells commented on the students' learning:

> Student literacy skills have improved, but they may have improved anyway, following a more conservative curriculum. But what I have seen is the growth in self-belief. Students are more confident, organized, independent, interested, motivated and involved in their learning.

Wells' hopes for the students exceeded normative approaches to improved literacy performance. While improvements were achieved, what she was seeking transcended what could be measured. She was ambitious in her aims to have the students understand but not fear change, understand people's attachment to places and institutions, and understand that the way buildings are designed is not neutral, that it makes a difference to what can be done there, that even the authorized plan can be contested. Such a pedagogical vision contrasts sharply with Foucault's (1979) critique of the school building as part of a wider apparatus for containing, measuring and managing the child subject—the disciplinary institution. In appropriating the discursive practices of oral history and memory telling, Wells and Trimboli hope to open up insider storytelling and knowing positions to their young journalists; their aim is to lessen the silencing and alienation that can accompany immigration and resettlement through ongoing activities designed to build the classroom as a meeting place and to develop a collective identity and sense of belonging.

Without romanticizing or overstating the effects of this small-scale collaborative research on immigrant students' literacy learning, it is instructive to return to a key tenet of critical literacy as captured some time ago by writing researcher Barbara Kamler, who argued that: 'Writing . . . is never simply a skill, but is deeply constitutive of subjectivity' (Kamler, 2001, p. 54). Kamler's insight is particularly relevant to the case made here. As Wells notes, the students' measurable literacy skills did improve quite markedly during the period of the study; yet equally, if not more significantly, there were the durable shifts in their learning dispositions and their sense of belonging. Ultimately, this is what will count for them in their educational trajectories and future lives.

The invitation to engage in writing about memories here is not motivated by a desire to bring the personal 'into the corrective space of the school' (Patterson, 1993, p. 66), nor to make it the object of surveillance, nor to make it the site for therapeutic activity (Kamler, 2001). Such are the criticisms that were made by feminist poststructuralist researchers of progressive approaches to writing pedagogy that made use of the writer's lifeworld in order that it could be seen, noted and repaired. Also informed by Foucault (1979), Hunter (1988) argued that child-centered pedagogies and normative social training operate together in forms of modern literacy pedagogy. As such, according to Hunter, they contributed to the management of increasingly diverse populations, where the relationship between the English teacher and students is a key site for disciplinary practices and training in technologies of the self. The result was that English teaching was reduced to a series of binary choices: freedom versus sophisticated social control, culture versus morality, and personal growth versus useful skill. The memories studied and represented here are the result of children engaging in interviews with people who have various historical and contemporary relationships with the school. They are not simply conjuring and repeating idealized and stereotypical nice and sanitized accounts. They are learning the rudimentary elements of life history interviews; small beginnings certainly, but learning to design questions and listen like a researcher. And this gives the children some distance on their material which does not necessarily happen in the writing of personal stories, critiqued by Foucauldian scholars and as discussed earlier. Place remains personal, but in making it the object of study, children learn also to bring different ways of knowing to phenomena and make a range of conscious decisions about which stories to tell.

In stark contrast, the place-based pedagogy developed by Wells and Trimboli in the school reported here made place and change the objects of study. Writers and text designers (teachers and students alike) enjoyed considerable freedom in contriving the stories to be told, and the representations to be included. Yet these stories were not simply romantic or essentialized versions of place as children investigated the dynamic politics between spaces. Rather than being stuck in the local, this version of *place*, in Massey's sense, is already global, as it is already relational.

> If we really imagine 'local places' relationally—as meeting places—then those relations may go around the world. In that sense 'the global' is just as 'real' and 'grounded', even just as 'everyday', as is the so-called local place.
>
> *(Massey, 2005)*

The inevitable thrown-togetherness of classroom and school populations in sites of urban renewal makes it an unpredictable, unmanageable arena for social action. While some educators may despair in the face of such uncertainty, and governments try to address diversity by insisting on common standards, other teachers are able to work with the 'interjecting trajectories' (Massey, 2005) in creative and productive ways. Switching the pedagogical focus is an 'evener': it serves to position people similarly. Everyone can speak and write about place. Focusing on the shared changing spaces of the neighborhood and the school itself further builds common ground for collaborative research, documenting and publication.

People's relationships with place(s) across time, including children's memories and those of family and community, can provide rich resources for developing literate repertoires. That does not mean that teachers or students pretend an innocence or homogeneity about memories or people's relationships with places or memberships of communities. The work done by Wells and Trimboli is more nuanced and because they are also involved in the ongoing politics of local and school change, there is recognition that people are differently positioned with respect to places and spaces. Yet constituting the individual and collective memories of people who work and learn in schools as assets is part of a wider agenda to contest deficit discourses which circulate about poor and culturally diverse communities and the schools located therein (Comber & Kamler, 2004). As Dooley (2012) has pointed out, how teachers attribute capability to learners becomes crucial to the curriculum and pedagogy that is enacted in the classroom and the range of learning opportunities young people are afforded.

If teachers continue to assume that immigrant and refugee children have no language or no experience from which to draw, or alternatively see their experience only in terms of a traumatic background to be forgotten, then the classroom learning community is subsequently impoverished. In the process of exploring memories, their own and those of their family and the wider school community, refugee children were able to accomplish positive identity work associated with respect for their histories. They were also able to forge improved connections with the school and neighborhood as they learned about the history of the school and its former and current inhabitants. Their positioning as autobiographers and journalists required their full intellectual participation in the classroom. They were no longer relegated to passive observation or seen as people without valuable knowledge to contribute.

10 Bronze Rules of Filmmaking—*Collaboration, Expertise and Induction Into Filmmaking*

Helen Grant, another teacher-researcher participating in the *New Literacy Demands in the Middle Years* project, decided to have her students explain to the research team what their film work involved by actually making a film about the process. They chose to create a parody in order to convey the key elements of making a good film. Grant is very much aware that critique of everyday media can colonize popular culture and, in bringing it into the corrective space of the school, work against student motivations (Burnett & Merchant, 2011). Hence, she works extensively on film production where students can play with what they already know and enjoy at the same time as they acquire new knowledge and techniques. Grant weaves the students' and her shared interest in filmmaking with her ongoing classroom inquiry projects and she involves the students openly in research. In providing as much access as she can to her ESL students to use cameras and microphones, Grant is aware that while her students may have been movie and television viewers, filmmaking technologies (such as digital video cameras and microphones) are 'placed resources' (Prinsloo, 2005, p. 94); that is, many of her recently arrived refugee students may not have access to such equipment at home. Her provision of opportunities and access to new production technologies is a fundamental aspect of her approach to social justice.

Another key principle in Grant's pedagogy is to involve students fully in the process of undertaking the research, not only as key informants, but also as researchers in their own right. Grant has demonstrated this consistently throughout her career. When journalists, politicians, academics or other visitors come to visit the school, her team of filmmakers and student coresearchers is likely to be ready at the gate with clipboards, digital cameras, microphones and an interview protocol. This is all part of demonstrating to students that they have agency and that they are already active citizens with contributions to make and questions to legitimately ask, despite apparent power differentials between themselves and prospective interviewees. It is also part of constituting the school as a site of serious learning, design and media production. Film, as we go on to discuss, has particular affordances in the study of place and people in places, with different potential for representation than that afforded by the production of print texts.

One of the challenges facing Grant as a teacher-researcher is the fact that as a teacher of students learning English as an additional language, she does not have a class of her own. Rather, she works with small groups of students with specific needs, as well as supporting the mainstream classroom teachers of culturally and linguistically diverse students. Her work yields important insights about how to make the best possible educational use of such educators in schools such that the school community as a whole, as well as individual learners and groups of students, have the benefit of expertise. In the examples provided here and in Chapter 3, Grant creatively and ethically exploits the affordances of particular situations to produce films that are educative in the making and educative in the product. Her films and other associated artifacts, such as *Afghan Newsstand*, various zines and installations for galleries are produced by groups of students working and negotiating throughout the process. As was the case with Wells and Trimboli, Grant is committed to collaborative multimodal text production. Like Wells and Trimboli, she cares about the quality and aesthetic of the artifacts and works with students to set very high production standards. Whenever possible (through artists in residence and other small grants), she invites filmmakers working locally to assist her and her students in the process, and she regularly helps her students to target state and national competitions for young filmmakers.

Involving filmmakers means that her students get access to actual models of practice rather than simulations and they accomplish a more professional product than they could possibly make alone. Over time, Grant has assembled many of the skills and techniques of professional filmmakers, which are now available to her students. The process of production of the film *10 Bronze Rules of Filmmaking*, discussed later, highlights key pedagogical principles. The following film, *Sudan*, is then used to explain how these principles of collaborative filmmaking were enabling for a particular group of students.

The *New Literacy Demands in the Middle Years* project comprised design experiments in place-conscious pedagogy as discussed with respect to Trimboli and Wells, subject-specific literacies (Morgan et al., 2014), and also youth cultures and new technologies. Grant's work focused on using students' interest in and knowledge of youth cultures and digital literacies as a bridge to Standard Australian English. It built on Grant's earlier research investigating her stated questions:

- How can filmmaking be used as a catalyst to examine personal, society and global issues?
- What do students need to know and use as part of literacy repertoires to produce high quality films?
- How can we collect information about their 'standards' of learning literacy to improve teaching techniques/methods/content?
- How could we run parallel research with students to mirror our own to encourage students' knowledge about language and how it works?

These questions indicate the complexity of Grant's approach. She went on to hone these further into an overarching research question:

Does my explicit teaching about multiliteracies and the language associated with multiliteracies, actually help my ESL students to understand the
filmmaking process? And the research process?

Her desire to induct students into the theoretically informed language and
the research process indicates her ambitious goals for the students' learning. Her
approach is highly informed by contemporary policy and wider research. Further
sub-questions in her planning for the research include:

- What are the negotiable and nonnegotiable literacies students need to be able
  to use these multimodal texts confidently? Is there a hierarchy of importance
  in texts valued and used?
- How are texts interwoven and used in contemporary technology? How do
  the ways of meaning-making interact? E.g. the visual and the audio in a film.
- Where are the genre valued and used in multimodal texts?

Such complex questions continue to intrigue researchers in literacy studies at
this time and are beyond what a single researcher might expect to address. When
Grant worked with students to write the script for the film (about a local art
gallery and shop), these big questions were modified to the following:

1. What is the topic?
2. How is it being presented? What themes and discourses are being used?
3. Who is writing to whom? Whose voices and positions are being expressed?
4. Whose voices and positions aren't being expressed?
5. What is the text trying to do to you?
6. What other ways are there of writing about the topic?
7. What wasn't said about the topic?

In evidence here is Grant's commitment to critical literacy and seeing literacy
as a socio-political process.

As she conducted her research with children, a colleague also interviewed
and observed some of the students to assess their understanding of the process.
When asked what she had learned from the first filmmaking session, one student,
Marisa, with limited oral English, responded, 'How to use the camera and take
angles, put the important things in'. After a few more workshops, she explained
to the interviewer where they were up to in the process of making the film:

We do all the talkings, you ends in asking question but we don't want the
question so we want to rid of them.

In dialogue with the interviewer, she explains the editing process in terms of
removing what is not needed—in this case, the questions. It is clear that in the

process of making the film with her costudents and teacher, Marisa is learning about editing. What interests us is that the student's facility with English does not limit her capacity for complex learning about language when given the chance to work collaboratively on a challenging and motivational task. Marisa also explained that she had learned 'manners' in the sense of how to appropriately request a filmed interview with the artists.

Another student expressed the deliberateness of filmmaking processes, saying, 'It's not an accident to make a film'. While these students may be looking for words to express their ideas, their insights are nevertheless visible. Their status as second language learners has not led to them being confined to basic or functional literacy. They use their developing English proficiency to learn about the ways in which decisions are made in filmmaking. Rather, Grant tends to assume a high level for capacity from learners and assists them in every way possible to meet her goals. This is an enabling curriculum that creates possibilities for these students as they negotiate their learner identities in a new context and, for many, a new country.

Two artifacts produced by Grant help explain her pedagogy. The first is a document titled 'How will you make the film?' (Figure 4.11), which Grant cowrote with the student filmmakers to share with the team and other teacher-researchers at a project meeting.

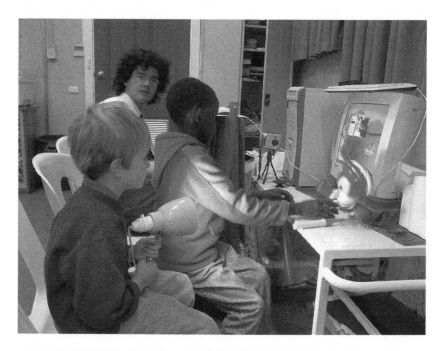

FIGURE 4.10 Filmmaking: collaborative, challenging and motivating

HOW WILL YOU MAKE THE FILM?

PURPOSE: For Helen to show research group on Sep 15 to give audience an idea about what our film work involves.
AUDIENCE: academics, teacher researchers, DECS/Ed Dept.
GENRE/STYLE: parody, comedy
MESSAGE: Making a good film involves complex skills, perspectives, angles, contrasts, English, ESL, multimedia, glossaries, foreground & background, talking...
FIRST THOUGHTS:
1. Planning-mood e.g. serious, idea-beginning, middle, end, roles-script, editing, director, sound, camera
2. Shooting/filming–James Bond 3 angles, shaky handheld, bilingual
3. Sound/music–Sound of Music, 3 sounds
4. Editing
5. Screening/sharing
Refined the idea: Film and tell a parody about making a film 'James Blond' where the main character is the director and group act out snippets from the fictitious film. Director states the 'bronze' film rule then we show good/bad examples.
After discussion the group came up with script breakdown:

GSPS' Ten Golden/Bronze Rules of Filmmaking

Include classification	Category: Ridiculous Include blurb about effect on adults viewing this ridiculous film, may cause laughter	
Rule 1	Always plan your production	Show opposite: confusion, chaos, wrong actors, argue over which scene
Rule 2	Make sure your crew can operate the equipment	Finger caught in the clapper board, 'did you get it' and camera films feet
Rule 3	Good communication is vital	Monica and John speaking in Mandarin to James Blond (Brennan) not understood
Rule 4	The mood must suit the scene. Music is important to set the scene.	James Blond death threat with inappropriate sound effects/music
Rule 5	Sound is paramount	Fisheye lens on JB, with 3 SFX
Rule 6	Devote time to editing, know the footage and have only one or two editing	All group saying their bit at the computer
Rule 7	Get the right angle	Axel shows right angle with clapperboard, James Blond from lots of angles
Rule 8	Frame your shots and pay attention to the background	Hands frame with JB 'shaken not stirred' and John knitting in the background still in shot
Rule 9	Maintain motivation to finish your project	Timing-clapperboard late, John knitting during fight scene
Rule 10	Promote your film to the world	Selling film in the yard
Credits	Clapperboard Axel with all group doing the conga off screen, run credits	
Serious group interview	Each group member gives points to support why filmmaking should be on the primary curriculum	

FIGURE 4.11 How will you make the film?

Several students involved in the film about the art and craft gallery and shop also participated in the making of the *10 Bronze Rules of Filmmaking*. Hence, they were building their knowledge across films and projects.

The Collaborative Process and Creation of 10 Bronze Rules of Filmmaking

The initial four headings are frames Grant uses each time she coproduces a film with students:

- Purpose
- Audience
- Genre/Style
- Message

The process of arriving at the descriptions of each of these concepts takes considerable time, including many lessons of brainstorming and discussion. In this case, the purpose is integral to Grant's participation in the research project as is the specified audience. This exemplifies the ways in which she includes students in her research and makes visible the goals of her work. Next, the genre/style is named as parody, comedy and the film's message is summarized:

> Making a good film involves complex skills. Perspectives, angles, contrasts, English, ESL, multimedia, glossaries, foreground and background, talking . . .

Here, the students work with Grant to document their own practice and their learning.

In writing the notes with Grant to report to the research team and other teachers, the students are of course revising the key concepts she wants them to understand about filmmaking and to be able to convey in their film. This is followed with a five-point summary of their thoughts so far. A reflection entitled 'Refining the idea' then explains that they will make a parody of a James Bond film, where the director will speak to the camera to illustrate good and bad examples of the 'bronze' (also sending up the notion of 'golden rule') rules of filmmaking.

Coauthoring such texts with their teacher in a group provides these students with modeling of the role of writing in planning and thinking and also provides textual traces of their discussions to which the group can return. This is an extremely rich linguistic environment for students to learn Standard Australian English for academic purposes, as well as draw on their own knowledge of popular culture. The final part of their text is a table naming the ten bronze rules. It ends with a note about credits and records a serious interview where each group member makes an argument about why filmmaking should be on the primary school curriculum.

Include classification	Students devised a new film classification: it was an R rating for *Ridiculous* Include blurb about effect on adults viewing this ridiculous film, may cause laughter	Humorous effect
Rule 1	Always plan your production	Show opposite: confusion, chaos, wrong actors arguing over which scene
Rule 2	Make sure your crew can operate the equipment	Finger caught in the clapper board, camera operator refers to good shots 'did you get it?' but camera is recording feet
Rule 3	Good communication is vital	Monica and John directingin Mandarin to James Blond who does not understand his role or what to act out
Rule 4	The mood must suit the scene. Music is important to set the scene.	James Blond has a death threat with inappropriate vaudeville style sound effects/music
Rule 5	Sound is paramount	Fisheye lens on James Blond firing his gun, with 3 SFX,e.g.: baby's squeaker toy
Rule 6	Devote time to editing, know the footage and have only one or two editing	All group leaning over computer giving their opinions simultaneously
Rule 7	Get the right angle	Axel shows right angle using the clapperboard followed by shots of James Blond from lots of extreme angles
Rule 8	Frame your shots and pay attention to the background	Hands frame with James Blond 'shaken not stirred' and John is looking bored, knitting in the background still in shot
Rule 9	Maintain motivation to finish your project	Timing is wrong showing clapperboard after camera is rolling, John seen knitting during fight scene
Rule 10	Promote your film to the world	Annoying students in the yard and fast talking
Credits	Clapperboard Axel with all group doing the conga off screen, run credits	
Serious group interview	Each group member gives points to support why filmmaking should be on the primary curriculum	

FIGURE 4.12 10 Bronze Rules of Filmmaking

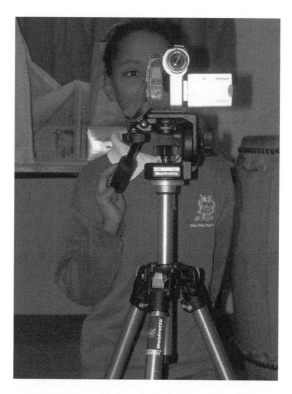

FIGURE 4.13 Bronze Rule 2—Make sure your crew can operate the equipment

FIGURE 4.14 Bronze Rule 6—Devote time to editing, know the footage and have only one or two editing

FIGURE 4.15 Bronze Rule 7—Get the right angle

FIGURE 4.16 Bronze Rule 8—Frame your shots and pay attention to the background

The *10 Bronze Rules of Filmmaking*, as outlined in Figure 4.12, and prepared for the research workshop, also acts as a written guide for the students as they work with Grant to produce the film. In the final column on the right hand side, the students summarize how they will be guided by these rules in producing this particular film. For example, they mention using inappropriate music, using a fisheye lens, showing a finger caught in the clapper board, and speaking in a language not understood by the audience, all as examples of what not to do. They understand that the art of parody is to show the unexpected with the actors doing the opposite to what the script will say.

A second artifact is helpful here to illustrate how Grant negotiates a particularly strong pedagogic relationship with these students even though she teaches them only for short periods of time across any given week. Figure 4.17 is a letter written by Grant to the student filmmakers a week after the research project meeting, where she presented their summary.

After addressing each of the 'fabulous filmmakers' by name, Grant summarizes in a series of dot points what they have achieved so far, in 'Where are we up to with our filmmaking?' As well as reminding students of what they have done, including five workshops with a filmmaker, finishing the *10 Bronze Rules of Filmmaking* and starting two other films, Grant also makes her position on the importance of filmmaking and multiliteracies clear to the students. This part of the letter works at multiple levels. It names and revises the work that has been done, but it also argues for a rationale for filmmaking as part of the curriculum.

In effect, within her letter, Grant is recruiting these students as her advocates. At a time when standardization and mandated testing threatens to close down spaces for teacher and student creativity, which is so necessary to complex literacy learning, Grant recognizes that she will have to fight for a curriculum space for media studies. Along with this agenda, she also wants students to understand the idea that a theory can be a 'resource'—in this case, with multiliteracies providing a language for them to talk about filmmaking. The teacher's semiotic work in the letter helps to create an enabling curriculum, where her textual practices become scaffolds for the students' learning. This also contributes to a group archive and a collective memory for the group that can be referred to again and again. Thus, students get to see the benefit once again of writing to communicate and organize activity. They come to understand fully that making a film is 'not an accident' and involves planning, negotiating, reflection, rehearsal, drafting, editing and so on and that writing can assist with managing this complex, but enjoyable, work.

In the second part of the letter, 'What next?', Grant lists some homework tasks and suggests some possible follow-up tasks for the group to consider. It is interesting to note that most of her suggestions involve specific communicative acts such as:

Dear fabulous filmmakers John B, John F, Monica, Axel, Declan, Aidan, Darren and Brennan!

Where are we up to with our filmmaking?
- Do you realize that we've had 5 workshops with Sam this term?
- We've started The Wall, Jamming with Gilles Street
- We've finished 10 Bronze Rules of Filmmaking featuring extras (interview with the filmmakers i.e. you) and got good feedback from your peers
- We've got resources to help us talk and learn about filmmaking including multiliteracies games
- I hope I've got you thinking about how important filmmaking is in the school curriculum: we can learn filmmaking as well as 'normal' class lessons... and it helps with literacy!
- We're really lucky to have professional filmmaker Sam Collins to teach us: this is not usual in primary school as Media studies is part of year 10 curriculum
- We are all learning together

What next?
- Use our journals in the holidays-log/note any films you make or view, new ideas that give you fire in the belly i.e. you feel strongly about
- Start emailing Dr Helen Nixon about filmmaking as she could be our mentor
- Make 10 Golden Rules of Filmmaking: still with a mix of school learning and home learning
- Think how you could tell your class about what you've learnt and still learning
- End of year reports
- Show films and give an update at assembly
- Write special features for newsletter
- Bring films to share with group

Any other ideas?

Love from Helen ☺

FIGURE 4.17 Letter from teacher to student filmmakers

- making journal entries
- emailing
- telling their classes about their learning
- giving an update at assembly
- writing special features for the school newsletter.

As well, she suggests the possibility of making a follow-up film, this time entitled *10 Golden Rules of Filmmaking*. The message here is that making a film is not an end in itself, but is part of wider cultural processes and practices into which these students are being inducted. The fact that Grant has used artist-in-residence funds to hire a professional, locally based filmmaker to work with her students demonstrates how seriously she takes this work. So the film club, and special filmmaking projects that Grant finds ways to resource, aim to support students to assemble complex discursive resources over time.

Sudan: Turning the Tables on Who's 'In the Know'

What Do You Know About Sudan?

This final example is one of the most significant films in Grant's current archive. *Sudan* (Grant & Walsh, 2003) is an eleven-minute documentary and was produced by Grant and a group of recently arrived Sudanese students. The film's key moves are provided and are followed by a focus on literacy, place and pedagogies of possibility.

The film opens with a black screen and the sound of African drumming. A series of questions in white text appear one at a time on the black screen:

What is the largest country in the continent of Africa?
What African country has hundreds of languages?
In what country is Dinka, Nuer, Ma'di, Kuku, Bari and Arabic spoken?
From which African country have hundreds of thousands of refugees escaped because of war and danger to their lives?

The next screen still with the quiet drumming simply reads:

SUDAN

At this point, the music changes to include other instruments with two boys and a girl dancing to African music, dressed in their usual Australian school clothes. While the dancers continue, in impressive style, several young girls appear holding embroidered textiles and woven artifacts from Sudan, made by family members.

The music continues and the camera moves between the dancers and the girls proudly displaying the items. The camera then pans to a classroom where the female Sudanese dancer, an upper primary student, is sitting on the teacher's chair and taking questions from the class of middle primary students. Students who want to ask her questions have their hands in the air. She points to a young white boy who asks:

Are there cars in Sudan?

Sudanese student replies:

Yes, of course. Why not?

The children laugh. The Sudanese student immediately points to another student, in effect dismissing his question.

The next set of scenes shows various groups of students in the school playground at lunchtime. The person holding the camera asks each group:

What do you know about Sudan?

Once again, Grant uses a vox pop style of presentation with short clips of students all addressing the same question. Mostly white and Anglo students respond in a variety of ways, but mostly displaying their ignorance:

Well, we know that you came from it. That's one thing.
It's meant to be very beautiful at this time of year.

There's a degree of complacency in the clichéd reply, yet the group's giggling perhaps suggest their discomfort in not being able to answer the question.

At this point, we return to the classroom, where the questioning of the Sudanese student continues:

Is there brown grass there?

The student answers, explaining the seasonal changes to the color of the grass, and still photographic images appear on the screen. The camera then turns to a male Sudanese student who reports 'tropical rain' in Sudan. Next, the camera turns to several teachers, each shown individually, and then to the school principal addressing the same question:

What do you know about Sudan?

Each educator adds a different fact or two:

Khartoum is the capital.
There are many different groups who live there.

Then, we are back in the yard again with student respondents. One shouts:

Nothing!

Two female high school students simply repeat the word,

Sudan?

Then they smile and move away from the camera.
The next respondent is the principal, who replies:

> *I know I've got thirty-three students in my school from Sudan. I know it's a very hot dry country. What else should I know about Sudan? Northern part of Africa.*

More students admit their lack of knowledge. Several look sheepishly back at the camera as they struggle for an answer:

> *I don't know anything about Sudan apart from the fact that it is called Sudan.*

Some groups of children and several teachers mention that they know that it is hot and that it is in Africa. This pattern of moving between showing responses from teachers and then students is repeated with many of the students either announcing they know nothing or not much, or awkwardly attempting to move away from the camera and the interviewer.

After the series of vox pops, the image of sticks and hands drumming returns. Almost half way into the film, this drumming marks a transition to a new section of the film. The next couple of minutes show two different boys using maps and globes to show the journeys they have made to come to Australia. They point to relevant places on the map. The first narrates his story:

> *Ten years ago, I was born in Khartoum and I went to Bal. I went to Ethiopia, and I went to Kenya, and I went to South Africa because of war.*

Both boys are still learning to speak English, but because they have rehearsed, their voices are clear and readily understood. We then see images of many different Sudanese students in various learning contexts: cross-age reading groups, a sleep-over at the zoo, eating lunch, in the yard, reading reference books on Sudan, answering the question concerning what they know about Sudan. Responses to the question include family, industries, foods, sports, the Nile and so on. As a transition, various images of African animals are shown with accompanying Sudanese music. One young boy says:

> *I know about cows, I know about my dad, . . . my brother . . . some*
> *sheep . . .*

The next two vignettes include an upper primary boy and a young female girl recounting humorous Sudanese moral tales told to them by family members, beginning:

> *Once upon a time, there was a fly and a frog . . . and*
> *Once upon a time, there was a man who lived with his son.*

This is an episodic story that goes on for over a minute. The little girl concludes the story with:

> *My dad told me that story. They decided to go for a ride on a donkey.*

The final scenes show the group of older Sudanese students who have made the film together with their tripod on the high point of the schoolyard, establishing themselves as the filmmakers. To conclude, each of the Sudanese students gathered in the school playground and simply say their names . . .

> *Nadia*
> *Patricia*
> *Samuel*
> *Mohammed*
> *Jodi*
> *Ruth, etc.*

Finally, there are several short Sudanese songs and proverbs—'Dinka sayings'—with translated subtitles on the bottom of the screen, which then goes to the credits, where each of the students are named for their specific roles in concept and research, scripting, filming, editing advice and so on.

The Power of Place-Based Pedagogy and Critical Literacies

Repositioning recently arrived refugees as experts and filmmakers is a powerful pedagogical approach. We see it as akin to Vasquez's (2004) approach to critical literacy in the sense that, as a teacher, she endeavored to take her cue from the students in terms of topics that needed to be studied and analyzed. *Sudan*, the film, is a student-produced documentary that acknowledges the prior knowledge

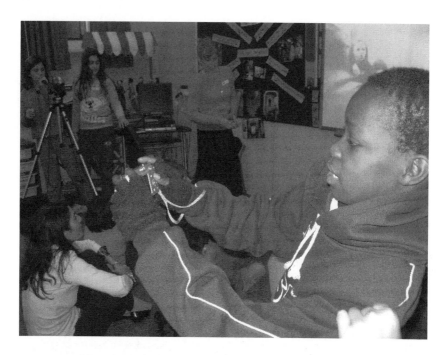

FIGURE 4.18 Negotiating learner identities in a new context

FIGURE 4.19 Critical and place-based pedagogies lifted the film beyond tokenism

and life experiences of the Sudanese students in the school about their 'place'. In a sense, it puts them in a privileged position. They are pointing the cameras, holding the microphones, asking the questions and giving their views.

However, they are also shown as still learning about Sudan: reading reference books in the library, learning about African animals at the zoo, finding stories and cultural artifacts by talking with family and community members. While the film celebrates elements of their cultural heritage, it avoids the tokenism so prevalent in some versions of multiculturalism (Kalantzis & Cope, 2008). Indeed Grant's use of humor problematizes any easy romantic views of culture, and having the older students recount their journeys out of Sudan, due to war, infuses the film with the gravity it deserves. There are several telling moments in the film that draw out key insights regarding literacy, place and pedagogies of possibility.

Because the Sudanese students are pointing the camera and asking the questions, their English-speaking peers are repositioned as respondents, and because they have little knowledge of Sudan, the tables are turned about who is in the know. No longer are the non-Sudanese able to take it for granted that their knowledge is paramount. The film records clear points of disruption where students use a range of strategies to try to repair their equilibrium and return to the normative status quo. Even the teachers answering the question, as to what they know about Sudan, struggle. The bodily awkwardness and lack of confidence in knowing what to say is a highlight of the documentary. Non-Sudanese viewers may have already experienced a lack of knowledge with the opening questions on the screen. When we watch the mainstream respondents struggle, there is a moment of knowing what it is like to be marginalized, to have no easy answers available. Non-Sudanese viewers are 'out of place'.

Grant's pedagogy enables Sudanese students to work with their existing languages, cultural repertoires and life histories at the same time as she introduces new ways of knowing and representing that knowledge. By valuing what they already know, she positions them as having significant cultural and educational capital. In Thomson's (2002) terms, she allows children to open their 'virtual back-pack' and to make use of their 'funds of knowledge' (Gonzalez, Moll & Amanti, 2005). Place is one of those resources, and includes even painful experiences in real places, and journeying through those places as refugees. Grant helps students revisit their homelands and their journeys with maps and globes, and gives them skills and confidence by rehearsing English language accounts of how they came to Australia.

Young people are recognized as having significant histories, but it is also clear that their knowledge is partial and she encourages them to do further research in their home and communities, as well as to access the library and other learning sites such as the zoo. In the process of building and sharing their knowledges, she also inducts them into a range of multimodal literate repertoires and develops their capabilities with spoken and written English. They are engaged in translation, reading complex reference books, writing scripts in English and learning all of the techniques and practices of filmmaking that were discussed earlier.

This is the epitome of pedagogy that brings together elements of critical literacy and place-conscious pedagogy, infused and strengthened throughout with respect for what students bring. Grant has introduced complex possibilities for negotiating something new, for trying out different ways of knowing and representing that knowledge and doing all of this while working in a group with their teacher and peers.

Conclusion

This chapter aimed to show that making place the object of study can provide opportunities for children to work together to make new meanings, imagine different possibilities, and in the process, to assemble complex literate repertoires. Such pedagogy does not pay tokenistic attention to place. As they study place, sometimes familiar places in different ways, learners are also introduced to ways of observing and knowing those places. Simultaneously, teachers introduce young people into new discursive and representational practices. As they learn specific literate practices and put together significant artifacts, they are also learning to collaborate in the production of multimodal texts for specific audiences and purposes.

The literacies evident here are a social accomplishment in every sense of that term. Children and teachers work as a collective to research and document places and to represent their complex knowledges and experiences in ambitious products destined for the wider school community and often beyond. They build an archive of their learning that becomes a resource for their peers and for future students. This is the knowledge-producing school in action. Here, literacy is not only a tool or skill for demonstrating given text-book knowledge, but a constantly evolving set of goal-driven practices designed to make knowledge and to represent people's experiences of places.

Textual practices are frequently used to govern populations (Smith, 2005), or to test the abilities of individuals in comparison to others. Yet school literacy learning has the potential to offer children so much more than this. A major plus for learning at school is the rich diversity of cultural and linguistic resources in most classrooms; yet if children are required to work alone on displaying literate practices with no social consequences beyond the self, we have missed one of the greatest affordances of schooling: namely, the capacity to work, learn, play and imagine together. A shared focus on studying and recording phenomena or changes in places can provide extraordinarily rich shared material to motivate children to make meaning together. In these classrooms, children learn together that places are constructed and that government and economic policies as well as vested private interests affect the design of, access to and use of different places. While they are learning about places, they are also assembling new literate repertoires. They are learning that they can produce different artifacts and meanings in partnership than they could make on their own. Monolingual English speaking students witness their multilingual peers reading gravesites written in Arabic, singing songs in other languages and writing in nonalphabetic scripts.

These vernacular languages and literacies are recorded in various modes, such as film, photos and artworks to be shared with the wider community. Such a curriculum is inclusive in every sense and works with the affordance of the local place, even as it pushes the cultural boundaries of the classroom.

Note

1. *New Literacy Demands in the Middle Years: Learning from design experiments* was an Australian Research Council (ARC) Linkage Project (No. LP0990692) with the Queensland University of Technology, the University of South Australia, and the University of Sydney, the Department of Education and Children's Services (DECS) (SA) and the Australian Education Union (AEU) SA Branch. The chief investigators were Barbara Comber, Peter Freebody and Helen Nixon. The partner investigator was Victoria Carrington (University of East Anglia). The research associate was Anne-Marie Morgan (University of South Australia). The views presented here are those of the author only.

References

Art Gallery of New South Wales 2011, *Artist talks series featuring Elaine Russell*, online video, accessed August 28, 2014, http://www.artgallery.nsw.gov.au/channel/clip/477/

Australian ABC 194-, Nucolorvue Productions, in conjunction with Photogravures, Melbourne. (Out of copyright, see National Library Catalogue, http://catalogue.nla.gov.au/Record/129059)

Baker, J 1990, *Window*, Greenwillow Books, New York.

Baker, J 2004, *Belonging*, Walker Children's Paperbacks, UK.

Baker, J 2010, *Mirror*, Walker Children's Paperbacks, UK.

Bautista, M, Bertrand, M, Morrell, E, Scorza, D & Matthews, C 2013, 'Participatory action research and city youth: Methodological insights from the council of youth research', *Teachers College Record*, vol. 115, no. 10, pp. 1–23.

Blommaert, J 2013, *Ethnography, superdiversity and linguistic landscapes*, Multilingual Matters, Bristol.

Burnett, C & Merchant, G 2011, 'Is there a space for critical literacy in the context of social media?', *English Teaching Practice and Critique*, vol. 10, no. 1, pp. 41–57.

Cobb, P, Confrey, J, di Sessa, A, Lehrer, R & Schauble, L 2003, 'Design experiments in educational research', *Educational Researcher*, vol. 32, no. 1, pp. 9–13.

Cochran-Smith, M & Lytle, S 2009, *Inquiry as stance: Practitioner research for the next generation*, Teachers College Press, New York.

Comber, B 1994, 'Critical literacy: An introduction to Australian debates and perspectives', *Journal of Curriculum Studies*, vol. 26, no. 6, pp. 655–668.

Comber, B in press, 2015, 'School literate repertoires: That was then, this is now', in J. Rowsell & J. Sefton-Green (eds.), *Revisiting Learning Lives—longitudinal perspectives on researching learning and literacy*, Routledge, London & New York, pp. 16–31.

Comber, B & Kamler, B 1997, 'Politicising the literacy classroom', *Interpretations*, vol. 30, no. 1, pp. 30–53.

Comber, B & Kamler, B 2004, 'Getting out of deficit: Pedagogies of reconnection', *Teaching education*, vol. 15, no. 3, pp. 293–310.

Comber, B & Nixon, H 2005, 'Children re-read and re-write their neighbourhoods: Critical literacies and identity work', in J. Evans (ed.), *Literacy moves on: Using popular culture, new technologies and critical literacy in the primary classroom*, Heinemann, Portsmouth, New Hampshire, pp. 127–148.

Comber, B & Nixon, H 2011, 'Critical reading comprehension in an era of accountability', *Australian Educational Researcher*, vol. 38, no. 2, pp. 167–179.

Commonwealth of Australia 1997, *Bringing them home: The 'stolen children'*, Report of the National Inquiry into the Separation of Aboriginal and Torres Strait Islander Children from Their Families, Sydney.

Dooley, K 2012, 'Positioning refugee students as intellectual class members', in F. McCarthy & M. H. Vickers (eds.), *Achieving equity in education for refugees*, Information Age Publishing, Scottsdale, Arizona, pp. 3–20.

Dudley-Marling, C & Michaels, S 2012, *High-expectation curricula: Helping all students succeed with powerful learning*, Teachers College Press, New York.

Dyson, A H 1989, *Multiple worlds of child writers: Friends learning to write*, Teachers College Press, New York.

Dyson, A H 1993, *Negotiating a permeable curriculum : on literacy, diversity, and the interplay of children's and teachers' worlds*, National Council of Teachers of English, Urbana, Illinois.

Dyson, A H 1997, *Writing superheroes: Contemporary childhood, popular culture, and classroom literacy*, Teachers College Press, New York.

Dyson, A H 2013, *ReWriting the basics: Literacy learning in children's cultures*, Teachers College Press, New York.

Foucault, M 1979, *Discipline and punish: The birth of the prison*, Vintage Books, New York.

Foucault, M 1988, *Technologies of the self : A seminar with Michel Foucault* (Trans.), University of Massachusetts Press, USA.

Freeman, C 2007, *Born to run*, Penguin Books, Camberwell, Victoria.

Gilbert, P 1991, *Fashioning the feminine: Girls, popular culture, and schooling*, Allen & Unwin, Sydney, NSW.

Gonzalez, N, Moll, L & Amanti, C (eds.) 2005, *Funds of knowledge: Theorizing practices in households, communities, and classrooms*, Lawrence Erlbaum, Mahwah, New Jersey.

Grant, H & Walsh, C 2003, 'Teacher research: What's it all about?', *Practically primary*, vol. 8, no. 2, pp. 4–6.

Greene, M 1988, *The dialectic of freedom*, Teachers College Press, New York & London.

Gregory, E & Williams, A 2001, *City literacies: Learning to read across generations and cultures*, Routledge, London. Gutierrez, K 2008, 'Developing a sociocritical literacy in the third space', *Reading Research Quarterly*, vol. 43, no. 2, pp. 148–164.

Hunter, I 1988, *Culture and government : The emergence of literary education*, McMillan, London.

Janks, H & Comber, B 2006, 'Critical literacy across continents', in K. Pahl & J. Rowsell (eds.), *Travel notes from the new literacy studies: Instances of practice*, Multilingual Matters, Clevedon, pp. 95–117. Reprinted in M. Mackey (ed.) 2007, *Media literacies: Major themes in education*, Routledge, New York.

Jewitt, C 2009, 'An introduction to multimodality', in C. Jewitt (ed.), *The routledge handbook of multimodal analysis*, London & New York, pp. 14–27.

Kalantzis, M & Cope, B 2008, *New learning: Elements of a science of learning*, Cambridge University Press, Cambridge.

Kamler, B 2001, *Relocating the personal: A critical writing pedagogy*, State University of New York Press, Albany, New York.

Kenway, J & Koh, A 2013, 'The elite school as 'cognitive machine' and 'social paradise': Developing transnational capitals for the national 'field of power'', *Journal of Sociology*, vol. 49, no. 2–3, pp. 272–290.

Kress, G 2010, *Multimodality: A social semiotic approach to contemporary communication*, Routledge, London & New York.

Kress, G & van Leeuwen, T 2006, *Reading images: The grammar of visual design*, Routledge, London & New York.

Luke, A, Cazden, C, Coopes, R, Klenowski, V, Ladwig, J, Lester, J, & Woods, A 2013, *A summative evaluation of the Stronger Smarter Learning Communities Project: vol 1 and vol 2*, Brisbane, Queensland, Queensland University of Technology, retrieved from http://eprints.qut.edu.au/59535/

Luke, C 1991, 'On reading the child: A feminist poststructuralist perspectives', *Australian Journal of Language and Literacy*, vol. 14, no. 2, pp. 109–116.

Massey, D 2005, *For space*, SAGE, London.

Morgan, A M 2013, 'Proof of concept: Beginning to use design-based research to improve science literacies for middle years learners', Australian Journal of Language and Literacy, vol. 36, no. 1, pp. 3–16.

Morgan, A, Comber, B, Freebody, P & Nixon, H (eds.) 2014, *Literacy in the middle years: Learning from collaborative classroom research*, Primary English Teaching Association, Newtown, Australia.

Morgan, S 1987, *My place*, Fremantle Arts Centre, Freemantle.

Patterson, A 1993, "Personal Response' and English Teaching', in D. Meridyth & D. Tyler (eds.), *Child and citizen: Genealogies of schooling and subjectivity*, Institute for Cultural Policy Studies, Faculty of Humanities, Griffith University, Brisbane.

Prinsloo, M 2005, 'The new literacies as placed resources', *Perspectives in Education*, vol. 23, vol. 4, pp. 87–98.

Rowsell, J 2013, *Working with multimodality: Rethinking literacy in a digital age*, Routledge, London & New York.

Russell, E 2000, *A is for Aunty*, Australian Broadcasting Commission, Sydney.

Russell, E 2011, *The shack that Dad built*, Random House, Sydney, Australia.

Smith, D E 2005, *Institutional ethnography: A sociology for people*, AltaMira Press, Lanham.

Smith, G & Sobel, D (eds.) 2010, *Place- and community-based education in schools*, Routledge, New York & London.

Thomson, P 2002, *Schooling the rustbelt kids: Making the difference in changing times*, Allen & Unwin, Sydney, Australia.

Vasquez, V 2004, *Negotiating critical literacies with young children*, Lawrence Erlbaum, Mahwah, New Jersey.

Vasquez, V 2010, *Getting beyond 'I like the book': Creating space for critical literacy in K-6 classrooms*, International Reading Association, Newark, Delaware.

Vygotsky, L 1978, *Mind in society: The development of higher psychological processes*, MIT Press, Cambridge, Massachusetts.

Wells, M & Trimboli, R 2014, 'Place-conscious literacy pedagogies', in A. Morgan, B. Comber, P. Freebody & H. Nixon (eds.), *Literacy in the middle years: Learning from collaborative classroom research*, Primary English Teaching Association Australia, Newtown, pp. 15–34.

Wheatley, N 1987, *My place*, Ashton Scholastic, Sydney.

5

REIMAGINING SCHOOL LITERACY

What If . . .?

Places . . . pose a challenge. . . . They require in one way or another that we confront
the challenge of the negotiation of multiplicity.

(Massey, 2005, p. 141)

Introduction

The aim of this book has been to gather together and illustrate rich, innovative and
enabling pedagogical practices in literacy education that in various ways exploit the
affordances of space and place as objects of study. In this final chapter, key principles
are revisited with reference to brief contemporary instances of classroom practices
that create pedagogies of possibility even in the face of mandated curriculum and
high stakes testing. The development of place-conscious pedagogies is seen as a
hopeful and distinctive direction in reconceptualizing critical literacy for the 21st
century as we engage with unprecedented changes to the world in which we live.
As Massey (2005, p. 141) observes, places 'pose a challenge'. Abstract phenomena,
such as superdiversity, economic instability, climate change, international conflicts
and injustices are experienced by people living in particular places and impact the
work of teachers and upon children learning. The dynamism of changing places
and populations also offer new possibilities, 'the negotiation of multiplicity' (Massey,
2005, p. 141). Classrooms, at their best, are sites for such negotiation.

The book is the outcome of an organic and extended process of documentation and synthesis. It reconsiders what it might mean in elementary schools to
'read the word and the world' in contemporary times (Freire & Macedo, 1987;
Luke, 2013). Researchers and teachers encounter theories and make sense and
make use of theories in our own educational landscapes—policy and practice
contexts. Nevertheless, the teachers' work documented here has been assembled

from over a period of several decades. These practices are enabling pedagogies which still have currency, but they may not be readily visible and available to early career teachers and researchers whose professional lives have been dominated by accountability (Dunn & Durrance, 2014). Hence, the intention is to capture in a modest way some exemplary practices that may evoke new iterations of enabling literacy pedagogies.

A recent education department recruitment campaign was advertised under the optimistic banner of 'Teaching is inspiring'. It can be! However, it can also be deflating and limiting, and perhaps that, in part, accounts for the high percentage of recent graduates who leave the profession within the first few years of their careers (Adoniou, 2013; Hong, 2010). During this period of implementation of high stakes testing and curriculum standardization, it must be remembered that it is the enacted curriculum that impacts student learning: that is, how it is conveyed through everyday classroom discourse, and negotiated in everyday learning environments which involve participants in socio-cultural and spatial relations, wherever they may be. As literacy educators and researchers, we need to strongly advocate to policy-makers and practitioners to ensure that consideration about what literacy is for, and how it can work in the interests of inclusion and justice, is not removed from public forums.

Soon, the baby boomer teacher and teacher-educator workforce will have all retired, including the teachers featured in this book, and the researchers who have engaged and collaborated with them. This book is designed to leave a legacy of practices and artifacts that have inspired teacher-educators and literacy researchers, and with any luck, it may act not only as a record, but also as a catalyst to inspire teachers setting out or still on their journeys. Hopefully, teachers will find something that captures their imaginations, something they cannot resist trying with their students, something that makes them look again and consider the resources they have in their classrooms and at their doorsteps.

To conclude, we offer some speculations and further questions for inquiry to researchers and teachers, along with some recent indicative glimpses of enabling and critical literacy pedagogies. While currently school literacy is often conceptualized as limited to the individual, to lessons and events, and increasingly to what can be assessed through normative assessment grids (Dyson, 2013), it does not have to be this way. What if these temporal and spatial frames were altered to take on literacy as a socio-spatial accomplishment of people working together? What if school literacy is considered as a collective accomplishment across time and place in Connell's (1993) sense of justice, where all participants share responsibility for each other's learning? Such an approach requires the situated analysis of the micro-practices of literacy learning to be considered over extended time periods and across places, and as relational and accomplished by people learning and working together. Such work would require long-term situated research (see Heath, 2012a; Rowsell & Sefton-Green, 2015).

Scholarly theoretical repertoires shift and change over time. As teachers and/ or researchers assemble the analytical tools for better explanations of educational phenomena, persistent trends (such as unequal educational outcomes) and sudden changes (digital technologies) shape classroom responses. Of course, lives in schools, and the places in which they are situated, are also continually changing. Teachers themselves gather knowledge, experiences and resources across their careers and then make these available in different ways to different cohorts of students. New waves of refugees change the face of a neighborhood or city, while new forms of poverty are created with the closure of industries or the loss of natural resources. And then, of course, there are times of significant material and environmental change, such as earthquakes and floods, terrorism and random violence.

Some change is more gradual, as populations age and demographics shift. Schools are demolished. New schools are built. Although schools are meant to be 'thinking and learning institutions' (Boomer, 1985), frequently they show signs of atrophy as the 'grammar of schooling' (Tyack & Cuban, 1995) takes hold and they become disciplinary institutions par excellence (Dixon, 2011; Foucault, 1979). But as Foucault argued, 'wherever there is power there is resistance' and 'spaces of freedom'.

The illustrations of teachers at work featured in this book are not provided in order that others replicate or simply adopt the same approach in other contexts. To the contrary, the intention is to distill key principles of their practices to contribute to the wider educational imaginary: to prize open what might be done in education and to suggest ways of operationalizing complex theory in the everyday world of classrooms, schools and neighborhoods.

Many literacy researchers, cited here, have in different ways foregrounded elements of

- time, space and place
  Barton, Hamilton & Ivanic, 2000; Burnett, Merchant, Pahl & Rowsell, 2014; Compton-Lilly, 2000; Green & Corbett, 2013; Green & Letts, 2007; Gutierrez, 2008; Heath, 1983; Hicks, 2002; 2013; Hull & Schulz, 2001; Jones, 2006; Leander & Sheehy, 2004: Moje, 2000; Nichols, Rowsell, Nixon & Rainbird, 2012; Pahl & Rowsell, 2010; Sefton-Green, 2009; Street, 1975; 2001; Thomson, 2002
- socio-cultural politics of literacy
  Dyson, 2013; Gee, 1990; Heath, 1983; 2012a; 2012b; Janks, 2010; Lewis, Enciso & Moje, 2007; Luke, 2012; Marsh, 2005
- discursive effects on pedagogy
  Cazden, 2001; Cochran-Smith & Lytle, 2009; Kress, 1997; Kress, 2003; Luke, 2000; Rogers, 2011

These bodies of work highlight the socio-political nature of literate practices in and out of school, and explore how literate practices are always relational, both in terms of the micro-visible activities of the present, but also historically and translocally, in that they are formed out of various traditions borne of particular times and places.

This theoretical corpus is vital to foreground the work of researchers collaborating with teachers in schools, or the teachers themselves, and especially those who are located or researching in areas of poverty. Place-conscious pedagogy deserves a place here (Green & Corbett, 2013; Gruenewald, 2008; Kerkham, 2007; Somerville, 2007; 2013) because the current era in which we are living and operating requires an urgent examination of the state of the planet and the relationships between people, as well as the relationship between people and the more-than-human world, including:

- significant climate change
- large-scale population mobility
- increasing gaps between rich and poor (which are racially and geographically correlated)
- escalating violence in many places
- other localized changes that threaten relationships.

These are teachers who have long histories in foregrounding place, language and identity in classroom practices in enabling ways, and many of these are not well known within the research field, or even recognized for their work in their local contexts, because they do so in a degree of isolation, even as they swim against the tide of standardization. This book is a gesture of consolidation with those teachers, as the work of Wells, Trimboli, Grant, Clifton and others are featured for their potential to inspire fellow educators. What they share is a capacity to collaborate with children to produce culturally significant artifacts that represent complex and contested ideas about place and identity. Although some instances of their teacher practices have been shared in different publications and forums previously, they have not, until now, been brought together and contextualized theoretically as they are in this book.

Our concern is that many early career teachers are leaving the profession in part due to the emphasis on standardized measures of student performance (Dunn & Durrance, 2014). This is not the profession that they thought they were joining. People who became teachers to work for social justice report feeling disappointed when they begin teaching and finding little space for pedagogical imagination and culturally responsive teaching in the face of directives to enact mandated and scripted curriculum. Lipman (2013) recently warned that these trends play out in particularly worrying ways in schools located in poverty.

Undermining teaching as a profession and breaking teacher seniority will certainly ensure the acceleration of teacher turnover in the least resourced and most test-driven schools. A revolving door of short-term, untrained novices supplied by privately run 'alternative certification' operations will constitute the staffs of the most desperate schools or schooling will be outsourced to private providers of online learning or learning modules synched to high stakes tests.

(Lipman, 2013, p. 566)

In such contexts, we are observing elementary classrooms where very little extended writing is created and very little drawing is undertaken, with very little multimodal text production of any kind, where the teachers have not managed to make spaces to teach beyond 'the basics' (see also Dyson, 2013). There is very little singing, and very little opportunity to create, imagine or play with semiotic resources. Such is the ubiquitous focus on targets that the bigger picture of what really matters is too often lost, and the sense of the local lives of children vanishes in the classroom. Young teachers tell us that they do want to learn how to design a curriculum based on an expanded view of literacy, but many of them cannot imagine what this might look like. Rather than 'big picture' pedagogy and curriculum design, too often they have been encouraged to view literacy education with tunnel vision, and the 'pedagogy of poverty' (Haberman, 1991) can result. Given these conditions, a key role for critical literacy researchers is to document pedagogies of possibility in places of poverty. The other side of interrogating injustice is being able to say 'which reading and writing positions and practices should be encouraged in the classroom' (Luke, 1995, p. 40); it helps the educational community imagine how it might be otherwise (Greene, 1988).

A flow-on effect of the return of pedagogies of poverty is that while many early career educational researchers want to document critical literacy, cultural responsive teaching, and ethical and inclusive practices, there appear to be fewer sites to suggest for their inquiries as the Global Educational Reform Movement spreads (Sahlberg, 2011). In other words, increasing standardization and insistence on closing the gaps in measurable performance comprises a juggernaut of neo-liberal performative discourses that reconstitutes the educational environment in terms of statistics and abstracts. These processes background actual children and families and take no account of their histories or present circumstances. Ultimately, this level of abstraction removes the teacher as curriculum designer and as professional pedagogue, thereby reducing them to a technician implementing programs of work and monitoring student performance. That is, the teacher agency, creativity and local place-based initiatives explored in this book have become more difficult to locate as the curriculum and pedagogical agenda has narrowed.

Some literacy researchers have advocated that the best solution for school literacies, in terms of motivation and relevance, is to replicate some of the conditions, purposes and audience of out-of school practices. By these accounts, many school literacies are remarkably predictable and without distinction. This is not surprising, particularly in periods of high stakes, mandated testing. However, it is important to understand *what* is being accomplished in particular places, and *how*, by theoretically informed talented teachers driven by equity and social justice. In other words, educators must consider seriously the positive affordances of the school as a meeting place, the students as a dynamic collective, and the classroom as a learning space where people can learn together and accomplish together tasks that they could not produce on their own. One goal of this book is to make available some accounts that show what enabling pedagogies and high expectations curricular look and sound like in different classrooms; and, in so doing, to foreground the sometimes neglected places where such pedagogies have been negotiated.

Given the current silences on context in educational policies with the emphasis on 'big data' and abstractions, as researchers, it is important to be able to present specific artifacts and the contexts of their production to instantiate the practice. Sometimes this can require long passages of descriptive writing and examples of student or teacher-produced work. Such detail is necessary because what teachers say and write is significant, and so too are the images that capture pedagogical and literacy repertoires. We need more 'thick description' (Geertz, 1983; see also Campano, Ghiso, Yee & Pantoja, 2013) to balance the tendency of contemporary textual practices to remove people and their doings (Smith, 2005).

In this spirit, this chapter offers brief glimpses of inventive ways in which principled school literacies can be reimagined in the contemporary context—enabling place-conscious pedagogies of possibility. If school literacy is considered as a collective accomplishment across time and place, teachers and students can work together to communicate significant ideas and knowledge beyond the school. School literacy education, including 'publication', 'purpose' and 'audience', can be reimagined if contextualized within broader projects with positive social consequences. Rather than conceptualizing literacy as a matter of individual educational achievement, it can be understood as a collective practice.

Classroom Messages About Learning and Literacy: What's School Good For?

The education community has long been preoccupied with what constitutes literacy (Gee, 1990). Yet, more than ever, educators need to think beyond definitions of literacy, especially those that reduce it to test scores, to reconsider Freire's call to read the world as well as the word (Luke, 2012). Questions worthy of consideration include:

* What is literacy for?
* Or, what might it be for?

- What might teachers have to do with this in the contemporary era?
- And relatedly, what is school good for?
- What kinds of graduates are we seeking to educate?

Almost three decades ago, as an early career researcher, Comber (1987) published a paper called 'Celebrating and analyzing successful teaching' in *Language Arts*. That paper described the common features of the practices of three teachers: one working in a high poverty suburb early childhood classroom in northern Adelaide, another in high school science in a regional working-class town in South Australia, and another in a small Catholic primary school in Tasmania. In all classrooms, teacher communication was found to be pivotal in conveying high expectations, modeling ways of approaching problems and enabling complex learning. Pedagogy is contingent upon how people talk to each other in situ.

Following the insights of researchers like Courtney Cazden (2001) and Shirley Brice Heath (1983; 2012a), the paper examined the ways in which these teachers addressed their students: the classroom discourse and the interactions between teachers and students. What was being talked about was of real interest to students and the teacher. Pedagogy is carried through teacher discourse and student engagement in things that really matter to them. The enacted curriculum, as experienced by students, is what counts for their learning. Working across the different stages of schooling, and across the curriculum, these teachers asked enabling questions and posed significant challenges:

- What else could you have done? Is there a way of solving this? (early childhood classroom)
- What makes a fairy or folk story a 'good story'? How would you evaluate our classroom reading materials? How helpful is this book? How would you use it? (primary classroom)
- See if you can work out what's going on. How are you going to do that? When will you be ready to share with the class? What else do you need to do? (high school science)

These questions require sophisticated and analytical reflection from students. Such questions open up space for inquiry and dialogue: the kinds of practices that lead to dynamic knowledge production (Johnston, 2012). Further, they demand that students take up active and responsible positions as learners. They are positioned as participants whose judgments count, and who can be invited to think about future practices. Innovative teacher-researchers, with strong understandings of curricular justice and student capabilities, demonstrate how it is possible to make a long-term difference to the learning lives and literacy practices of different children, in different kinds of schools, in different kinds of places.

Inevitably, the discursive practices of teachers do more than inform children intellectually: they also send messages about moral, social and political values. The extent to which teachers communicate to all young people their respect, their positive expectations and their reflections on classroom practices and processes plays a significant part in children's development of sustainable learner dispositions and therefore their learning lives and their lifelong capacities to participate in their families and communities. As Luke (2012) recently reiterated, face-to-face classroom discursive relations between teachers and students are key sites where inequality is reproduced. That is, what teachers say and write and read in the classroom in part constructs what is possible in terms of the micro-politics of classroom life in which learning, including literacy learning, is embedded. In a similar vein, in the UK, Robin Alexander (2012) has recently argued:

> The quality of classroom talk has a measurable impact on standards of attainment in English, mathematics and science.

Citing robust international evidence, he reiterates the importance of high quality talk for children's learning. He mentions Lauren Resnick's (2010) notion of accountable talk, or disciplined interactive discussion:

> Accountable talk is talk that is orchestrated by teachers so that students learn to formulate responses to problems, interpretations of text that are correct in disciplinary terms and go beyond what was actually written there, just give back the answer you see on the page.

She elaborates that cognitive psychology has demonstrated that 'when you explain things you learn them.' Alexander (2012) and Resnick's (2010) combined points here are that teachers' talk and teacher-produced artifacts tell learners who they are and who they can be within the micro-politics of the classroom. Simultaneously, the discourse also carries key information about the kinds of academic learning to be done. These messages cannot be separated. So how teachers speak with students and linguistically frame tasks and feedback is more than contextual, more than about support or relationships: it is, in fact, fundamental to learning processes and classroom identity work.

It is equally important to consider the productive discursive work that teachers do, as it is to expose how classroom discourse maintains or extends inequities. Teachers can and should play a pivotal role in enabling young people's learning about social inclusion and active citizenship. As we have seen in Grant's film production of *Kissing Babies and Pressing the Flesh*, learning about democracy in action can begin in elementary school (see also Vasquez, 2004). The work teachers do is not only socio-cultural and discursive in making, but also spatial, material and embodied. Who gets to communicate with whom, where and when, and about what, really matters! Frequently, children begin their school lives with very different life, language, and cultural experiences and some children have already lived in many places before they start school. The global financial crisis, population mobility, and the changing nature of regional and rural communities and workplaces has meant that schools are increasingly diverse. Classrooms inevitably become meeting places for children with very different life histories, as well as linguistic and cultural capital. No longer can we take it for granted that the local school serves a single stable community; it is more likely that any one local school will educate children from many communities. In addition, the neighborhood or region itself, and indeed even the school, may also be undergoing physical change associated with urban renewal, natural disasters and changing economies.

Following Massey (2005), we understand place 'as an arena where negotiation is forced upon us', where people are 'thrown together' (p. 109) and that they must negotiate how they will interact in those places. Teachers know this in an everyday embodied sense. Their classroom communicative work involves orchestrating dynamic and changing socio-spatial relationships between people and objects of various kinds in semi-confined places. To some degree, classrooms have always been sites of throwntogetherness and negotiation. Viewing this as an asset rather than a drawback, and building the English literacy curriculum around the notion of the classroom as a meeting and belonging place, may foster a generation of critically literate graduates who are inclusive citizens, even in the face of standardization.

Working Critically and Creatively With Mandated Curriculum

In this era of standardization of curriculum and high stakes testing, teachers need to be creative and critical readers of the authorized curriculum in order to make space for inclusive and locally responsive pedagogies, perhaps informed by questions such as the following:

- What happens if our goals for English literacy are building classroom communities where students and teachers are motivated by an ethics of inclusion, belonging and respect?
- Are inclusive pedagogies possible in an era of competitive individualism, the marketization of schooling and payment by measurable outcomes?
- What has inclusivity and citizenship got to do with literacy and English education?
- What about high stakes testing and common curriculum?
- What difference does it make to think about classrooms as meeting and belonging places?
- What is the potential for curriculum and pedagogy?

The seven general capabilities in the current Australian Curriculum do allow some room for creative teachers. They include:

- Literacy
- Numeracy

- Information and communication technology capability
- Critical and creative thinking
- Personal and social capability
- Ethical understanding
- Intercultural understanding. (ACARA, 2014b)

Similarly, the three cross-curriculum priorities provide a mandate for the kinds of cross-curriculum innovation and local pedagogical design illustrated throughout this book:

- Aboriginal and Torres Strait Islander histories and cultures
- Asia and Australia's engagement with Asia
- Sustainability. (ACARA, 2014a)

Australian teachers have been fortunate. However, as this manuscript nears completion, a review of the Australian Curriculum commissioned by the current federal conservative government has recently been released (http://docs.education. gov.au/system/files/doc/other/review_of_the_national_curriculum_final_report. pdf; accessed November 20, 2014). Even prior to this review, there had been relentless attacks from journalists in the national paper, *The Australian*, of the cross-curricular priorities, especially focusing on Aboriginal and Torres Strait Islander ways of knowing and numeracy, for example. Not surprisingly, the review concluded that the curriculum was overcrowded and that the early years should focus on literacy and numeracy, with more explicit teaching of structured phonics and attention to the Western literary cannon. The priorities survived this review.

Yet internationally, there may yet be opportunities in national curriculum or curriculum standards for teachers to design or modify curriculum in ways that allow for place-conscious pedagogy and critical literacy. For instance, the New Zealand National Standards for Reading and Writing includes examples of textual practices that could be considered critical in orientation and that also include exemplar texts and questioning regarding the health of local environmental ecologies and species (Ministry of Education, New Zealand, 2014).

Similarly, the US Common Core State Standards may be read creatively, critically and strategically by experienced teachers and scholars. Whether standards come to be toxic in their effects depends on the extent to which they are placed alongside other policy ensembles that undermine teacher autonomy. Teachers have indicated a willingness to embrace literacy standards and acknowledge that literacy teaching is the task of all teachers across the curriculum and year levels. However, they argue that they need time to build their knowledge and collaborate with their peers and access knowledgeable educators in order to understand standards and data and plan accordingly (National Center for Literacy Education, 2013).

It is of considerable concern that there may be many inexperienced teachers who have not been inducted at all into critical and creative approaches to literacy, and that the time and space for appropriate mentoring may be limited. Current research in Australian schools indicates a paucity of critical and inclusive teaching of literacy (see also Luke, 2012). We need to know where the effects of standards lead to a reductive curriculum. For these reasons, it more important than ever to document and assemble the work of experienced teachers in classrooms with diverse learners. The intention of this book is to provide glimpses of ways school pedagogies and literacies might be designed for contemporary and future citizenship. Recent sociologies of youth conducted in Australia have indicated that 'learning about democratic processes involves practice and active participation' (Fyfe & Wyn, 2007, p. 116). Citizenship involves practice. Literacy education has always had and still has a significant role to play in ensuring that young people graduate from schooling with the capacities to contribute as ethical, inclusive and critically literate citizens. What teachers say and how they say it matters; how they negotiate the classroom as a belonging and meeting place is crucial.

The next section of this chapter highlights brief vignettes of recent and current ways in which educators in different contexts foster inclusive literate citizens through the communal production of texts and artifacts of various kinds. In each of these sites, students are positioned as researchers and journalists using a range of media to tell shared stories, and collectively represent their diverse experience and knowledges. In each of these cases, educators have exploited the particularities of material change to negotiate a curriculum that is of the place, of the moment, and of the people. They are engaged in principled enabling pedagogies that produce ethical graduates who wield complex multimodal literate repertoires beyond the so-called basics.

Milpera—Meeting Place of Brothers and Sisters

The first of these illustrative vignettes concerns Milpera State High School in Queensland, Australia. This is a school community literally built around the notion of meeting-place, where the school's mission is devoted to helping ESL students and recently arrived young refugees to belong and to achieve highly as learners. On its website in 2012, the school was described as:

> a special purpose state high school which teaches English language across curriculum areas. It also provides settlement services to newly arrived immigrant and refugee background young people to prepare them for living and studying in Australia. All of the students who come to Milpera are speakers of languages other than English when they arrive. Some are children of business or work migrants, some are joining family already in Australia, and some are victims of war and/or political unrest in their home countries. Most of the students are permanent residents who are starting a new life in Australia, but some may have temporary visas, be waiting

for visas or be on bridging visas. All of the students are approved by the Minister for Education to attend school in Australia.

(Milpera State High School, Queensland Government, 2012)

Each year, the principal and teachers sought out or created forums and occasions for young people to represent their experiences of resettling in Australia and learning at Milpera. For example, a number of significant learning and celebratory events are held across the year, providing a sense of how schools can become meeting and belonging places, even as they negotiate learning spaces, for young people. The principal, Adele Rice, shared her archive of films with researchers, and these capture some of the history of the school and how leadership, teachers and students collectively respond to change and trauma.

In 2011, the school was inundated during the Brisbane floods and many classrooms, offices and educational resources, including the principal's, were destroyed. The school needed to be closed for repairs for over a term, and students were temporarily relocated to other schools. Rather than letting this incident become a source of further trauma for students, the principal won a grant to produce a film with ABC journalists, *Milpera and the Floods*. The day the school reopened, the principal and students participated in a radio program. A small section of transcript is provided from ABC radio's *The World Today* program, broadcast on May 23, 2011:

ELEANOR HALL: To Queensland now where the last of the schools that was closed by the summer floods reopened in Brisbane today. Milpera State High School at Chelmer in the city's west was the most flood-damaged school in the state. But as Debra Nowland reports teachers at the school for refugee and migrant children turned the disaster into a learning experience.

(Sound of teacher talking to students)

DEBRA NOWLAND: It's a foggy misty morning at Milpera State High and students are being shown where to go.

TEACHER: All good? Let's keep walking.

DEBRA NOWLAND: Four-and-a half months ago Milpera State High was the worst of Queensland's 212 flooded schools. Today it's the last to be reopened. It's attended by students learning English before they go to mainstream schools. Many children are refugees who've survived camps in Africa, Bangladesh and Afghanistan, like 17-year-old Amin Alizada.

AMIN ALIZADA: When I come here I had no English and I had no friends. Now I met lots of friends. I have many, many new friends here from Korea and from Australia, and yeah, many friends.

DEBRA NOWLAND: Some of those friends joined together to make a documentary about their flooded school, with the help of the Australian Film Television and Radio School.

AMIN ALIZADA: We made a film about flooded Brisbane, especially our school. Milpera is flooded completely on the first floor. Flooded, we lost everything and we moved to Yeronga and then Milpera's made a new building and everything is okay. We come back here. We are very happy today. Today's the first day in Milpera come back after flood.

DEBRA NOWLAND: Principal Adele Rice says the floods have been used as a learning experience.

ADELE RICE: They worked very hard at scripting, taking photographs, structuring the interviews, filming, and of course in a week they didn't get a chance to do a lot of the editing. So there's a lot of unedited material. It's another vehicle and a tool for learning English. And it was a good vehicle so that we've just put in for an application to Arts Queensland because I can see that film-making is a great way to hear the students' voice and to give them that chance.

(Australian Broadcasting Commission, ABC Radio, 2011)

As principal, Rice actively brokered opportunities for her students to engage with professional artists working with various media. This school regards its people and their places as serious resources for learning. This is a school creating and narrating its own histories, both those of individual learners and the collective. This is a school looking outwards and to young people's possible futures, even as they help them address the traumas of the past and the immediate challenges of the present, including many students who are establishing actual citizenship. This outward-looking approach means that even though their focus is firmly upon helping students learn Standard Australian English literacy, including academic literacies, they make time to engage in community projects.

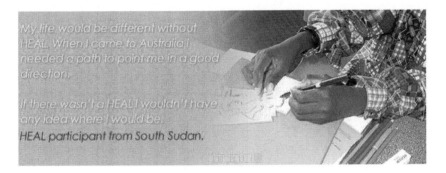

My life would be different without HEAL. When I came to Australia I needed a path to point me in a good direction.

If there wasn't to HEAL I wouldn't have any idea where I would be.

HEAL participant from South Sudan.

FIGURE 5.1 Screenshot 1 from FHEAL website (http://www.fheal.com.au/)

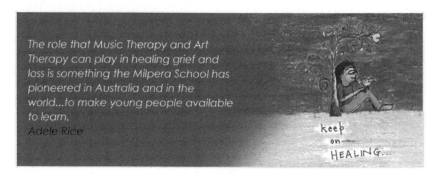

The role that Music Therapy and Art Therapy can play in healing grief and loss is something the Milpera School has pioneered in Australia and in the world...to make young people available to learn.
Adele Rice

keep on — HEALING...

FIGURE 5.2 Screenshot 2 from FHEAL website (http://www.fheal.com.au/)

During Refugee Week in 2012, an art exhibition titled *Through Their Eyes* was held in Brisbane under the auspices of Art from the Margins (AFTM). As the publicity made clear:

> the students of Milpera State High School (an English language settlement school at Chelmer) come from all the far corners of the world. HEAL (Home of Expressive Arts in Learning) is the well-being service at Milpera, offering *Art for Relaxation* in many forms. These artworks speak of belonging, of a sense of place and of identity.

There is a great deal that could be said about such events, yet what is clearly evident is that this program and exhibition reiterate the importance of young people contributing to cultural events that draw on their expertise and experiences, allowing them to work in new modes and media and to contribute to a larger collective cultural event beyond what they could do as individuals. Schools can foster and broker student cultural participation. Indeed, they have a responsibility to do so. The reason for including an account of this school's work in this final chapter is to reiterate once again that attending to the specificities of place, time and the student population allow place, diversity and even the challenges of the flood to become resources for new learning.

Studying Place Across a School Year

Complex and Durable Understandings of Power and Language

In Chapter 3, the work of Marg Wells and her colleagues and their students was considered, including the pedagogical creativity that integrated the design and building of a new *superschool* and the subsequent demolition of their old neighborhood school, Ridley Grove. The fact that their built environments were changing was certainly the impetus for their focus on the school as a built environment.

Yet all schools and neighborhoods are situated in particular places and change of one kind or another is ongoing. For all children, beginning school represents a new meeting-place; for 5-year-olds, the school is a very strange place indeed; each year it is a new social space and, often, a new classroom configuration. The classroom as a material and social space can be explored rather than seen as a static backdrop for the real action. So what is involved in helping children to understand change, and how can they be supported to develop a sense of belonging in a place, and what have these questions got to do with inclusive literacy and active citizenship?

Wells designed the curriculum to construct the classroom as a meeting-place, a dialogic space, as a negotiable learning site and to practice inclusive literacies and active citizenship. Her overarching goal for 2010, the final year of the old school, was to position her students as researchers and help them to be more prepared for change, and as we have discussed earlier, to produce a book of 'Memories'. Again, Wells grasped the opportunities afforded by unavoidable change. Like Rice, she is attuned to the material and socio-spatial circumstances that construct everyday life in the school and broader community. Being tuned in to students' lived experiences allows her to explore the possibilities and to demonstrate ways of taking agency even in the face of major transformations.

The following summary of the year's plan illustrates how Wells conceptualized the curriculum in terms of space, time and place:

> **Term 1—Setting the scene:** Establishing a belonging environment where relationships, interactions and expectations are made clear, a place where communication, respect and getting along are important and where all students can be successful.
>
> **Term 2—Living windows:** Looking at the new schools from our side of the fence; observing and questioning what was happening.
>
> **Term 3—Talking walls:** Conducting interviews to collect and record 'memories' from the staff and students at RGS in 2010, and making them into a book.
>
> **Terms 4—Growing grounds:** Planting native plants and observing their growth at the same time that the new school is being landscaped and the grounds prepared.

Consistent across Wells' curriculum design is making time to teach children how to research, including the demands of observation, questioning, collecting data in different media, data analysis, reporting and producing artifacts. This means that their literacy tasks are framed more broadly as part of assembling researcher repertoires. Often, Wells explicitly talks with children about 'their research', and sometimes she speaks of them as 'journalists'. The key thing here is that they are investigating what is going on. The study of place, however defined, is ideal for children to learn how to do this work. It is 'right there'. We just have to learn to see it.

In a series of activities, Wells invited the children to describe everyday objects such as a clock or a computer. She assisted them to look for and describe details: the materials things were made from (not always easy to answer), the shape, the size, the texture, the color, the sound, the placement, and then to find the most useful vocabulary to describe and explain. They considered where people and things were placed in relation to each other spatially.

When they tried to give each directions for how to get to a particular place, Wells found that the children struggled, so she spent time with them in the drama room working in small groups with blindfolds experimenting with what happened when their language was imprecise. In the context of the redevelopment of the school, children chose viewing places where they could record changes in a particular location of the school over time. As children observed the new school buildings being constructed, Wells and her colleague, Trimboli, booked fortnightly class meetings with the project manager so that the students could question him about any aspects of the build and the design.

As children hit the middle years of primary school, they are expected to read and write to learn across the curriculum, and their writing is expected to display details of that learning. In a longitudinal study of children in Grades 3–5, it was found that teachers wanted children to include detail, facts and understandings to expand their writing and give it depth. Building content or field knowledge is crucial to producing good writing (Comber, Badger, Barnett, Nixon & Pitt, 2002). Writers have always known this. Yet so often in classrooms, children have thin knowledge and little vested interest in learning more about the topics at hand.

Critical and inclusive literacies are vital for nurturing and developing active citizens, and critical literacy has always involved children being positioned as researchers. It is one of the ways to avoid versions of critical literacy that are simply exercises in political correctness. This is key in students learning about the way things work, why things are organized the way they are, and the processes for making change. Developing complex and durable understandings of power and language cannot be done through simulation. If students do not learn the practices of 'research' by doing it and assembling interpretive resources, they may be limited in their repertoires for learning and acting independently in everyday life and in academic situations.

Our Belonging Places

A key feature of Wells' place-based pedagogy is that children undertook research and publication both as individuals and as part of a collective. They reflected and wrote about the qualities of those spaces where they felt they 'belonged'.

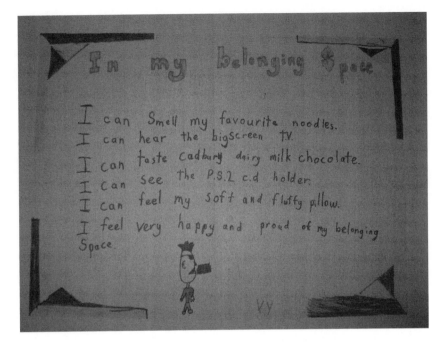

FIGURE 5.3 'Belonging space' as a concept—Tan's belonging space

Wells and the children produced two different Photo Stories reflecting on *Our Belonging Places*: the first with spoken voice-over, and the second with music. Students identified and discussed their preferred places in the school environment where they felt they belonged and then recorded that place. The students went about photographing the place itself, deciding the frame and the angle they wanted, then populating it with the people and the activities they associated with that place. At the end of the year, they produced a third Photo Story archiving, through photographs, their experiences of being a class member of Room 15 in 2010.

The final Photo Stories were in some respects not remarkable. Each child represented a place through a photograph or artistic representation, and then depicted or captured themselves in that place. They explained why that place in the school was where they felt a sense of belonging. In the process of producing the Photo Story, each student produced a small set of three slides along with their voice-over. However, the informed discussion and decision-making between the children themselves and their teacher was every bit as important as the final product, even though the discussion and decision-making are not always immediately visible in the final product.

Collecting the diverse perspectives of class members ensures that students have multiple opportunities to learn about and from each other. The accomplishment

At the new school I like the library.   Vincent

I like my school to have a swing.

At the new school I want new friends.

FIGURE 5.4 Imagining belonging space in the new school from reception and Year 2 children

of class-produced texts has been underresearched in the past few decades. Since teachers stopped having time to publish class sets of student writing or locally customized versions of big books, literacy has become a solitary practice in many schools and classrooms. This emphasis on individual display of competence is of course an artifact of standardized testing as argued elsewhere (Comber, 2012; Comber & Cormack, 2011; Comber & Nixon, 2009).

Because Wells' focus is on places in the school where children feel as though they belong, and then exploring why that is the case, each student can participate fully. It does not depend on prior knowledge or preexisting cultural or linguistic capital; there really are no right answers, but the perspectives the children do give are important information for their teacher to have as part of building knowledge of her class and their learner identities. It is also important for a school community to understand how its children relate to the school as a built environment that allows for and limits their activities in time and space. Place and the spatial relations that are negotiated in, through, and across space can become important resources for students' learning about themselves, their environments and other people.

In Wells' classroom, the children and the teacher finish the year with a body of work they have produced in the context of their learning together. Often it is aesthetically very satisfying. The writing is always the result of significant research, drafting, feedback and editing. Producing a corpus of high quality artifacts in different media is an important achievement. This collective approach to literacy work contrasts sharply with moves across all levels of education, which foster competitive individualism. For example, the national tests of literacy and numeracy are shrouded in secrecy, supposedly to prevent teachers or school leaders cheating or having an unfair advantage.

When paying close attention to those aspects of the authorized curricula which, rhetorically at least, give permission for critical and creative thinking, personal and social capability, ethical behavior and intercultural understanding and prioritize Indigenous perspectives, multiculturalism and sustainability, then literacy teaching and learning may be a serious site for such work. It must be reimagined as a field constituted beyond what can be measured in standardized tests. In order to produce graduates who take responsibility for the community, contribute and participate in collective action, then young people need to practice such engagement in the safety of classroom and school spaces where they feel like they belong.

Assembling the complex multimedia, multimodal discursive practices needed for contemporary active citizenship should be at the heart of what schools are for. Yet to capture young people's imaginations, and harness their energies, such work cannot be done in a vacuum. It cannot be about just any content. Massey's

FIGURE 5.5 Collective engagement and activity in the classroom

work (2005)—the notion that people are thrown together in places and must negotiate being together in a space—is certainly obvious when it comes to schools.

Wherever possible, Wells tries to capitalize on the collective histories, different language and cultural resources of the young people in the classroom. She tries to design curriculum that will include all children. In making *place* the object of study, she ensures that they will be able to share a common focus. The classroom becomes a 'research center' for ongoing investigations of what is going on and producing reports in various modes and media to record those changes and experiences. It is no wonder that Wells' graduates, like those of Rice and, as discussed later, Grant, come back to visit her and to acknowledge the role she has played in their long-term educational successes.

Filmmaking and Media Studies

The final vignette takes us very briefly back to Helen Grant, English as a Second Language teacher and filmmaker. Like many filmmakers, Grant is a serious 'cultural worker', in Freirian terms (Freire, 1998). Once again, it is important to reiterate that place-conscious pedagogy does not leave students where they are or limit them to the local. Instead, young filmmakers can connect with other student-producers elsewhere.

Beeban Kidron, a UK-based filmmaker who directed *Bridget Jones: The Edge of Reason* and *Oranges Are Not the Only Fruit*, is one of a group of filmmakers who founded FILMCLUB, which organizes screenings and discussions of great films with school children. FILMCLUB now boasts 7,000 clubs across the UK, and Kidron makes a number of inspiring observations which have resonance here. She begins:

> Evidence suggests that humans in all ages and from all cultures create their identity in some kind of narrative form. From mother to daughter, preacher to congregant, teacher to pupil, storyteller to audience. Whether in cave paintings or the latest uses of the internet, human beings have always told their histories and truths through parable and fable. We are inveterate storytellers.
>
> But where, in our increasingly secular and fragmented world, do we offer communality of experience, unmediated by our own furious consumerism? And what narrative, what history, what identity, what moral code are we imparting to our young?
>
> *(Kidron, 2012)*

As literacy teachers, we need little persuasion about the importance of narrative, but Kidron goes on to explain the particular affordances of film. She describes young people's extraordinary responses to FILMCLUB, which allowed them to select, view, discuss and review from a historical archival selection; in addition, she explains how her own life in various ways was integrally shaped by great films. First, she argues that '[t]he films provided communality across all manner of divide'. She explains how in watching films together and debating their preferences for particular films, young people began to 'see themselves'. She elaborates on the unanticipated effects of FILMCLUB:

> We guessed that film, whose stories are a meeting place of drama, music, literature and human experience, would engage and inspire the young people participating in FILMCLUB. What we could not have foreseen was the measurable improvements in behaviour, confidence and academic achievement. Once-reluctant students now race to school, talk to their teachers, fight, not on the playground, but to choose next week's film— young people who have found self-definition, ambition and an appetite for education and social engagement from the stories they have witnessed.

This highlights the importance of the school as a meeting place, as a place of belonging, as a site of possibility for more than can be accomplished through home or online schooling, where the teacher orchestrates inclusive participation in exciting inclusive cultural events, whether that be watching truly great films, reading fabulous literature, enjoying popular culture or running the school assembly. In FILMCLUB, children displayed empathy, critical questioning and analysis, high motivation for debate and involvement. Kidron goes on to argue against views of young people as feral, consumerist and self-absorbed, but she throws out a telling challenge. If we want different values, we have to tell a different story, a story that understands that an individual narrative is an essential component of a person's identity, that a collective narrative is an essential component of a cultural identity, and without it, it is impossible to imagine yourself as part of a group.

Once again, it is the emphasis on a collective narrative and belonging to which we wish to draw attention. Recent surveys of young people have found that friends and family are most important to their sense of well-being and that 'being connected to a place may have become of heightened significance' (Harris, Wyn & Younes, 2007, p. 24). Schools and classrooms, when they work well, become key sites for positive identity work, connection and friendship-making.

It is not surprising then that Grant's graduates, now many of them at university or working, make time to return to visit her at Gilles Street Primary School. At the time of sourcing photographs and permissions, Grant reported that a young boy from her class who directed the *Sudan* (2003) film had made contact, now as an adult, via text message to ask how she was and to say hello (see Figure 5.6). This is a fortuitous reminder that the sense of connectedness, belonging and community does not disappear when students leave school. In fact, for the student-director of *Sudan*, it is eleven years later that the text message is sent, received and responded to with great delight. Many young people take these long-term learner and citizen dispositions, learned in relationship with their peers and teachers, with them into adulthood.

FIGURE 5.6 The student-director of *Sudan* (2003)

We have seen a similar phenomenon at each of the other schools whose work we have reported here, where young people go back to see their primary school teachers, sometimes as high school students, sometimes as university students, sometimes as young parents. They are able to explain in hindsight what they have learned from their elementary or early childhood teachers, not only in terms of academic breakthroughs, but also about themselves as citizens, about learning lives and responsibilities. Hence, even though place-conscious critical literacy may begin with the here-and-now, it develops repertoires and dispositions that go beyond a project, a school year. The scale of impact of such educators is yet to be fully understood.

Enabling Pedagogies—Key Pedagogical Principles

At a 2013 conference for teachers in Broome in northern Western Australia, we shared stories of teachers' literacy work that we had gathered over time and in different places. Not surprisingly, place-conscious pedagogy resonated with many of the Indigenous educators who already know the importance of country in children's learning and identity formation. Indeed, place as pedagogical is at the heart of their community ways of knowing; country underpins identity (see also Somerville, 2013). The artifacts, especially the films made by students and filmmakers at Milpera about the Brisbane floods, were warmly welcomed as the region had recently experienced Cyclone Rusty.

A young teacher from one of the schools excitedly shared her documentary film, *Cyclone Rusty, 2013* (see Mills, Comber & Kelly, 2013), to huge applause. The teacher had worked with the senior class to tell the story of Cyclone Rusty from the perspective of different members of the community. They collected news items about the impending cyclone, captured footage during the actual cyclone and interviewed people after it had passed. In the process, students learned about interviewing, filming, editing, credits and so on. This moment is mentioned here because creative practices deserve wider attention. When shared, as the Cyclone Rusty film was, they can create their own momentum and provide rich alternatives for teachers seeking to break out of the performative regimes associated with high stakes literacy testing.

Christchurch, in 2014, the site of recent earthquakes and storms, is a place of change and trauma for communities and their students. Learning to live with the threat of major disasters, unfortunately, is an ongoing issue in some places. Building resilience out of trauma is complex and it is clear that there are significant psychological dimensions involved. However, engagement in creative place-conscious projects with the associated collective production of aesthetically satisfying artifacts is academically and therapeutically positive for students affected by trauma. The opportunity to engage with actual places, remembered places and imagined places allows forms of reconnection, identity work and new forms of belonging.

Recently, some of the teachers whose work has been described here met to catch up and discuss what is going on now in their classrooms and schools. As usual, they are continuing to invent place-conscious pedagogies that include their students on exciting paths. Wells, for example, recounted a recent unit of work where she had taken her class to IKEA in order for them to develop more concrete ideas about 'designing their dream bedroom'. While on the one hand this could initially seem quite commercial and uncritical, it is important to understand this work in context. Wells has always recognized that an important dimension of teaching is to explore elements of pleasure and desire, not to immediately rule it out. The affordances of the IKEA experience for her students, from her perspective, outweigh the risks of consumer culture. These are not children who get to experience housing renovations and the spatial literacies and discourses that go along with that at home. The IKEA excursion could be seen as somewhat like going to a play or a concert. It provides an opportunity for the children to play in a different space and to imagine themselves and their home spaces differently.

In 2014, Wells was working with the local council and their artists. In a recent email, she writes:

> I am continuing my work with the local council about the development in Murchison St. They will be employing three artists to work with the

students next term to create mosaic tiles. They will be used to decorate low walls/seats instead of as pavers in the paths as in stage 1. I am linking this to the new Geography curriculum.

To set the scene we have revisited Street 1—looking at the site, taking photos and posing questions, such as: What is happening? Why is there a trench with plants in it? Where will the water come from? Why is it here? We are going to explore our thoughts and ideas about these questions and I'm also going to invite the Project Officer from the council to come out and the students can pose their questions to him. Streets 2 and 3 will happen this year. This will continue the channeling of water (in different ways) down the street until it gets to the local park where the lower level will be planted out as a wetland. Posing questions, reading maps, making observations, envisaging what they think will happen next is where we are at, at the moment. I want students to come up with their own plans for Street 2 (and reasons/ recommendations) before we look at the council approved plans. They will use scale and mapping skills, model making and computer programs to create street images. And the council thinks we are only making tiles!

Wells' curriculum design is propelled by possibilities to position her students as researchers and as people who can imagine a better place. She is always on the look-out for opportunities. In a classroom just next door, her colleague, Trimboli, starts by considering the students who comprise her class. Trimboli is designing a unit of work, linked with the Australian curriculum for Grade 5, focusing on reasons people migrate to Australia. She plans for students to interview their parents or someone they know who migrated to Australia who has settled within their local community. First of all, they will take time to develop the questions. She recognizes the resources she has in the student community, stating:

I have kids from Poland, Pakistan, India, China, Vietnam, Liberia, Uganda, Guinea, Somalia, Greece, that's just what I can remember . . . There might be a couple of others. However, I would like for the kids to tap into other people at the school. I think it has the possibility for interesting reading.

Evident here is the pattern of these teachers supporting student learning to research change, to formulate critical questions, and then to develop an archive of reports which contribute to a larger report.

The projects of these teachers continue to be designed around the particular students who arrive in the classroom. They continue to work creatively with the affordances of the changing local place, and demonstrate their capacities to imagine pedagogies of possibility, and projects that will bring young people together, fostering a sense of belonging and a sense of responsibility for each other and their places. Hopefully, their projects will trigger the educational imaginations of readers working in different places.

FIGURE 5.7 Pedagogies of possibility fostering a sense of belonging and responsibility

The pictures of practice portrayed in this book are as rich, complex and detailed as possible. Because teachers and principals lead busy lives, they are constantly looking for big ideas that can be summarized in dot points, or captured within the boundaries of a page or a screen. For this reason, the dot points to follow capture the essence of *place-conscious pedagogy* and *critical literacies* fused together to form *enabling pedagogies* for diverse student communities.

Three assumptions underpin these principles. First, that knowledge of place is an enabling resource for literacy learning, and, relatedly, that place can be known in many ways. Second, that it is within the teacher's power to ensure that their classrooms become belonging places. Third, this is part of curricular justice where the teacher's central role is to build student repertoires for knowing, representing and communicating.

To summarize, key principles of these enabling pedagogies include:

- building conceptual knowledge (using necessary subject-specific language)
- positioning and educating students to be researchers (observation, note-taking, interviewing, transcribing, interpreting, reporting)
- exploring the reasons for and effects of physical and social change in places
- working on complex multimodal tasks as a collective
- imagining the ways in which places might be changed for the better
- ensuring student products have social consequences and public outcomes.

These principles clearly underpin the examples of practice shared in this book. These processes and practices take time to develop and implement. This is not a surface-level, neat-and-tidy curriculum which can be covered according to a schedule, but a dynamic curriculum that can and must be negotiated with the students in the classroom, based on what they already know, what is going on, and the resources that can be called upon to support new learning.

This book provides illustrations of ways that teachers can create discursive and material spaces for rich communal learning projects which highlight literacy as socio-cultural political practices. This underscores the importance of teacher learning—indeed, teacher research—in supporting powerful analytically fearless teachers, who are not afraid to consider the effects of their practices on different students, who could create responsive, challenging and engaging curriculum. Improving the quality of student learning is contingent upon ensuring teachers' ongoing learning. Attending to the politics of the embodied contexts of teachers' work is a key step in building durable critical and collaborative research alliances. Recognizing and experimenting with the affordances of school locations in particular places can help educators realize, in Foucault's (1988, p. 10) terms, that we are 'freer than we feel'.

Increasingly, the ways in which literacy is constituted by politicians, policy-makers, principals and practitioners rings alarm bells. Too often, it is about fixing deficits, raising scores, and bolt-on classes. The vision is narrow. The literacy is reduced. In times when educators are increasingly under pressure to produce measurable standardized outcomes in short periods of time, it is crucial not to lose sight of the bigger purposes of schooling. Indeed, producing inclusive critically literate graduates is more urgent than ever. However, ensuring the space and time for this work is not a given. Leaders, teachers and researchers must consider what literacy is for, and how to educate young citizens who can read the world and the word, and who can negotiate positive and inclusive learner identities. The abiding importance of classroom discourse, and the quality of engaging shared experiences, and the concept of the classroom as a meeting and belonging place must be considered and addressed.

To see classrooms as sites of multiplicity which must be negotiated is to acknowledge the materiality of teachers' work and the relational aspects of pedagogy. Enabling pedagogies help students to become researchers who can observe and question, see patterns and interrogate inequities, even as they engage in satisfying and enjoyable learning. Working with connectedness to place and design of spaces are hopeful practices in a world where young people are constantly assaulted with the world's problems. Place-conscious approaches to critical literacy open up ways of seeing and shared objects of study whereby teachers and children can work together to come to know and represent their collective understandings.

References

Adoniou, M 2013, 'Preparing teachers—The importance of connecting contexts in teacher education', *Australian Journal of Teacher Education*, vol. 38, no. 8, pp. 47–60.

Alexander, R 2012, 'Improving oracy and classroom talk in English schools: Achievements and challenges', presentation given at the DfE Seminar on Oracy, the National Curriculum and Education Standards, February 20, 2012, accessed March 5, 2014, http://www.ukla.org/news/story/spoken_language_in_the_new_national_curriculum_radical_reform_or_business_a/

Australian Broadcasting Commission, ABC Radio, 2011, The world today: Last of flooded Queensland's schools reopened, broadcast May 23, 2011, accessed March 26, 2014, http://www.abc.net.au/worldtoday/content/2011/s3224281.htm

Australian Curriculum, Assessment and Reporting Authority (ACARA) 2014a, Cross-curriculum priorities, accessed March 1, 2014, http://www.acara.edu.au/curriculum/cross_curriculum_priorities.html

Australian Curriculum, Assessment and Reporting Authority (ACARA) 2014b, General Capabilities, accessed March 1, 2014, http://www.acara.edu.au/curriculum/general_capabilities.html

Barton, D, Hamilton, M & Ivanic, R 2000, *Situated literacies: Reading and writing in context*, Psychology Press, London.

Boomer, G 1985, *Fair dinkum teaching and learning: Reflections on literacy and power*. Boynton/Cook, Upper Montclair, New Jersey.

Burnett, C, Merchant, G, Pahl, K & Rowsell, J 2014, 'The (im)materiality of literacy: The significance of subjectivity to new literacies research', *Discourse: Studies in the Cultural Politics of Education*, vol. 35, no. 1, pp. 90–103.

Campano, G, Ghiso, M, Yee, M & Pantoja, A 2013, 'Toward community research and coalitional literacy practices for educational justice', *Language Arts*, vol. 90, no. 5, pp. 314–326.

Cazden, C 2001, *Classroom discourse: The language of teaching and learning*, Heinemann, Portsmouth, New Hampshire.

Cochran-Smith, M & Lytle S (eds.) 2009, *Inquiry as stance: Practitioner research for the next generation*, Teachers College Press, New York & London, pp. 326–342.

Comber, B 1987, 'Celebrating and Analyzing Successful Teaching', *Language Arts*, vol. 64, no. 2, pp. 182–195.

Comber, B 2012, 'Mandated literacy assessment and the reorganisation of teachers' work: Federal policy and local effects', *Critical Studies in Education*, vol. 53, no. 2, pp. 119–136.

Comber, B, Badger, L, Barnett, J, Nixon, H & Pitt, J 2002, 'Literacy after the early years: A longitudinal study', *Australian Journal of Language and Literacy*, vol. 25, no. 2, pp. 9–23.

Comber, B & Cormack, P 2011, 'Education policy mediation: Principals' work with mandated literacy assessment', *English in Australia*, vol. 46, no. 2, pp. 77–86.

Comber, B & Nixon, H 2009, 'Teachers' work and pedagogy in an era of accountability', *Discourse: Studies in the cultural politics of education*, vol. 30, no. 3, pp. 333–345.

Compton-Lilly, C F 2000, 'Staying on children: Challenging stereotypes about urban parents', *Language Arts*, vol. 77, no. 5, pp. 420–427.

Connell, R W 1993, *Schools and social justice*, Our Schools/Our Selves Education Foundation, Toronto.

Dixon, K 2011, *Literacy, power, and the school body*, Routledge, New York & London.

Dunn, A & Durrance, S 2014, 'Preparing [or prepared] to Leave? A professor-student dialogue about the realities of urban teaching', *Teachers College Record*, August 15, 2014, accessed August 25, 2014, http://www.tcrecord.org, ID Number: 17645.

Dyson, A H 2013, *ReWriting the basics: Literacy learning in children's cultures*, Teachers College Press, New York.

Foucault, M 1979, *Discipline and punish: The birth of the prison*, Vintage Books, New York.

Foucault, M 1988, 'Truth, power, self: An interview with Michel Foucault October 25 1982', in L. Martin & P. Hutton (eds.), *Technologies of the Self: A Seminar with Michel Foucault*, University of Massachusetts Press, Massachusetts.

Freire, P 1998, *Teachers as cultural workers: Letters to those who dare teach*, Westview Press, Boulder, Colorado.

Freire, P & Macedo, D 1987, *Literacy: Reading the word and the world*, Bergin & Garvey, Westport, Connecticut.

Fyfe, I & Wyn, J 2007, 'Young activists making the news: The role of the media in youth political and civic engagement', in K. Edwards, M. Print & L. Saha (eds.), *Youth and political participation*, Sense, Rotterdam, pp. 113–132.

Gee, J 1990, *Social linguistics and literacies: Ideology in discourses*, Falmer Press, London.

Geertz, C 1983, *Local knowledge: Further essays in interpretive anthropology*, Basic Books, New York, New York.

Green, B & Corbett M (eds.) 2013, *Rethinking rural literacies: Transnational perspectives*, Palgrave McMillan, New York.

Green, B & Letts, W 2007, 'Space, equity, and rural education: A trialectical account', in K. Gulson & C. Symes (eds.), *Spatial theories of education: Policy and geography matters*, Routledge, New York & London, pp. 57–76.

Greene, M 1988, *The dialectic of freedom*, Teachers College Press, New York & London.

Gruenewald, D 2008, 'Place-based education: Grounding culturally responsive teaching in geographical diversity', in D. Gruenewald & D. Smith (eds.), *Place-based education in the global age: Local diversity*, Lawrence Erlbaum & Associates, New York & London.

Gutierrez, K 2008, 'Developing a sociocritical literacy in the third space', *Reading Research Quarterly*, vol. 43, no. 2, pp. 148–164.

Haberman, M 1991, 'The pedagogy of poverty versus good teaching', *Phi Delta Kappan*, vol. 73, no. 4, pp. 290–294.

Harris, A, Wyn, J & Younes, S 2007, 'Young people and citizenship: An everyday perspective', *Youth Studies Australia*, vol. 26, no. 2, pp. 19–27.

Heath, S B 1983, *Ways with words: Language, life, and work in communities and classrooms*, Cambridge University Press, Cambridge, Massachusetts.

Heath, S B 2012a, *Words at work and play: Three decades in family and community life*, Cambridge University Press, New York.

Heath, S B 2012b, 'Seeing our way into learning science in informal environments', in W. F. Tate (ed.), *Research on schools, neighborhoods, and communities: Toward civic responsibility*, Rowman & Littlefield Publishers for the American Educational Research Association, New York, pp. 249–267.

Hicks, D 2002, *Reading lives*, Teachers College Press, New York & London.

Hicks, D 2013, *The road out: A teacher's odyssey in poor America*, University of California Press, Berkeley.

Hong, J Y 2010, 'Pre-service and beginning teachers' professional identity and its relation to dropping out of the profession', *Teaching and Teacher Education*, vol. 26, no. 8, pp. 1530–1543.

Hull, G & Schultz, K 2001, 'Literacy and learning out of school: A review of theory and Research', *Review of Educational Research*, vol. 71, no. 4, pp. 575–611.

Janks, H 2010, *Literacy and power*, Routledge, New York & London.

Johnston, P 2012, *Opening minds: Using language to change lives*, Stenhouse, Portland, Maine.

Jones, S 2006, *Girls, social class & literacy: What teachers can do to make a difference*, Heinemann, Portsmouth, New Hampshire.

Kerkham, L 2007, 'Teaching in a place: Locating teacher identity', paper presented at AARE, Fremantle, Western Australia, November 25–29, retrieved from http://www.aare.edu.au/07pap/ker07373.pdf

Kidron, B 2012, The shared wonder of film, TED video, TEDSalon London, May 2012, accessed June 27, 2012, http://www.ted.com/talks/beeban_kidron_the_shared_wonder_of_film.html

Kress, G 1997, 'Visual and verbal modes of representation in electronically mediated communication: The potentials of new forms of text', in I. Snyder (ed.), *Page to screen: Taking literacy into the electronic age*, Allen & Unwin, Sydney, pp. 53–79.

Kress, G 2003, *Literacy in the new media age*, Routledge/Falmer, London & New York.

Leander, K & Sheehy, M (eds.) 2004, *Spatializing literacy research and practice*, Peter Lang. New York.

Lewis, C, Enciso, P & Moje, E B (eds.) 2007, *Reframing sociocultural research on literacy*, Routledge/Taylor & Francis, New York & London.

Lipman, P 2013, 'Economic crisis, accountability, and the state's coercive assault on public education in the USA', *Journal of Education Policy*, vol. 28, no. 5, pp. 557–573.

Luke, A 1995, 'Text and discourse in education: An introduction to critical discourse analysis', *Review of Research in Education*, vol. 21, pp. 3–48.

Luke, A 2000, 'Critical literacy in Australia: A matter of context and standpoint', *Journal of Adolescent & Adult Literacy*, vol. 43, no. 5, pp. 448–461.

Luke, A 2012, 'After the testing: Talking and reading and writing the world', *Journal of Adolescent and Adult Literacy*, vol. 56, no. 1, pp. 8–13.

Luke, A 2013, 'Regrounding critical literacy: representation, facts and reality', in M. Hawkins (ed.), *Framing languages and literacies: Socially situated views and perspectives*, Routledge, New York, pp. 136–148.

Marsh, J 2005, 'Ritual, performance and identity construction: Young children's engagement with popular cultural and media texts', in J. Marsh (ed.), *Popular culture, media and digital literacies in early childhood*, Routledge/Falmer, London, pp. 21–38.

Massey, D 2005, *For Space*, SAGE, London.

Mills, K, Comber, B & Kelly, P 2013, 'Sensing place: Embodiment, sensoriality, kinesis, and children behind the camera', *English teaching: Practice and critique*, vol. 12, no. 2, pp. 11–27.

Milpera State High School, Queensland Government 2012, accessed July 1, 2012, http://www.milperashs.eq.edu.au/about-us.html

Ministry of Education, New Zealand 2014, Reading and writing standards, accessed March 5, 2014, http://nzcurriculum.tki.org.nz/National-Standards/Reading-and-writing-standards

Moje, E 2000, 'Critical issues: Circles of kinship, friendship, position, and power: Examining the community in community-based literacy research', *Journal of Literacy Research*, vol. 32, no. 1, pp. 77–112.

National Center for Literacy Education 2013, NCLE Report: Remodeling Literacy Learning, accessed August 28, 2014, http://www.literacyinlearningexchange.org/remodeling

Nichols, S, Rowsell, J, Nixon, H & Rainbird, S 2012, *Resourcing early learners: New networks, new actors*, Routledge, New York.

Pahl, K & Rowsell, J 2010, *Artifactual literacy: Every object tells a story*, Teacher's College Press, New York.

Resnick, L 2010, 'How does accountable talk improve learning?', Institute for Learning, University of Pittsburgh, Pennsylvania, accessed March 5, 2014, http://ifl.lrdc.pitt.edu/index.php/resources/ask_the_educator/lauren_resnick

Rogers, R 2011, 'The sounds of silence in educational tracking: A longitudinal, ethnographic case study', *Critical Discourse Studies*, vol. 8, no. 4, pp. 239–252.

Rowsell, J & Sefton-Green, J (eds.) in press, 2015, *Revisiting learning lives—longitudinal perspectives on researching learning and literacy*. Routledge, New York.

Sahlberg, P 2011, *Finnish lessons: What can the world learn from educational change in Finland?* Teachers College Press, New York.

Sefton-Green, J 2009, *Location, location, location: Rethinking space and place as sites and contexts for learning*, Beyond Current Horizons, London, UK.

Smith, D E 2005, *Institutional ethnography: A sociology for people*, AltaMira Press, Lanham.

Somerville, M 2007, 'Place literacies', *Australian Journal of Language and Literacy*, vol. 30, no. 2, pp. 149–164.

Somerville, M 2013, *Water in a dry land: Place-learning through art and story*, Routledge, New York.

Street, B 1975, 'The Mullah, the Shahname and the Madrasseh', *Asian Affairs*, no. 6, vol. 3, pp. 290–306.

Street, B (ed.) 2001, *Literacy and development: Ethnographic perspectives*, Routledge, London.

Thomson, P 2002, *Schooling the rust-belt kids: Making the difference in changing times*, Trentham Books, Stoke-on-Trent.

Tyack, D & Cuban, L 1995, *Tinkering toward utopia: A century of public school reform*, Harvard University Press Cambridge, Massachusetts.

Vasquez, V 2004, *Negotiating critical literacies with young children*, Lawrence Erlbaum, Mahwah, New Jersey.

INDEX